Praise for *Danc.*

"For each of the Four Noble Truths there are three aspects, which form a paradigm of reflection, investigation, and insight. Thus, there are Twelve Insights contained within the Four Noble Truths, which free one from suffering. This investigation Phillip calls 'dancing with life.' As he reveals, in order to dance with life, you need to give yourself completely to the dance, and the way to do this is through the development of mindfulness. I welcome Phillip's excellent book."

—*Ajahn Sumedho, founding abbot, Amaravati Buddhist Monastery*

"The ancient practice of mindfulness is increasingly being shown in scientific studies to have remarkable consequences for healing and well-being across the life span. *Dancing with Life* systematically maps out a rigorous and profoundly loving choreography for cultivating mindfulness in the service of embodying our full potentiality as human beings, utilizing whatever circumstances we happen to find ourselves in. It is a practical and reassuring dharma guide for a great many people in the ongoing development of their practice and lives. It is very different from most dharma books in that it has such an elaborate and friendly structure to it, nested within and around the Four Noble Truths and Ajahn Sumedho's lovely voicing of dharma. I love the precision of Phillip's teaching of the embodiment of each insight; the stories about his students and their challenges; and also, his willingness to share his own trials, travails, and openings along the path."

—*Jon Kabat-Zinn, author of* Full Catastrophe Living
and Arriving at Your Own Door

"I just want to say how much we have appreciated your book on the Four Noble Truths. It is a wonderful commentary and explication of Ajahn Sumedho's teaching and for several weeks we had our teatime readings from it. Great job! I hope it is found to be useful to many people and that it receives the plaudits it deserves."

—*Ajahn Amaro, abbot, Amaravati Buddhist Monastery*

"Phillip Moffitt has given us a clear and practical guide to dealing with the unhappiness and frustration that come our way in life. He leads us on a path of connection rather than isolation, and compassion rather than fruitless anger and self-judgment. Everyone could benefit from reading this book."

—*Sharon Salzberg, author of* Lovingkindness:
The Revolutionary Art of Happiness

"Dharma for Phillip Moffitt is alive and practical, not theoretical or abstract, and he anchors the teachings in everyday life examples. *Dancing with Life: Buddhist Insights for Finding Meaning and Joy in the Face of Suffering* is Moffitt's gift to us, a handbook for those of us who wish to lessen our suffering. The book has grown out of Moffitt's life experience both as a student of the dharma and as a teacher. It is replete with concrete examples, ones the reader can relate with and apply to his or her individual situation.

—*Rick Hanson, PhD, neuropsychologist and author of* Buddha's Brain

DANCING
WITH LIFE

BUDDHIST INSIGHTS FOR FINDING MEANING
AND JOY IN THE FACE OF SUFFERING

PHILLIP MOFFITT

PREFACE BY VENERABLE AJAHN SUMEDHO

RODALE

First published in hardcover by Rodale Inc. in 2008.
This paperback edition published in 2012.

Printed in the United States of America
Rodale Inc. makes every effort to use acid-free ♾, recycled paper ♻.

Excerpts from "Burnt Norton" in FOUR QUARTETS by T. S. Eliot, copyright 1936 by Harcourt, Inc., and renewed 1964 by T. S. Eliot, reprinted by permission of the publisher. Excerpts from "East Coker" in FOUR QUARTETS, copyright 1940 by T. S. Eliot and renewed 1968 by Esme Valerie Eliot, reprinted by permission of Harcourt, Inc. Excerpts from "The Dry Salvages" in FOUR QUARTETS, copyright 1941 by T. S. Eliot and renewed 1969 by Esme Valerie Eliot, reprinted by permission of Harcourt, Inc. Excerpts from "Little Gidding" in FOUR QUARTETS, copyright 1942 by T. S. Eliot and renewed 1970 by Esme Valerie Eliot, reprinted by permission of Harcourt, Inc. Excerpts from the *Samyutta Nikaya* are from *The Four Noble Truths*, Amaravati Publications, 1992.

Book design by Joanna Williams

Library of Congress Cataloging-in-Publication Data

Moffitt, Phillip.
    Dancing with life : finding meaning and joy in the face of suffering / Phillip Moffitt.
      p.   cm.
    Includes bibliographical references and index.
    ISBN-13 978-1-59486-353-0 hardcover
    1. Four Noble Truths. 2. Suffering—Religious aspects—Buddhism.
    3. Buddhism. I. Title.
    BQ4230.M65 2008
    294.3'4—dc22   2007047263
    ISBN-13 978-1-60529-824-5 paperback

Distributed to the trade by Macmillan

    10 9   paperback

We inspire and enable people to improve their lives and the world around them
For more of our products visit **rodalestore.com** or call 800-848-4735

Dedicated to the monastics,
who have kept the tradition of vipassana alive
for more than 2,500 years.

"THERE ARE TWO KINDS OF SUFFERING: THE SUFFERING THAT
LEADS TO MORE SUFFERING AND THE SUFFERING THAT LEADS TO
THE END OF SUFFERING. IF YOU ARE NOT WILLING TO FACE THE
SECOND KIND OF SUFFERING, YOU WILL SURELY CONTINUE TO
EXPERIENCE THE FIRST."

—AJAHN CHAH, A STILL FOREST POOL

CONTENTS

BOOK THREE: THE THIRD NOBLE TRUTH

BOOK FOUR: THE FOURTH NOBLE TRUTH

PREFACE

by Ajahn Sumedho

Phillip Moffitt's *Dancing with Life* is a clear and well-written explanation of how to apply the Four Noble Truths to daily life based on his own experience and insights and the insights of his students. For each of the Four Noble Truths there are three aspects, which form a paradigm of reflection, investigation, and then "insight" (a profound recognition). In the Pali language this paradigm is described as *pariyatti* (theory or statement), *patipatti* (actual practice), and *pativedha* (the result of the practice). Thus, there are twelve insights contained within the Four Noble Truths, which free one from delusion and suffering. This investigation Phillip calls "dancing with life." As he reveals, in order to dance with life, you need to be able to move and flow and give yourself completely to the dance, and the way to do this is through the development of mindfulness. Mindfulness is the path to the deathless—the underlying joy and love that is consciousness without delusion. It is through the surrender of the illusory self that enlightenment is realized.

When I first became interested in Theravada Buddhism while living in Malaysia more than four decades ago, there was a dearth of available literature on the subject in English. So I would send for tracts and books from the Buddhist Publication Society in Kandy, Sri Lanka. One of the books I received was Venerable Nyanatiloka's *Word of the Buddha*, which was a succinct synopsis of the Four Noble Truths. The quotations were all taken from the Pali scripture and organized under the appropriate headings of each of the Four Noble Truths.

This small booklet was the only teaching material I took with me when I began a yearlong retreat at a monastery in Thailand after becoming a *samanera* (novice monk). None of the monks spoke English and I had no grasp of the Thai language, so I could not understand the dharma talks or engage in discussions with other monks. All I had for inspiration and instruction was that synopsis of the Four Noble Truths. I spent the year in a little hut reading and rereading the booklet and putting the teachings into practice.

That year, 1966, that I spent reflecting on and practicing the Four Noble Truths was the most significant and powerful year of my life. Living alone with nothing to do, no one to talk with, only one small book to read, and only a beginner's experience of meditation, I could easily relate to the First Noble Truth—the Noble Truth of Suffering. My daily life without its usual distractions presented me with a lifetime supply of suppressed anger and fear. For the first three months, I had to endure an almost continuous flood of hatred, rage, anger, and fear. This deluge of negativity was not at all what I was expecting. I had been looking forward to a life of tranquility.

It became apparent after several weeks of fumbling resistance to this turmoil that the only way that I could survive was to endure these emotional storms by watching them. This insight arose after contemplating the First Noble Truth—there is suffering. It was clear that the suffering was not due to any external circumstances because all the conditions affecting me were kind and benevolent. This suffering was created through my mental habits.

Reflecting on the Second Insight of the First Noble Truth that suffering "should be understood," I found that the only way that I could understand my hatred and anger was to "stand under" it—in other words, to observe the feeling, the mood, and the emotional atmosphere with patient endurance. Through practicing nonresistance and paying noncritical attention to the quality of my emotional conditions, I experienced the Third Insight of the First Noble Truth that suffering "has been understood."

After about three months of practicing "standing under" my suffering, I awoke one morning to an experience of total bliss. At that moment I did not sense any trace of negativity. Everything was touched by luminous beauty. This state lasted for five days, and I thought I was enlightened.

When the intensity of this beautiful experience diminished, I felt longing for it. I wanted to have it again, and I wanted to have it all the time. At that point, the Second Noble Truth that suffering is caused by attachment to desire began to interest me. I noticed that my longing to recapture the luminous beauty I had experienced was the result of clinging to a memory. So for the remainder of that year, my meditation practice was a continuous reminder to let loose of clinging to desire.

Living the Four Noble Truths as a daily practice and understanding them as a profound reflection provides a context for your entire life. But to sincerely live in this manner is not easy in modern life with its conflicting push/pull forces and confusing cultural messages as to what is valuable. For this reason *Dancing with Life* is a significant contribution to the plethora of Buddhist literature that has been published over the past 50 years. Phillip has created an important guide to working with this most profound of the Buddha's teachings for contemporary practitioners. It honors the Buddha's words while providing fresh examples of how a layperson can skillfully live the Four Noble Truths today. The challenge for each person is to realize the insights in your life rather than merely accepting them as concepts. The lucid way in which Phillip has written about how to actualize the twelve insights is a real achievement.

In 1967, after practicing by myself for a year, I took higher
ordination, and became a Bhikkhu. I went to live in the remote
forest monastery of the great Thai teacher the Venerable Ajahn
Chah, where I became his devoted student and stayed for the
next 10 years. Ajahn Chah's approach to meditation practice
was very practical. The traditional monastic form and discipline
were taught and practiced in daily life. The Dhamma teachings
were always about the Four Noble Truths. We were expected to
memorize in Pali the *Dhammacakkapavatana Sutta*, the first
sermon the Buddha gave on the Four Noble Truths after his
enlightenment. It is a complete description and an accurate
road map to freeing oneself from the delusions that cause
human suffering.

I have observed how rarely the practical use and application
of this essential teaching of the Buddha are taught and practiced in Theravadin countries. Even the vipassana movement in
the West seems to only pay lip service to it when, in fact, the
Four Noble Truths are a lifetime's reflection. I find it quite
mind-boggling that in the Buddhist world this really profound
teaching has often been dismissed as primitive Buddhism. In
making the Four Noble Truths accessible and contemporary,
Dancing with Life illuminates many of the subtle and advanced
realizations contained within the teaching. Phillip offers a variety of views for understanding and living the insights without
ever asking readers to embrace any particular view of his own.
In Buddhism we never believe in doctrines or teachings that
come from others; we want to find out the truth for ourselves.

It is with much joy and enthusiasm that I welcome Phillip's
excellent book. It is, indeed, a marvelous work. May it be a
guide and a blessing to those beings committed to the cultivation of mindfulness.

—*Amaravati Buddhist Monastery*
Hertfordshire, England
July 2007

INTRODUCTION

MY DANCE WITH LIFE

On the very last day of 1986, soon after my 40th birthday, I did something that many people have since told me they long to do. I completely abandoned my professional identity, with all its security and privileges, in order to devote myself to finding more joy and meaning in my life. It was a good life that I left—some would even say a great one. I was editor-in-chief and chief executive of *Esquire* magazine, having bought it with some colleagues when it had fallen on hard times and slowly nourished it back to financial health and prominence. I liked what I did, was reasonably good at it, and as both creative and operational leader, I got to do things my way—a rare situation. Through the articles I published and the monthly column I wrote in the magazine, I had a voice in the national debate around social issues relevant to my generation. And as a business leader I got an adrenaline charge from being the underdog competing against much larger media companies and finding creative ways to hold my own.

Although I felt very fortunate to have these experiences, they did not ultimately provide me with a deep sense of purpose. Whenever I imagined spending the rest of my life continuing on the same path toward worldly success a strong feeling of disappointment in myself arose. So to the astonishment of people in the New York publishing community I gave up all that I had accomplished in order to dedicate myself fully to exploring the inner life and to understanding the mystery of this human existence, with all its joyous possibility and its endless suffering.

When I walked out of the door at *Esquire*, I had no plans. I did not know what city or even what country I would be living in, let alone what I would be doing with my time. Had I known that I would spend most of the next few years living in various meditation centers in rooms so small that I often could reach out and touch both walls, I might not have so cheerfully left my comfortable Manhattan apartment.

And yet I was not completely naïve about such matters. At the age of 23, I had begun a hatha yoga practice in which I learned to put my body into various poses and to hold them for long periods of time. I soon added the breathing exercises called *pranayama*, and within a year, a meditation practice. By the time I turned 26, I was doing yoga for at least an hour and a half each evening. In fact, I became so immersed in my practice that I came close to withdrawing from the conventional world at age 30 to live in an ashram, but then I backed out at the last moment due to what I call a "failure of imagination." I couldn't see how my life would unfold once I became a renunciate. I also hadn't surrendered that dream many young people have to test themselves in the world—"to run against the fast horses." So I chose to continue building the publishing company I had started in graduate school. Groping for a way to challenge myself led me to purchase *Esquire*, a magazine that I had always admired for its literary quality and hip style. I hoped that I could continue my spiritual development while testing myself.

In my naïveté I had not realized when I bought *Esquire* that it had lost most of its readers as well as its advertisers and was practically moribund. I worked incredibly long hours, seven days a week, under great pressure to keep the magazine going when no one believed it had a chance of surviving. During those early years at *Esquire,* I lost the momentum of my spiritual practice. After a while, despite my best efforts, I could not access the impulse to do yoga or meditate. Perhaps this was due to my conflicted feelings about not pursuing the inner life full-time. Or perhaps it was because I misused certain yogic concentration and breathing techniques in order to energize myself to work ridiculously long hours. It was a painful and humbling experience to go from having such a strong practice full of ecstatic states to being someone who could not even make himself do a yoga pose. I felt exiled from my own heart.

After three years and nearly going bankrupt twice, *Esquire's* circulation and advertising finally started to grow and it became clear to me one day that the magazine was going to be a success. It was a satisfying and confirming moment after so much doubt and stress. So imagine my dismay when, only a few nights later, while sitting in my apartment editing manuscripts, an unnamed but very disturbing thought started rushing through my body with a buzz as it tried to voice itself into consciousness. I knew that I did not want to hear it, but I also knew that there was no stopping the undeniable realization that I had come to a turning point in my life, that despite the excitement and ego satisfaction of my job, I could not stay in publishing any longer. I had to follow my heart, to surrender myself to a calling—what traditionally would be referred to as a spiritual calling, but I could not identify it so clearly at the time. I could only describe it to my friends and advisors as an intuitive knowing, very strongly felt in my body, that I must engage in an exploration of the inner life.

How I resisted this urge—not just that night, but for several years afterward as I tried various plans to have my cake and eat it too. I delegated more responsibility for the business to my colleagues; I hired a private yoga teacher; I went on two- and three-day self-retreats. But my life never coalesced into a unified experience around a sense of purpose. Thus, I had a real dilemma because I was and remain a very practical person (to this day, many of my friends refer to me as "the practical mystic"). I did not relish abandoning everything I had gained from years of hard work and going off into some unknown life without a plan.

But there was no denying the call. The end finally came while I was sitting in a Magazine Publishers of America board meeting. I suddenly realized that if I did not act right then I might never leave. My mind was calm and very clear, and I finally knew what I had to do. I excused myself from the meeting, went to a phone, and called an investment banker. Six weeks later, the magazine was sold and I was gone!

Stunned by the suddenness and seeming irrationality of my decision, the *New York Times*, *Vanity Fair*, and the *New Yorker* all assigned writers to find out what had gone wrong. Was there a financial scandal? Did I have cancer? There had to be a reason for my behavior. They couldn't imagine why I'd just walk away. But none of the stories were ever published. One reporter confided that when he turned in his piece, the editor told him that she could not publish it because the story was too boring! None of them realized that it was not a personal story of loss or tragedy, but a far greater story of forsaking the pursuit of money, power, and glory in order to seek out a more meaningful life, something that many others in my generation would soon be doing in their own style.

Leaving *Esquire* so abruptly was disorienting initially because I no longer had a defined role or an identity in the world. When I interacted with former colleagues they treated me as though I'd had an unfortunate accident. I had no simple explanation to offer people when they asked what I was doing, nor did I want to proclaim that I was undergoing some noble quest when I had no assurance that I wouldn't change my mind any day! I was repeatedly tempted by opportunities to get back in the game that were quite appealing, especially those in the nascent world of internet media. These offers were attractive because, on one hand, what was I going to fill my time with? On the other hand, I knew I had bought my time back from the marketplace at a great cost and that gave me the perspective to repeatedly say no.

As I embarked on my new life, the teachings and meditative practices of the Theravada Buddhist lineage, the so-called "forest tradition" or "tradition of the Elders," became my primary practice. My first significant teachers were Joseph Goldstein and Sharon Salzberg, who along with Jack Kornfield are the three Westerners considered most responsible for bringing these teachings from Thailand, Burma, and India to the U.S.

Because I had worked so intensely in the life I left behind, redirecting that energy into an intense meditation practice was relatively easy. However, sitting long hours day after day without moving was quite painful, until my body finally started to adjust. Plus, I was impatient. I did not necessarily think I was practicing the right way, and I craved more action in my life. But the pain and emotional turmoil became grist for the mill as I continued my exploration.

I spent much of my time either in meditation centers sitting long silent retreats or practicing on my own. I also became interested in the body-mind connection and studied aikido and somatic healing techniques. Also, because of my past, a number of individuals who were leaders and who were struggling with questions about what to do with their lives began to seek my advice. I gradually evolved a system to help them sort out their priorities, which I ultimately called "life balance work."

One day after I'd been practicing vipassana for seven years, I received a phone call from Jack Kornfield, the founder of

Spirit Rock Meditation Center. He asked me if I would like to become a member of the Spirit Rock Teachers Council and participate in the three-year teacher training program he conducted. I was surprised by his offer as I had not once thought about becoming a full-time meditation teacher. After telling Jack I needed to think about it, I went to see him a few days later and explained that while I was honored by his invitation I didn't think I was the right person because I had not spent years studying in monasteries in Southeast Asia. Jack laughed and said that it was when people acted like it was about time they had been chosen to teach that he worried about their readiness. Although I still wasn't sure teaching was my calling, I was attracted by the opportunity to be part of a community of fellow seekers and was excited about learning from the senior teachers. It also offered a structure for my life, which I had been living without. As it has turned out, teaching the dharma is the most satisfying activity I had ever done in my life.

I now travel throughout the United States leading silent residential meditation retreats of varying lengths, usually with one or more co-teachers. I also teach daylong retreats and have a weekly sitting group. I've written numerous articles on the wisdom that is contained in the Buddha's teachings, including a regular column for *Yoga Journal*.

During the vipassana meditation retreats and the life-balance seminars and private sessions, I've conducted individual interviews with thousands of practitioners and clients, listening to them describe their agonies, the many realizations they've experienced, and the personal transformations they've undergone. Through their experiences as well as my own, I've come to a deep personal and intellectual understanding of the role that suffering plays in our lives and how we can free ourselves from it. These are the lessons I offer here. I do not write as a

Buddhist scholar, nor am I claiming to be enlightened; I am simply giving witness to what I've seen really makes a difference in people's lives.

You Can Find Freedom from Your Suffering

Why do you suffer? Is there a purpose to your pain? What about the amount of suffering you experience—is it fair, based on some understandable system of cause and effect, or is it simply arbitrary? Can you affect how much you suffer? If so, how?

For thousands of years, questions such as these have confounded human beings trying to make sense of the seemingly random and unfair distribution of gain and loss, joy and unhappiness in every person's life. All people are united in their common desire for happiness and their common experience of suffering. As you grow from childhood to adulthood, you inevitably experience life's difficulties, whether it is through a physical limitation or illness, emotional anguish, fear or disappointment, loss or separation from a loved one, or the anxiety and stress surrounding all your wants and needs. No one is spared.

In a sense, then, you are already an expert on suffering. You remember it from your past, and you easily recognize it in yourself and others. You have an array of skills for averting it when possible and surviving it when it is unpreventable. But do you have a conscious relationship with your suffering? Do you utilize it to enrich your life? Or is it merely something you try to avoid? When you suffer, do you experience it as failure, an embarrassment, something shameful? If so, how √ much of your life is unacceptable or alien to you because it contains suffering?

The Buddha asked himself such questions 2,500 years ago, and he came to the following realization: The path to happiness and a sense of well-being in this very life lies not in *avoiding* suffering but in using the *conscious, embodied, direct experience of it* as a vehicle to gain deep insight into the true nature of life and your own existence. Instead of being a reactionary slave to the inevitable pain, frustration, stress, and sorrow in your life, which the Buddha called *dukkha*, you can free your mind such that you have a sense of well-being even when dukkha is present, and you create the possibility of finding complete freedom. Why not dance with the constant vicissitudes of life in a manner that is joyful and liberated, rather than feeling like a victim or being flooded with fear and stress?

The Buddha discovered a path for finding freedom from dukkha or suffering, which he called the Four Noble Truths. This set of attitudes and practices he prescribed doesn't require you to create some new and improved version of you—one that you can only hope will someday emerge. You can take these steps as the "you" who exists right now—the one who gets lost, afraid, angry, and caught up in desire, despite good intentions. All that's required is that you let go of your preconceived notions about suffering and open yourself to exploring the role that it plays in your life.

If you are new to meditation practice, you may well think that you have no choice about how you experience suffering. You may have some problem from your past or in your current situation that seems as though it can be understood only as unrelenting pain—an abusive family history, a tortuous marriage, economic woes, a hideous wrong done to you, a disabled child whose affliction breaks your heart. But if you give yourself the chance to investigate your suffering more deeply, you will discover that being "with" your pain can lead to wisdom and happiness. The event or circumstance itself does not lose its unpleasant or unfortunate quality, but by going through it consciously you arrive at a peaceful and luminous state of mind. In this "enlightened" state, your mind experiences difficulty in a very different manner.

THE BUDDHA'S TWELVE INSIGHTS

The Four Noble Truths was the Buddha's first teaching after he found freedom from his own suffering. Understanding the meaning of these Noble Truths—that your life contains moments of dukkha; that the cause of your dukkha is clinging to desired objects and states of being; that you can release dukkha by letting go of clinging to those desires; and that there is an Eightfold Path to freedom from dukkha that you can follow in order to accomplish all this—is the foundation of Buddhist wisdom.

If you currently have an established meditation practice in any of the three *yamas*, or schools, of Buddhism—Theravada, Mahayana, or Tibetan—then you may believe that you already know all you need to know about the Four Noble Truths. This was certainly my attitude some years ago when my teacher, the Venerable Ajahn Sumedho, first started to talk about the Noble Truths in a new way during a silent meditation retreat that I was attending. Referencing the long discourses in a collection of the Buddha's teachings called the *Samyutta Nikaya*, he began describing the Four Noble Truths as consisting of a set of Twelve Insights, three for each Noble Truth, that are to be realized through practice.

It seems that few people are familiar with the Twelve Insights that lead to full understanding and integration of the Four Noble Truths. And yet these insights are revolutionary because they transform the Truths from a philosophical statement about suffering into a method for directly coping with suffering in your life. They elucidate not only the Truths themselves but also the way you can experience the Truths on an emotional as well as an intellectual level, and then integrate these experiences into your life. In other words, the Four Noble Truths is not just a summary guideline, a creed, or a statement of philosophy, but an actual practice of insight and realization in and of itself. *It is a teaching in how to live wisely.*

First in discussion with Ajahn Sumedho, then by going to the original text, reading many commentaries, and researching for similar insights in modern depth psychology, I developed an integrated view of the Buddha's teaching of the Twelve Insights of the Four Noble Truths, a vision that combined the practical and the mystical. I made the insights my primary focus for some years, and doing so changed both my own practice and what I teach. Thus this book represents my experience of living the Buddha's teachings in daily life. It builds upon the traditional teachings to offer a contemporary, integral view of how to live your life—one that asserts both the value of finding peace and joy within the context of your suffering and the possibility of purifying the mind so that it no longer collapses into suffering.

Dancing with Life is a teaching of the wisdom that is to be found in being consciously and fully present with your suffering until what is called "pure awareness," or "Buddha nature," or "emptiness" that lies beyond your personality is revealed. It points to the opportunity you have to make a radical inner shift in how you view your existence. Whatever the source of your suffering may be, this inner shift will provide a new, deeper context for interpreting your experiences that brings clarity and equanimity to your mind. *The result of this inner transformation is that your life—with all its pain, disappointment and uncertainty, as well as all that you cherish, love, and work hard for—is radi-*

cally enriched. You will discover, as so many others have before you, a feeling of aliveness, something mystical, palpable in your daily life. You may have a long journey to your final and full liberation, but peace and freedom of mind are available to you right now in ever-increasing measure.

A Mother's Suffering

In the private interviews I conduct with participants during the vipassana meditation retreats I lead, I hear endless variations on the theme of how suffering manifests itself in a person's life. What happens on these retreats is that you develop a genuine understanding about the suffering in your own life. (This same understanding can come from a steady daily life practice of mindfulness and inquiry.) You are changed by these insights, sometimes in small ways and sometimes in a very dramatic fashion. One particular student's story provides a typical example of how direct insight into your suffering can lead to immediate liberation from it.

Sarah (all students' names in this book have been changed to protect their privacy) had an adult autistic son who had been violent all his life. She had suffered greatly for more than two decades because of this child, whom she loved dearly, and was heartbroken over his condition. I listened to her story with tremendous sympathy, for is there anything worse than caring for a child whose suffering you cannot relieve? And yet at the same time, I pushed her to consider a different perspective: She—not her son—was responsible for her misery. Therefore she could choose to do something about it. By viewing her life circumstances in a different light, she could free herself from the bonds of suffering.

Over the course of the two-week retreat, Sarah and I discussed the nature of her suffering in depth. Eventually, she came to a startling realization: For 20 years, she had denied herself joy because she felt that it was somehow not right for her to be happy when her son was ill. She kept trying to help him get better, all the while waiting for her time to come. But as the years and then decades passed, she became resigned to a life without sparkle.

Slowly, I confronted Sarah's assumptions. In what way did her not being happy serve her child's well-being? Didn't her unhappiness in fact hinder her efforts by draining away her energy? Could she conceive of her child wanting her to be unhappy because of his difficulties? Anyway, what right did she have to be living out his struggles? His life was tormented in many ways, but it was the only life he had, and it was his to live, not hers. Just as the glory of a child who achieves great success belongs to the child and not the parent, doesn't the same hold true of an affliction? She could honor him most by acknowledging that this was the nature of his life—difficult though it was—and celebrating him just as he was.

The longer Sarah stayed at the retreat practicing mindfulness and compassion, the more the story of her suffering broke apart. This is what makes meditation retreats so powerful. You are there alone on the cushion with yourself day after day, and so you have a precious opportunity to directly know the truth of your own life. The teacher is only there to inspire, clarify, and hold out the possibility of your realizing your own true nature until you can feel that possibility for yourself.

One day, Sarah came into the interview room and announced, "I'm ready to allow myself joy, right now." She was smiling and crying. "I don't know why I so strongly held onto the idea that my son had to be happy before I could ever be. Maybe I will figure that out with therapy. But regardless, I am through holding onto it." I was excited for her. Sarah had had her very first taste of freedom. She had collapsed under her suffering. Now she was ready to bear it and open to the joy of her own life.

You can find this freedom for yourself. It will expose you to an entirely new way of being. It was Sarah's willingness to open to life's gifts in spite of her trials—not her long-suffering sacrifice—that was truly heroic. Do you see this distinction and how it might apply to your own life?

Even under the best of circumstances, life is challenging, and much of the time it is difficult. It is always uncertain, constantly changing, and mostly out of your control. Whether it is taking you on a wonderful ride or stepping on your toes, life will move you with the rhythm and in the direction of its own unfolding, irregardless of your best intentions. *Life dances and you must dance with it*. This is the necessary price and mysterious gift of being incarnate—alive in a body.

If life is going to dance with you, then what kind of dance partner do you wish to be? Can you have a conscious, peaceful relationship with your own life's dance as characterized by a sense of ease, empowerment, and meaning? Certainly it is possible to affect the course of your life. Hard work, discipline, and self-development enable you to be a better partner when life comes to dance, but finding a way to be at ease with the dance itself is a crucial skill in finding freedom and meaning in life.

CHAPTER 1

DANCING LESSONS: HOW TO USE THIS BOOK

The Twelve Insights of the Four Noble Truths are instructions for the practice of self-liberation. They will not protect you from experiencing dukkha—loss and difficulty are an unavoidable reality in our everyday human existence. Even the Buddha experienced pain and loss during his life, such as back pain and grief at the deaths of close friends. However, these Twelve Insights will enable you to relate to your suffering in such a way that it does not define you. It is possible to fully experience the precious and beautiful moments in life as they occur, yet not be desperate for them. Likewise, you can fully experience the difficult in life without being filled with stress and anguish. These Twelve Insights teach you to dance with both the joy and the pain, finding peace in a balanced mind and calm spirit. As the most specific, practical life instructions I have ever encountered, they serve as an invaluable tool for anyone who seeks a life filled with meaning and well-being.

When the Buddha taught the Twelve Insights of the Four Noble Truths, he first presented the *problem*: There is dukkha, which is a *result* of how the untrained mind reacts to ever-changing conditions (the First Noble Truth). Then he presented the *cause* of the problem: Your mind falls into clinging and grasping because of wanting (the Second Noble Truth). Next he presented the *solution*: A different *result* is possible, which is the cessation of suffering (the Third Noble Truth). And finally he presented the *cause* of this radically different *result*: The Eightfold Path (the Fourth Noble Truth). Thus, the Buddha, like a doctor, tells the patient what the *illness* is, *diagnoses* the cause, tells the patient the *cure* for the condition, and recommends the *medicine* needed to bring about the cure.

There are three insights associated with each Noble Truth, and they follow a similar pattern: first *reflecting*, then *directly experiencing*, and finally *knowing*. The Buddha taught that in order to completely understand a Noble Truth, you first reflect on it as a conceptual description of a general truth in life. Hence, to gain the First Insight of each Noble Truth, you critically examine it in your mind to see if it makes intellectual and common sense. When you intellectually know that a given Noble Truth is at least logical and theoretically possible, then the Buddha directs you to the second insight of each Truth. This insight requires you to consciously seek to realize the Truth. You immerse yourself in the truth and therefore experience its validity for you personally. Practicing the Second Insight for each Truth means seeking direct experience of it in your own life through mindful, compassionate awareness. (In Chapter 2, I offer detailed instructions for how to practice each insight using mindfulness meditation.) It is tempting in meditation practice to skip this step in relation to the first two Noble Truths, to jump into a detached, witnessing state about suffering and its cause without knowing the "felt experience" of the Truth. But if you do, you can easily get stuck in your practice. I have witnessed this many times, even in students with years of experience. Their lives don't change and they become disappointed in themselves, but have no understanding as to why they are getting stuck.

The Second Insight of each Truth is not theoretical; you are to experience it in your body, to know both the "wow" and the "ouch" of it. This direct experience is what makes the Buddha's teaching a living wisdom, rather than a philosophy or ontology. The Buddha's offering is not a theory about being, but the actual felt experience of being in your life. That is its liberating power.

Finally, having carefully thought about the Noble Truth and known the embodied experience of it, you are ready for the Third Insight—knowing. Ajahn Sumedho refers to this insight as the call to "know that you know."[1] It involves mindfully integrating what you've just learned and felt into your daily life. People often leave this step out of their spiritual (and psychological) work, as well. And yet, without it, you are likely to lose your grasp on the Truth and return rapidly to your old habits. Soon you'll be living the way you've always been living, in spite of your recent revelations. In my view, knowing is a vital step in each Noble Truth because without it, nothing is really accomplished.

Let's take the First Noble Truth as an example of how these three insights work. First, you examine what the Buddha means by the teaching, "There is dukkha." Does this statement ring true in your life? Is there suffering in the lives of those around you? Second, you open yourself to the experience of suffering. You penetrate it by seeing, tasting, and touching it in a heartfelt manner. Rather than being an uninvolved witness, you seek to directly experience suffering within the body and the mind by staying present with it. You feel the pain, the "ouch" of it, in effect. Third, you realize that you now know for yourself the

---

[1] Many times this third insight is interpreted as meaning, "what needed to be done has been done," or, in other words, that you've had the realization of that particular truth. However, this perspective is not always so helpful as you proceed along the path, because it doesn't point to the practice aspect of the Third Insight of each Truth. This is an example of how hearing the Four Noble Truths as practice requires a mind shift. Throughout this book I use language that describes what it's like to practice the truth from an unliberated state of mind, as opposed to the perspective of a mind that has already achieved liberation.

implications of the Truth, in this case that "there is dukkha." You start to live your life from this known truth, letting go of judgment, of the belief that when you suffer, you somehow fail. Instead, you're willing to meet your suffering and view it as an opportunity for personal growth. You mindfully *respond* to rather than emotionally *react* to it.

Naturally, as with any practice, there are layers of understanding and ability. You dig deeper and become more skillful over time. You do not gain each insight separately and serially, but through a spiraling process of ever-deepening self-knowledge. With every step, you achieve greater peace and understanding.

A FRESH PERSPECTIVE ON AN ANCIENT WISDOM

Dancing with Life is a teaching about moving from suffering to joy in your life. This teaching involves your learning each of the three practice insights for each of the Four Noble Truths. These insights, when directly realized, bring you to the experience of wholeness and unity in your life.

The practices for each of the Noble Truths are treated like a self-contained book. Therefore, you can read *Dancing with Life* as four books, each complete in itself. Each "book" contains an overview and four chapters. In the overview for each book, I provide an interpretation of that particular Truth. The overview is followed by three chapters that explore the three insights related to that Truth: The First Insight for each Truth is to be understood by *reflecting* on the Truth; the Second Insight is to be practiced by *directly experiencing* the Truth; and the Third Insight is gained by *knowing that you know* the Truth. Finally, a summary chapter on the Truth helps you apply these insights in everyday life. Preceding Book One are instructions on mindfulness practices that you will need to investigate the Twelve Insights. Even if you are a longtime meditator, I recommend that you not skip over these instructions because they contain certain key concepts that you may not have learned elsewhere. (See Appendix 1 for a complete list of the Twelve Insights.)

I ask that you be sensitive to the fact that although there are Twelve Insights, the Buddha's teaching is in no way a "twelve-step program," through which you must progress one by one. On the contrary, the insights are fluid and interrelated. It is like being a porpoise in the ocean that suddenly gains consciousness and wonders, "What is the nature of this water that I swim in, from which I am not separate?" You may skip some chapters and come back to them later, or return to certain insights over and over again. You may find that what is most relevant to you are the practices in the book on the First Noble Truth, the Truth of Suffering, for this is where you are in your life. Or you may find that the practices in Book Two around the causes of suffering are most helpful. Or you may find intellectual reflection on each of the Truths to be your starting point. Feel free to proceed as you see fit.

Throughout each chapter, I refer to modern psychological perspectives that support the insight and make it more understandable to the Western mind. These references come primarily from the evolving vision of Jungian psychology that I studied for many years with analyst Dr. Joseph Henderson and from years of extensive reading and exploration on my own. The writings of the analyst and classicist Helen Luke, which I discovered while serving on the board of the C. G. Jung Foundation in New York and the Jung Institute in San Francisco, have been very valuable to me.

To convey the feelings associated with practicing particular insights, I also offer excerpts from the poetry of T. S. Eliot. Eliot, who in midlife became a devoted Anglican Christian, once said that he could just as easily have become a Buddhist. His poetry captures the essence of spiritual realization that unites Buddhism and the Judeo-Christian tradition. In working with students, I often base entire teaching sessions around just a few lines from Eliot's *Four Quartets* because they so perfectly capture the feeling of the truth of inner experience. In a lecture in 1947, Eliot stated: "If we learn to read poetry properly, the poet never persuades us to believe anything. . . . What we learn from Dante or the *Bhagavad-Gita* or any other religious poetry is what it *feels like* to believe that religion." *Dancing with Life* holds forth the possibility that you can feel the truth of your own liberation, not as a concept but as a direct experience of your true nature; Eliot's poetry proves highly suitable for this purpose.[2]

DANCING WITH YOUR LIFE, JUST AS IT IS

This book does not offer academic theories, vague promises of enlightenment, or repetitions of general ideas about the Four Noble Truths. Rather it presents a practical approach for dealing with pain and hardship. It leads you along the path of exploring suffering—all suffering, but yours in particular—in order to reach a destination where you can experience what is called a "direct" or intuitive knowledge of the meaning of suffering in your own life. Through this intuitive knowledge, you

---

[2]   I am not presenting either C. G. Jung or T. S. Eliot as examples of fully enlightened beings. Biographers still debate flaws in each man's character. But I have come to the conclusion that at a certain point in each of their lives, they experienced remarkable insights. In part, each had these insights in response to their own struggles, and so it is with us. Being less than perfect, we can benefit from their gained wisdom, and suspend opinions and judgments for now.

can find a new relationship with your suffering that will bring you increased meaning, joy, and liberation, no matter how difficult your life may be.

Other spiritual teachers have offered advice on how to deal with pain and hardship. But it was the Buddha who specifically focused on liberation from suffering as the path to liberation in life. Other religions and methodologies (such as therapy) may offer techniques for coping with suffering and examining its origins, but they do not offer freedom from it in this manner. I have witnessed thousands of people—including psychotherapeutic professionals and their clients—successfully find their way along this path, opening themselves to unanticipated joy.

Let me be perfectly clear that in order to take the Buddhist approach, it is not necessary for you to adopt a creed, sacrifice your religion, or transform yourself into some new person. You simply must have faith in the possibility that understanding your suffering can bring about a radical change in how you experience life. In other words, you must suspend your doubt long enough to see for yourself what you are capable of realizing. At the same time, you should not underestimate this challenge, as it demands that you voluntarily show up for your own suffering with no agenda other than knowing the truth of it.

Dancing with Life is a very personal book in that every individual suffers through his or her own life experiences in a unique way. At the same time, it is a very impersonal book in that suffering—like happiness—is a universal stream flowing through each of us. Standing in the stream, we only experience the suffering that flows around us. Our view is only through our eyes—our context, body sensations, and emotions are unique. But all humans share suffering. Therefore the practices of mindfulness and meditation presented here can apply to and be harnessed effectively by everyone, regardless of age, gender, religion, or national background.

I feel confident that the Twelve Insights provide a way—not *the* way, mind you, but *a* way—into a more meaningful relationship with life. I base this judgment on my experiences over the last 37 years with my own meditation and yoga practice, as well as my experiences as a vipassana teacher. I can honestly say that I know of no better method of reflection and practice than that contained in the Buddha's teachings of these twelve insights. Penetrating suffering to this level spontaneously brings freedom and profound peace of mind.

May this book help you learn to dance with life—your life just as it is.

CHAPTER 2

MINDFULNESS
AND COMPASSION:
TOOLS FOR
TRANSFORMING
SUFFERING INTO JOY

The Buddha taught that suffering comes from ignorance. "Ignorance is the one thing with whose abandonment clear knowing arises," he said. By "ignorance" he meant the misperceptions and delusions that your mind has about its own nature, in short, being ignorant of the Four Noble Truths. Thus, the way to free the mind from suffering is through gaining *insight* into what truly is. Insight is a profound level of understanding that transcends mere intellectual cognition and can only be known by experiencing it. One of the tools the Buddha taught for gaining insight is *mindfulness*, the ability to be fully aware in the moment.

Mindfulness enables you to go beneath the surface level of moment-to-moment life experience, which is clouded with emotions, to clearly see the truth of what is happening. The untrained mind is just the opposite of mindfulness. It is often described as "monkey mind" because it is continually distracted by one thought, emotion, or body sensation after another. The monkey mind repeatedly identifies with the surface experience and gets lost in it. The insights that arise through mindfulness release the mind from getting caught in such reactivity and can even stop the cycle from beginning.

An important aspect of practicing mindfulness is "sampajanna," which translated means "clear comprehension"—the ability to see clearly what needs to be done, what you are capable of doing, and how it relates to the larger truth of life. Obviously it is not easy to be mindful in such a manner, let alone experience the deep insights that lead to full liberation, but you can develop mindfulness through the practice of meditation.

In this book, I use "mindfulness" to refer to both mindfulness in daily life and mindfulness meditation practice. You practice realizing the Twelve Insights by being mindful in your daily life activities and in meditation. As your practice of the Twelve Insights of the Four Noble Truths matures, the two blend together and you have less and less of a sense of separation between being meditatively mindful in daily life and practicing mindfulness in meditation.

MINDFULNESS IN DAILY LIFE

First let's look at how the insight from mindfulness might manifest in daily life. Suppose someone at work says something that upsets you and you become angry or defensive and react by saying something you later regret. The incident ruins your day because you can't stop thinking about it. Of course you are aware of your feelings; they have registered in your brain. But this kind of "ordinary awareness"—simply being conscious of your emotional reaction to an experience—is not what the Buddha meant by mindfulness.

Mindfulness enables you to fully know your experience in each moment. So when your colleague upsets you, if you are being mindful, you witness that her words generate thoughts and body sensations in you that lead to a strong emotion with still more body sensations. You have the insight that these feelings are being created by a chain reaction of thoughts in your mind. While this chain reaction is going on, you acknowledge how miserable it makes you feel. But instead of reacting with harsh words when you feel the impulse to speak unskillfully, you choose not to. Your mindfulness allows you not to identify with the impulses of your strong emotions or act from them. Moreover, because you witnessed the impersonal nature of the experience, you don't get stuck in a bad mood for the rest of the day. It is an unpleasant experience, but you are not imprisoned by it. When you are being mindful, you are aware of each experience in the body and mind and you stay with that experience, whether it is pleasant or unpleasant, such that you see what causes stress and harm to you or another and what does not.

MINDFULNESS AS A MEDITATION PRACTICE

It truly is possible to experience this wise awareness in your daily life, but you need to train yourself to do so, and mindfulness meditation is the most effective means to accomplish this. Through the practice of mindfulness meditation you develop your innate capacity to:

- Collect and unify the mind (at least temporarily)
- Direct your attention
- Sustain your attention

- Fully receive experience no matter how difficult
- Investigate the nature of experience in numerous ways
- Then let go of the experience, no matter how pleasant or unpleasant it may be

Formal meditation practice involves sitting in a chair or on a cushion in a quiet space with your eyes closed for a period of time and slowly training the mind. You can do so by simply sitting, doing nothing special, and just watching what happens, but the more common approach is to direct the mind by cultivating your power of attention. By being mindful, you train or condition your mind to be more mindful. It is not unlike training the body and mind to play the piano, dance the tango, speak a foreign language, or play a sport. You learn forms in order to train the mind, in the same way that a pianist learns scales. You learn what to pay attention to in the same way a dancer learns to feel the music and to be aware of her body and her partner's.

Mindfulness meditation training begins with practicing techniques for concentrating your attention on an object, which enables you to notice how your mind is reacting to what it is experiencing. Concentration is the ability to direct your attention and to sustain it so that it becomes collected and unified. It is a skill everyone already has, but for most people it is limited to only certain specific tasks and is not within their control. When concentration and mindfulness are combined, the power of attention is transformed into a spotlight that illuminates a particular experience in the same way that a theater spotlight holds steady on a single actor until it's time to focus the audience's attention elsewhere. You learn how to direct and sustain your attention on a single experience, rather than letting the mind jump from one thought or feeling to another as it usually does. In Pali the ability to direct attention is called "vitakka" and the ability to sustain it is called "vicara." The Buddha referred to these skills as "Factors of Absorption."

Traditionally, in vipassana meditation you use your breath initially as the object of concentration to collect and unify the mind. You typically stay with the experience of the breath as it touches the body in a single spot, such as the tip of the nose as it moves in and out, or the rise and fall of the chest, or the in-and-out movement of the belly, or the feeling of the breath in the whole body. There are many ways to follow the breath, including counting, noticing its speed, and making mental notes of what is happening, using labels such as "in" and "out" or "rising" and "falling." You can also learn to stay with the breath by coupling a word with each breath. Some teachers insist on a particular method of developing concentration, while others are more flexible. (A list of meditation instruction books is included in Appendix 3 of this book. Silent residential meditation retreats, which are the best way to learn mindfulness meditation, even for those who already have other meditation practices, are also listed.)

At first you won't be able to stay with the breath, but soon you will at least be able to be with one or two breaths throughout the complete cycle of inhalation and exhalation. You will also develop the ability to notice when your mind has wandered and to firmly and gently bring it back to the breath.

When your mind starts wandering, the breath becomes your anchor to which you return in order to stabilize and focus your attention. This anchor object is important because meditation is so hard to do. You may get distracted by what's worrying you or by some longing, or you may get bored, sleepy, or restless, or you may start doubting the whole process. Staying with the breath calms the mind, collects your scattered attention, and unifies the mind so that you are able to continue. It is never a mistake or a bad meditation if all you do is work on staying with the breath. Even when you constantly struggle and don't actually spend much time with the breath, it's good practice. By repeatedly returning to the breath, you are learning to just start over. Starting over is a key step in meditation. It expresses your intention to be present, and *the power of your intention is what determines your ability to be mindful in daily life.*

The manner in which you stay with the breath in meditation is called "bare attention"—you simply feel the movement of the breath and the body's response and notice whether the breath is warm or cool, long or short. You observe the arising of a breath, its duration, and its passing. You might stay with only one of these experiences or a combination of them. In practicing bare attention you don't judge the breath or think about how you might improve it. You simply register the experience of the breath without reacting to the experience with mental commentary or physical action.

MOVING BEYOND THE BREATH IN MEDITATION

Once you're somewhat able to stay present with the breath, you start to open your field of attention to ever-more-subtle objects of experience that arise in the mind. This process continues until you are able to respond to all of your experiences as opportunities for mindfulness. In order to meditate in this manner, the Buddha taught what are often called the Four Foundations of Mindfulness, in which you systematically learn how to pay attention to and investigate what arises in your mind, whether the experience comes from one of your five body senses or from the mind generating thought. The four modes of investigation he prescribed are:

- Knowing how any experience feels in the body (First Foundation),
- Noting the pleasant-, unpleasant-, or neutral-feeling tone that accompanies every moment's experience (Second Foundation),
- Witnessing your mental state and your emotions in the moment (Third Foundation), and finally:
- Opening to the impersonal truth of life that is revealed in this moment (Fourth Foundation).

These Four Foundations of Mindfulness and all the practices associated with them are described in depth in the Buddha's *Satipatthana Sutta*. By building your awareness utilizing these four foundations, you gradually develop clear seeing (sampajanna), the ability to be mindful in the present moment. In so doing you begin to have insight about what is true and how to respond skillfully in any situation.

When you are just beginning this practice, you serially investigate all Four Foundations of Mindfulness. For instance, if the mind is pulled away from the breath by a strong body sensation, then you temporarily abandon the breath as an object and let that body sensation become the object of your attention. When the mind gets tired of staying with the body sensation and starts to move to other objects, return to the breath. At this stage of practice you do not investigate your emotions or your mind states, only body sensations. The challenge is to sustain your attention on a particular body sensation in such a way that you can feel it. Is it a pulsation or a wave? Is it expanding or contracting? If it's painful, what kind of pain is it? Does it twist, stab, burn, pinch, and so forth? If it's pleasant, is it sweet, warm, tingly? In the First Foundation of Mindfulness the attention is to be focused on the body from within the body, meaning that you are not training your mind to be a distant, indifferent observer of your body; rather, you are being with your aching back.[3] This same method of keeping attention within the experience is used for all Four Foundations of Mindfulness.

The Buddha started vipassana practice with mindfulness of the body because for most people it is far easier to stay present with the body than with the mind and because the body participates in all other experiences you have in ordinary consciousness. He said, "If the body is not mastered [by meditation], then the mind cannot be mastered, if the body is mastered, mind is mastered."[4] He went on to say, "There is one thing, monks, that cultivated and regularly practiced, leads to a deep sense of urgency, . . . to the Supreme Peace . . . to mindfulness and clear comprehension, . . . to the attainment of right vision and knowledge, . . . to happiness here and now, . . . to realizing deliverance by wisdom and the fruition of Holiness: it is mindfulness of the body."[5]

Many experienced students of meditation tend to skip over the body and focus on the emotions and mind states, thinking they are getting to the really juicy part of practice, but as the Buddha's quote indicates, this is a significant misapprehension. Throughout this book I will encourage you to develop an almost continual awareness of your ever-changing body experience. I have found that cultivating this body-awareness is the surest way for most students to start to impact their daily life with their mindfulness practice. Therefore, as you move from the First Foundation of Mindfulness of the Body to the Second Foundation, remember that throughout the practice, you use the breath

---

[3]   Analayo. *Satipatthana: The Direct Path to Realization.* Windhorse Publications, 2006, p. 32.

[4]   Thera, Nyanaponika, *The Heart of Buddhist Meditation.* Weiser Books, 1966, p. 158.

[5]   Ibid.

as an anchor to collect and unify the mind while expanding your mindfulness to an ever-greater range of experience.

After you develop mindfulness of the changing nature of body experience, you are ready to work with the Second Foundation—the feeling tone of your experience. You start to include the pleasant, unpleasant, or neutral flavor contained in each moment of body sensation in your field of attention. You don't try to control these sensations but simply to know them. For instance, you notice how pleasant the warm sun feels on your face on winter mornings or how an aching leg feels unpleasant from within the experience. When body sensations are neither pleasant nor unpleasant, they are neutral. Ordinarily you don't notice the neutral sensations, but with mindfulness they become part of your awareness and expand your experience of being alive. Developing awareness of pleasant, unpleasant, and neutral sensations and how they condition the mind is a critical factor in finding peace and well-being in your life.

After you have worked with body sensations, you are ready to work with the Third Foundation, mental events (your emotions, mental processes, and mind states), in your meditation. At first just take emotions as a field for investigation. Notice when your mind is pulled away from the breath by an emotion. What is the nature of the emotion? How do you feel it in the body? In my experience, all emotions are accompanied by body sensations. What is an emotion, really, when you deconstruct it? Is it not an internal image, or words, or a pleasant or unpleasant feeling accompanied by many coarse or subtle sensations? I'm not referring to what caused the emotion, which is a combination of perception, belief, intent, and response, but rather to what happens when the mind registers an emotion. Does the mind keep feeling the emotion, or does it arise and pass like a body sensation? Remember to continue to use your anchor object so that you don't get lost in your emotions.

Many times you will discover that you do not know what emotion you are feeling or that there is more than one emotion competing for attention. In these instances, just be aware of emotions; do not try to name them. Likewise, sometimes you can't name a body sensation, so it only feels like numbness; numbness then *is* the body sensation. Don't insist on specificity; just be aware that there is a body.

Now you are ready to examine your mental processes. You will quickly notice that the mind is almost always thinking and that much of this thinking is based on the past or future in the form of remembering, planning, fantasizing, and rehearsing. Observe each of these. Are they pleasant or unpleasant? What happens to them as you turn your attention on them? Do they stop or intensify? Or do you get lost in them and lose your mindfulness? What underlies your constant planning? Is it anxiety? When you bring up a fear or worry over and over again, is it really unpleasant or does it induce a kind of reassurance? What happens if you stop? Is the constant worrying really a false reassurance? Does it actually induce a habit of anxiety? Remember to feel your mental processes from within them— the fuzziness and excitement of fantasy, the heaviness of worry and fretting, and the speed of planning. Notice what it is and how it then changes.

Finally, you are ready to experience the Buddha's insights as they manifest in your life—the life you have been examining until now, which includes your body sensations, emotions, mind states, and mental processes and the pleasantness and unpleasantness that accompanies each of them. With the Fourth Foundation of Mindfulness, you see how each moment constantly changes and that most of what you take personally is actually impersonal and is not about you. For instance, in our earlier example, the person at the office who upset you was not really focused on you, but was reacting to her own inner turmoil, and you just happened to receive the eruption. You also notice which mind states lead to suffering and which don't, and you begin to live more wisely.

WALKING MEDITATION IN MINDFULNESS PRACTICE

In daily life a continuous sense of body-awareness greatly facilitates knowing your emotions and remembering your true priorities. One effective technique for cultivating continuous mindfulness of the body is the practice of walking meditation. In the Theravada tradition, walking meditation is often done walking back and forth on a path that is 10 to 30 steps in length, either indoors or outdoors, for 5 to 45 minutes. You begin by standing at one end of your designated path and turning your attention to the body just standing still. Then you realize your intention to walk and to be present during the walking such that you directly experience the sensations in the leg and foot that you are moving. From this intention you mindfully start to walk your path. You can walk at a slow stroll, a very slow stroll, or at an extremely slow speed. Depending on the speed you are walking, you practice noting a certain level of detail in the body that comes from the movement. "Noting" means that you actually feel the sensation as sensation and make a mental note that you are doing so in order to keep yourself focused. Thus, if you are walking at a normal strolling pace, you might note, "right moving, left moving." If you are going at a very slow stroll, you might be able to feel the sensations of "lifting and placing" the feet and make a mental note as you feel them. If you are walking extremely slowly, you may have time to be aware of the sensations of lifting the foot, swinging the leg, and placing the foot, or maybe even more detailed sensations.

Again, you would use mental noting to keep yourself focused, although you do not have to always do the mental noting if the mind is really focused on physical sensation. For instance, you might notice the weight shifting in the foot or the thighbone moving in the hip socket. Walking meditation serves your mindfulness in many ways: It is a concentration practice that helps collect and unify your mind; it balances the energy buildup and emotional pressure that can sometimes arise in sitting meditation practice; it creates continuity of awareness; and through body-awareness you can experience insight that is just as profound as in sitting practice.

IMMEDIATE AND LONG-TERM BENEFITS OF MINDFULNESS MEDITATION

Being present or awake empowers your life. It gives you a presence that you feel and others can feel, and it opens you to the experience of being fully alive. Many people complain that something is missing in their lives or they have some vague sense of incompleteness, dissatisfaction, or unease with life. As you wake up, such emotions start to diminish and lose their hold on you. You also begin to realize you have more choice in how you react to whatever arises and you discover that it is genuinely possible to dance with life.

Mindfulness meditation strengthens the mind so that you can more easily be with difficult emotions or uncomfortable physical sensations that cause your mind to abandon the present moment. Mindfulness also strengthens the nervous system such that physical and mental pains don't have the same degree of "hurt" because the mind isn't contracting in anticipation of more pain in the future. For the first few years of practice you are literally reprogramming your nervous system to free it from habitual reactivity. This alone will bring much ease and flexibility to your mind.

The most life-changing benefits of mindfulness meditation are the insights, which arise spontaneously the way a ripened apple falls from the tree of its own accord. Insight is what changes your life. Through insight you realize what brings well-being to yourself and others as well as what brings stress, discomfort, and dissatisfaction into your life. Such insights can be small or quite dramatic. Moreover, they have a cumulative effect such that previous insights become building blocks for still more insights.

Each insight is a direct knowing or "intuitive knowing" of the truth of your experience as contrasted with the conceptual perception, which comes from your usual way of thinking. This direct knowing is what enables mindfulness meditation to have such impact in your life—you feel the truth of your experience, instead of conceptualizing it, reacting to it, or being lost in the past or the future.

During meditation, you will most often have personal insights about your life and how it has been conditioned. Such insights help you grow and understand yourself better, leading to a fuller life. For this reason, many psychotherapists teach their clients a simple form of mindfulness practice.

Less frequent, but having far greater impact when they arise, are the insights about the nature of life itself. These are universal insights about the ever-changing and impersonal nature of your life experiences. These universal insights are what constitute the Buddha's teachings of *dhamma* (in Pali) or *dharma* (in Sanskrit), which is often translated as "truth." For example, mindfulness meditation helps you realize the impersonal nature of difficult experiences, that they are just part of life. This is known as *anatta* or "not-self," the realization that much of what you previously identified as "you" is actually "neither me nor mine." Therefore you do not take defeat or loss as personal failures, and you are much less reactive to them. You also become aware of *anicca*, the rapid and endlessly changing nature of all things in life. Not-self and the constancy of change are basic characteristics of life, but the truth of them, in the sense of being life altering, can only be known through direct insight, which comes from mindfulness.

LIVING IN THE SACRED NOW

Another major benefit of mindfulness meditation practice is that it brings you into what is sometimes called the "sacred now." This is a state of being fully present such that you are both "in time" and "not in time." Mystics in most contemplative traditions throughout the ages have extolled this as an exalted state, but have seldom given instructions for how to achieve it. What most people discover once they start meditating is that they ordinarily spend much of their time not in the present, but lost in thoughts about the past and the future, whether planning, daydreaming, anticipating, remembering, or just spacing out. Your life isn't in the past or the future because at this moment you are not there to live it; both are just mental constructs based on the mind's ability to remember, conceptualize, and imagine. When you are stuck in either past or future thinking, you create suffering for yourself and miss much of the actual experience of the gift of having embodied consciousness. For instance, you go for a hike and see a beautiful sunset. At first you feel really alive and fully present as you watch the sky change colors, but then your mind starts judging and planning. You say to yourself, "I don't do this enough. I'm too lazy, I've got to be more disciplined and take time for myself. Now, if I would just do this once a month. I remember taking this hike a year ago and saying I would do this more. I really need to . . ." On and on the mind goes. Meanwhile, you're not actually experiencing the beauty that initially enthralled you. You have lost this moment to pointless judging, reminiscing, and fantasizing.

As shocking as it may be to realize, you spend most of your time some distance removed from what is actually happening in the present moment. You are lost in past associations, future planning, or caught in judging yourself or another. Or you've split from the experience and distanced yourself by conceptualizing it, constantly moving your attention, or daydreaming. This is true for body sensations, whether they're pleasant or unpleasant, as well as all the other senses and your thoughts themselves. Most of the time you do not stay with the music or even the friend you are listening to; you don't even stay present for your own thoughts, and certainly not your emotions. By developing mindfulness, however, you gain the power to be more fully present for your life and to have keen insight about it.

It is not that evaluating, planning, and remembering are unskillful activities—they are useful and are all part of a rich experience of life—but you obsess or get lost in them at the expense of being present for your own life. Mindfulness meditation establishes this capacity for being present. It retrains the mind and breaks it of its old, unskillful habit of tuning out.

T. S. Eliot describes the power of being present in the sacred now in this manner in *Four Quartets*:

You can receive this:
"on whatever sphere of being
The mind of a man may be intent
At the time of death"—that is the one action
(And the time of death is every moment)
Which shall fructify in the lives of others:
And do not think of the fruit of action.

Eliot is saying that there is only *this* moment in your life, and each moment is a death and rebirth. You only exist as a string of moments and you are new and different in each moment. It is only when you are present in a moment that you are capable of affecting your life or another's. You fail to notice this truth because life is constantly changing and because of the power of memory and association.

When Eliot cautions not to think of the fruit of your actions, he is echoing the Buddha's teaching of nonattachment. To be nonattached is "to care" and "to not care" simultaneously, which can only be realized as an insight, not as a concept. Through meditation and practice of the Twelve Insights in daily life, you slowly come to understand this paradoxical wisdom, which is the way to dance with life.

BOOK ONE

THE FIRST
NOBLE TRUTH

THE FIRST NOBLE TRUTH

WHAT IS THE NOBLE TRUTH OF SUFFERING? BIRTH IS
SUFFERING, AGING IS SUFFERING, AND DEATH IS SUFFERING.
DISASSOCIATION FROM THE LOVED IS SUFFERING, NOT TO GET
WHAT ONE WANTS IS SUFFERING . . .

THERE IS THIS NOBLE TRUTH OF SUFFERING: SUCH WAS THE
VISION, INSIGHT, WISDOM, KNOWING, AND LIGHT THAT AROSE
IN ME ABOUT THINGS NOT HEARD BEFORE.

THIS NOBLE TRUTH MUST BE PENETRATED TO BY FULLY
UNDERSTANDING SUFFERING . . .

THIS NOBLE TRUTH HAS BEEN PENETRATED TO BY FULLY
UNDERSTANDING SUFFERING . . .

—SAMYUTTA NIKAYA LVI, 11[6]

---

[6] Ajahn Sumedho. *The Four Noble Truths*. Amaravati Publications, 1992.

CHAPTER 3

YOUR LIFE IS INSEPARABLE FROM SUFFERING

The Buddha's teaching of the Four Noble Truths begins with the injunction that if you are to attain liberation, you must understand and fully experience how your life is entwined and defined by "dukkha," meaning your *mental experiences* of discomfort, pain, anxiety, stress, instability, inadequacy, failure, and disappointment, each of which is felt as suffering in your mind. This teaching is often referred to as the "Truth of Suffering."

Understanding the First Noble Truth involves the practice and realization of three specific insights about dukkha: first, realizing that the philosophical description that life seems to elicit feelings of dukkha at every turn is correct; secondly, gaining insight into your suffering by penetrating it with conscious awareness day by day, moment by moment; and finally, deeply accepting this truth as part of your life and that it affects how your mind reacts to all your experience.

The Buddha was a great pragmatist. As a spiritual teacher, he was interested in teaching what could be achieved through a persevering and patient practice; he was not interested in teaching metaphysics. A story tells of how the Buddha was walking through the forest one day with his students when he stopped to pick up a handful of leaves. Holding his hand out with the leaves in it, he asked, "Are there more leaves on all the trees in the forest or in my hand?" Naturally, they answered, "There are more leaves in the forest." "What I know is as great as the leaves on all of these trees," the Buddha replied, gesturing around the forest. "But what I teach is equal to this handful of leaves." What did the handful of leaves that the Buddha was holding represent? On numerous occasions he made it perfectly clear by declaring, "I teach only suffering and the end of suffering."

Oftentimes, the First Noble Truth is misquoted as "All life is suffering," but that is an inaccurate and misleading reflection of the Buddha's insight. He did not teach that life is constant misery, nor that you should expect to feel pain and unhappiness at all times. Rather, he proclaimed that suffering is an unavoidable reality of ordinary human existence that is to be known and responded to wisely.

The Buddha really understood the human predicament, didn't he? Even when your life is going well, you always feel the pressure to keep it going, the anxiety that it won't, the endless wanting of "more" or "different," and the frustration of being upset by life's constant little traumas and challenges. There is no lasting resting point for the unliberated mind, only some brief moments of appreciation and immersion, and then the mind starts worrying, planning, feeling tension all over again. Life is a never-ending dance between moments of feeling good and moments of feeling bad. The pleasant moments may be mildly enjoyable, positively joyful, or even ecstatic. Likewise, the unpleasant moments may be boring, irritating, painful, or overwhelmingly awful. While you, like all beings, may try your hardest to experience only the good and avoid the bad, there is simply no way for any of us to escape unpleasant experiences. They are part of the dance, life being true to its own nature.

It is vital to your experience of the Twelve Insights that you interpret "suffering" in the sense that the Buddha originally intended, as an umbrella term whose true purpose is to invite you to reflect on the *entire range of negative human emotional reactions*. The stress or unease that is dukkha—alienation, despair, uncertainty, lack of control, grief, frustration, fear, anger, longing—constitutes your mind and heart's resistance to life being simply as it is. Dukkha can also be understood as the *discomfort of inhabiting a body*, with all its physical vulnerabilities and pain. And it can refer to the *unease* you experience because you have conscious knowledge of how scary and uncertain life is and the inevitability of death. Sometimes the words *unsatisfactory* and *unreliable* are used to describe dukkha, for the way life can let you down when things don't go as you'd hoped and planned.

There is suffering that originates from external events and the suffering you experience because of how you process those events in your own mind. It is an *objective* fact that your life is filled with challenges, from illness to conflict with others to the death of loved ones. An outside observer witnessing your life would be able to confirm that this is so. But in addition to—or more accurately, in reaction to—these objective painful experiences, you also have an internal experience. Your mind is filled with a seemingly endless stream of emotions that arise in reaction to what's going on around you. It is this *subjective* type of suffering that the Buddha is primarily addressing in the First Noble Truth. As you deepen your understanding of this richer and more complex meaning of dukkha, you will find opportunities for freedom and well-being that you never even knew existed.

THE FIRST INSIGHT:

There is this Noble Truth of Suffering.

CHAPTER 4

HOW SUFFERING GOT A BAD NAME

REFLECTING ON THE FIRST NOBLE TRUTH

The First Insight empowers you to notice and investigate dukkha in your life and to be completely honest with yourself about the suffering you experience, which you may ordinarily ignore, or suppress, or blame on circumstances.

The first challenge you may face in knowing the Truth of Dukkha is resistance to the very idea of your own suffering. One of my students, Sasha, a married professional woman with children, maintained for years that she did not relate to the Four Noble Truths because there wasn't any suffering in her life! Sure, she had a few health and financial problems, and some emotional worries and disappointments, but these were not really suffering. In her view suffering only occurred if you experienced some devastating loss such as the death of a child. Her life was great, so how could she be suffering? She found the very idea humiliating, although she could not say why she felt that way.

Upon hearing the teaching of the Twelve Insights, Sasha realized just how much her mind suffered from all her wants, needs, and responsibilities. She saw that in denying the dukkha in her life, she actually prevented herself from responding wisely to it. She tended to perpetuate it rather than make changes, because to consider change was to admit the extent of her suffering. For Sasha, it was a personal defeat to make such an admission. I find that this holds true for many people. If you have a reasonably good life, you may strongly resist acknowledging the constancy of stress, uncertainty, and dissatisfaction that life inevitably brings for fear that it will diminish your self-esteem, lead to a loss of confidence or collapse, or turn you into a pessimist. You may feel it is important to hide your daily suffering from others for fear that they would think less of you, see you as a loser or a victim or someone not emotionally "together."

Such negative opinions are understandable because suffering has a bad name in Western society. Many, maybe most, people have a conscious or unconscious bias against the idea that their suffering is noble. It is ironic that this attitude prevails when just the opposite is true: Your suffering presents an opportunity for the most relevant, sophisticated, inspiring, and useful inquiry you could conduct in your life. The Buddha called the Truth of Dukkha "noble" precisely because suffering requires that which is most magnificent in you to come forth.

I sometimes joke with my students that our modern interpretation of suffering is so distorted that for the Buddha to teach the Four Noble Truths today he would have to rename them "One Crummy Truth and Three Noble Truths" or "The Horrible Truth of Suffering and Three Great Solutions." When restated in self-help jargon, it is easy to see the degree to which suffering has gained a bad reputation. We view it as a mistake, something shameful, or a sign of powerlessness and inadequacy.

Our culture's debasement of suffering represents a major loss to you. It denies the validity of many of the major emotional events in your life. It narrows your life such that you are constantly reacting to a set of questions: How do I get and keep what's pleasant and avoid or get rid of that which is unpleasant? Am I winning or losing? Am I being praised or blamed? It locks you into worrying about the future when the future is always uncertain and each day is made up of hundreds of small future moments that can bring up anxiety, excessive aggression, fear, and anxiousness. Look to your own life to see if this is true. Do you want the meaning of your life reduced to these teaspoon-sized measurements of attempting to gain control over what in the end cannot be controlled?

It wasn't always like this in Western culture. The Greek philosophers and playwrights understood the ennobling power of suffering. In fact, they placed it in high esteem, giving it context in their art and mythology. Just think of Homer's *Odyssey* and Odysseus's epic struggle to return home, and the Greek tragedies, such as *Oedipus*, in which the hero's suffering is portrayed as noble, even glorious. For hundreds of years, the Western mind took comfort in this Greek view of suffering, which gave it meaning and did not equate it with failure.

What happened? How is it that suffering no longer seems worthy of being considered noble? First of all, our culture evolved into one that is pleasure-based and ego-identified, and that emphasizes immediate gratification. It also began to define success as your ability to control outcomes. Today, we teach our children that if you are an effective person, you can control your life. You can get and do what you want. If you do, you win in life. This modern image portrays "winners" as people who have it all together. You are not supposed to have internal conflicts, stress, or anxiety—that means you are incompetent. You're a loser. This was the unrecognized view of the student who kept saying that she did not suffer.

Furthermore, our culture teaches you to constantly judge yourself based on superficial measures: How much money you make, the car you drive, the clothes you wear, the level of recognition and reward you attain at school and at work, how beautiful and athletic you are. But this perspective flattens life. It denies the possibility of finding a deeper meaning to your experience. If you measure your self-worth and effectiveness according to these superficial cultural standards, then each time you suffer you are forced to interpret suffering as humiliation. Why would you choose to acknowledge suffering if it only stands for failure?

Sasha, the student who denied her suffering, now reports that she feels more effective as a person because she is able to focus more directly on her internal experience of outward difficulties. She discovered that these internal reactions are much more responsive to her attention than the external circumstances over which she has little control. "It's like finally having a real relationship with myself," Sasha explained.

Recognizing the Dukkha in Your Own Life

Now that you have a broad understanding of what the Buddha meant by the Truth of Dukkha, and a context for seeing it as noble, you are ready to begin reflecting on how suffering manifests in your life. The Buddha identified three kinds of suffering: the dukkha of physical and emotional pain; the dukkha of constant change; and the dukkha of life's compositional nature, which creates a kind of pressure and unease that is constantly present, even in the best of times.

The first kind of dukkha is the obvious suffering caused by physical discomfort, from the minor pain of stubbing a toe, hunger, and lack of sleep, to the agony of chronic disease. It is also the emotional suffering that arises when you become frustrated that things don't go your way, or upset about life's injustices, or worried about money or meeting others' expectations. Each day you have many experiences that cause you to be disappointed, anxious, and tense, from getting stuck in traffic to forgetting to complete an important task to snapping at a loved one during an argument. Isn't this true? In matters of love, family, work, and self-acceptance, do you not experience these sorts of negative emotions over and over again?

In addition to the dukkha you experience as a result of painful, traumatic, and uncomfortable events, there is a second type of dukkha that you confront on a regular basis. That is the suffering caused by the fact that life is constantly changing. Doesn't it often seem as though the moment you have found happiness, it disappears almost at once? Something really good happens at work, or you and your partner spend an intimate morning in bed, or you share a precious laugh with your child, and then bang! It's over. Now you're worried about a deadline, or fighting with your significant other, or coping with your child's needs, and all those pleasant feelings are replaced by worry, fatigue, and the weight of responsibility. In truth, no moment is reliable because the next moment is always coming along fast on its heels. It is like a constant bombardment of change undermining every state of happiness. It is paradoxical, isn't it, that the one constant in your life is change.

Like everyone else, you do what you can to try to prolong, enhance, and increase the number of pleasurable moments in your life, but nothing consistently works. There is always the next moment of the dance. No matter how much you attempt to distract yourself (and you may be one of those people who are great at creating distractions), your nervous system still perceives the changing dance, even when you are not aware of it, and it suffers, oftentimes even more so because you are trying to ignore it.

No doubt you have felt the pain, confusion, and stress that this constant flux brings to your own life. The implications are vast: You make many choices every day within this context. You cannot escape from the continuous dance. It is an impersonal, universal truth of life. None of us—not even the wealthiest, the wisest, the most powerful—gets to be an exception. We all feel pain, we all lose loved ones, we all get ill, and we all die.

Furthermore, every day, even during the pleasant moments,

do you not experience an underlying unease about the future? This worry and anxiety is a manifestation of the third type of suffering the Buddha identified—life's inherent unsatisfactoriness due to its insubstantial compositional nature. Each moment arises due to certain conditions, then it just disappears. There is not a lasting or substantial "there there" in daily life, thus it is often described as being like a dream.

How often in your adult life have you experienced the queasiness and unease that come from a sense of meaninglessness in your life? Think of all those occasions when you felt as though you were wasting your life, or sleepwalking through it, or not living from your deepest, most heartfelt sense of your self. Remember the times when you've felt as though there is little you do each day that has any real, lasting significance. We've all fallen prey at some point in our lives to such dark times of self-doubt and existential angst.

What the Buddha is pointing to is that suffering is an experience of the mind. He's not offering you relief from pain; he's offering you relief from the extra mental reactivity that causes your misery. At first this can seem foreign, but in fact it's consistent with the roots of Western understanding of suffering. We've just lost our connection to it. Our ancient wisdom-bearers knew life was hard, and they too discovered that there was a difference between the pain of life and your reaction to it.

What the Word "Suffering" Really Means

Suffering is derived from the Latin word *ferre*, which means "to bear" or "to carry." Helen Luke, the late Jungian analyst and classics scholar, likens the true meaning of conscious human suffering to a wagon bearing a load. She contrasts this definition of suffering with *grief*, from the Latin word *gravare*, which refers to "the sense of being pressed down," and *affliction*, from the Latin word *fligere*, which means "to be struck down, as by a blow." When you deny or resist the experience of your own suffering, you are unwilling to consciously bear it. It is this resistance to accepting your life just as it is that makes suffering ignoble, despicable, and shameful. It is a mistake in perception that can cause you additional suffering. In the First Insight the Buddha asks you to carry your suffering without judgment and without resistance in just this manner, to bear it with compassion and mindfulness in your heart.

When you are overcome with resentment and aversion to suffering, your resistance is indeed an affliction. When you feel ashamed, depressed, and defeated by your suffering, it presses you down, causes you to contract. But if you can learn to separate your resistance to suffering from the actual pains and difficulties in your life, an incredible transformation takes place. You are able to meet your suffering as though you were a wagon receiving the load being placed on it. Paradoxically, the effect is that your load is lightened, and your life can roll forward, whatever its destination.

The first insight of the Truth of Dukkha is realized when you are able to distinguish between carrying the weight of your life with all its loss and pain, and collapsing underneath these difficulties. You nobly accept your suffering and acknowledge that your life is being characterized by it, despite your preference for it to be otherwise.

When you learn to be with the truth of your suffering and the suffering of those for whom you care in a mindful, compassionate manner, you are *ennobled*. Being able to bear your pain with dignity empowers you to examine your suffering and bring an end to it. This is why the Buddha starts the Four Noble Truths with suffering, because only the *noble ones*, those who can stay with the Truth of Dukkha, are able to realize the Twelve Insights.

THE SECOND INSIGHT:

This Noble Truth must be penetrated to by fully understanding suffering.

CHAPTER 5

FEELING THE "OUCH"
OF YOUR SUFFERING

DIRECTLY EXPERIENCING
THE FIRST NOBLE TRUTH

Now that you have gained some understanding of the nature of suffering from your mental investigation of the Truth of Dukkha, you are ready to explore it directly as a felt experience. "Suffering is to be known," the Buddha said. This is the practice of the second insight of the First Noble Truth—penetrating dukkha directly. Penetration occurs when you consciously choose to be mindful of the actual experience of pain, stress, and emotional distress as it manifests in your body, mind, and heart.

What we ordinarily lump together under the label "suffering" the Buddha called a "tangle," meaning a complex of physical and emotional stimuli registering in your brain and your mind's reaction to these stimuli. The Buddha taught that to penetrate suffering you must deconstruct this tangle, but you can't conduct this practice as a detached observer, as though you were a barcode scanner that reads the prices of groceries in the supermarket. On the contrary, in order for you to *know* its true nature you must be with your suffering as a lived physical experience and willingly feel the "ouch" of it in your own life. These two different ways of *knowing* also have historical precedence in Western culture. The ancient Greeks had one word for direct or intuitive knowing, *gnorizo*, and another, *exero*, for knowing with the mind.

It's Not Easy to Feel Suffering

In his core teaching on the Four Foundations of Mindfulness, the Buddha gave explicit instructions on how to use mindfulness techniques to penetrate and free yourself from suffering (see Chapter 2). He says that you must know every experience of the body and mind from within the experience itself: The breath is to be felt within the breath, the body within the body, the feelings of pleasant, unpleasant, and neutral within these feelings, the state of the mind within the actual experience of the state of the mind.

Even experienced students of meditation and the dharma are often confused about the Buddha's instruction to penetrate dukkha as an embodied experience. They mistakenly think that *mental* recognition of their difficult emotions and physical pain suffices for them to begin their journey to freedom. "After all," a student named Rick told me recently, "I've had plenty of suffering in my life, and of course I've felt the suffering; otherwise I wouldn't know that I've suffered!" Although Rick's statements are true enough, they miss the Buddha's point entirely: Intellectual recognition of emotional and physical discomfort or misery isn't sufficient to penetrate suffering; you must learn to be with what I call the "felt sense" of your suffering.

Rick understood his experience of suffering only on a surface level as physical and mental events that registered in his mind as unpleasant and stressful. He had not penetrated the tangle of his mind. As a result meditation had brought him little relief in his daily life, despite the fact that he had attended meditation retreats for a decade. Rick was very disappointed that he continued to get caught up in his emotional issues. Recently, when he learned that he had a serious physical ailment, he became bitter about the distress it caused him. "Why isn't my practice helping me to not be discouraged?" he demanded to know.

I suggested to Rick that he practice *being with* his suffering rather than trying to make it go away. After two more silent meditation retreats, during which he struggled greatly, Rick finally opened to the pain, anger, and unease that his health challenge was causing him. "I had no idea that I was veering away from my suffering so much. Boy, was I ever making myself miserable," Rick told me during an interview at the end of the second retreat. He had not been able to see what was going on in his own mind. He had been deluded, caught in the hidden demand that things be other than they are.

Like Rick, you may resist the direct knowing of your suffering because the knowing itself is often unpleasant at first. You may have developed a habit of turning away from it. Emotional pain in particular is difficult to confront head-on. It is much easier to react to your discomfort by turning it into anger or frustration with another or yourself, to distract yourself from it through recreation or work, or to just shut down that part of your mind.

When something difficult arises, the mind often wants to jump in to comment on it, or try to fix it, or move away from it—anything but stay with it. This may seem like healthy, self-protective behavior, but the truth is that if you can't be fully present with the difficult moments, chances are you won't be present with the best moments of your life, either. In other words, when you work directly with your capacity for being with pain, you are also working directly with your capacity for being with joy.

This Moment Is Like This

Ajahn Sumedho repeatedly says, "This moment is like this," which sums up the sense of being fully present that you are trying to capture with the second insight of the First Noble Truth. Making "this moment is like this" a focus of your mindfulness practice can be an effective technique for understanding the difference between skillfully observing a difficult experience from within and unskillfully getting lost in the content of that experience. So when you're meditating, you would practice noticing, "Back pain [or any other body sensation] feels like this," and "Disappointment [or any other emotion] feels like this." But you can also focus your meditation inquiry on a particular life issue. Take for example a painful situation at work. You find out that your company is planning to lay people off, and your first thought is, "Oh, what if it's me?", followed by the mental anguish of imagining getting fired. This is accompanied by a physical reaction. Perhaps you feel nauseous, or your body becomes flushed with heat and your heart starts pounding. Very quickly you start telling yourself a story about how difficult your life will be once you've lost your job, and your mind replays the story 100 times. When that happens you are getting lost in an imagined story about the experience and creating dukkha for yourself. Instead, turn the situation into the focus of a mindful meditation inquiry and return to your actual experience, which is your physical and mental unease. Your only possibility for release is to acknowledge, "My work situation feels like this in this moment." In time you will see that just being with the experience brings dramatic relief.

In all aspects of your life, you come to fully know your experience of suffering by noticing its specific qualities. Back pain may be felt as throbbing, piercing, or contracting, whatever the experience is in the moment when it is occurring. "Back pain is like this," you tell yourself, which points to the impersonal nature of suffering. This is simply the experience that emerges when certain causes and conditions come together. Likewise, you may know anger as a sensation of heat and tension in your body and a feeling that your mind is fixated and confused.

You have a personal, unique experience of suffering in knowing that "anger feels like this." But the underlying difficulties that cause you to become angry are universal. As with back pain, when anger arises there is no need to identify with the experience, to become more miserable by taking the events personally. It is just another moment of life dancing, and you respond to it as best you can.

When you are able to be fully present in this way and to say, "This moment is like this," you will experience a new kind of confidence. It is not that you immediately become fearless in the face of suffering, but your fear becomes just one more naturally arising experience, and so your suffering loses some of its power to control your life.

The Inner Fire We Call Suffering

The Buddha frequently used the image of fire when explaining suffering. In one well-known teaching, he describes how to the untrained mind every sense gate can be a source of suffering: "The eye is burning," he said, "visible things are burning, the contact of the eye with visible things, be they pleasant or unpleasant, is burning." In other words, anything you become identified with will burn you. It is either immediately a cause of suffering or will become one in time.

Ironically, exposing yourself to the heat is how you begin the journey that will eventually put out the flames. If you don't submit yourself to the fires of your dukkha—your pains, losses, frustrations, as well as your likes and dislikes—they will consume you. It took Rick a decade to learn this inescapable truth.

Only by experiencing your internal responses to life's inherent stress around getting and keeping what you like and avoiding or enduring what you don't like can you know suffering in a manner that will ultimately free you from its grip. The Buddha referred to this state when the mind is no longer consumed by suffering as *nibbana*. The pains of life do not disappear, but rather their ability to burn you ceases. What you see with your eyes, touch with your body, taste with your tongue, smell with your nose, hear with your ears, and think with your mind may be pleasant and enjoyable, or unpleasant and quite painful, but they no longer burn; you are not in a state of suffering.

In the poem *Four Quartets*, T. S. Eliot's description of the process of transforming suffering into joy by embracing the suffering echoes that of the Buddha. He was writing as a Christian, yet he too pointed to the necessity of penetrating suffering, as paradoxical as it initially seems.

The only hope, or else despair
    Lies in the choice of pyre or pyre—
    To be redeemed from fire by fire.

When Eliot says "pyre or pyre," he is referring to two ways of experiencing suffering—mindful versus reactive. Similarly, Ajahn Chah points to this same freeing insight when he says, "There are two kinds of suffering: the suffering that leads to more suffering and the suffering that leads to the end of suffering."

If you try to deny the truth of dukkha or run from it, you will be consumed by your desires, dislikes, and fears. The sole solution is to open to the fires created by the discomfort of your mind and body in such a way that you are transformed by the heat, softened, and made stronger by it.

Being present with your dukkha is a daunting task because it means that you must abandon many of your mental defenses (including denial, rationalization, blaming, and judging) against life's assaults. Essentially, the Buddha is asking you to embrace your own unease, to submit to the undeniable reality of your vulnerability in this human form, and to open your heart to the truth of life just as it is. In Buddhism, this recognition of "the way things are" is referred to as *tathata* or the "suchness" of the moment.

At first, being with the suchness of your own suffering may seem a pointless, uncomfortable, indulgent, or self-pitying practice. But you'll be surprised to discover that rather than being morose or unpleasant as most people anticipate, it is actually calming, relieving, and empowering. *Long before you find final liberation from the cause of your suffering, just learning to be with it brings enhanced peace and meaning to your life.* By simply choosing to be present with your pain, you signal your willingness to be transformed, to allow the purification process to begin. When you embrace life just as it is and just as you are, it ignites a mysterious process of inner development. You are voluntarily submitting to the purging fire of the felt experience. You will feel more authentic and be aware of a fuller, richer, more vital presence in yourself; others will notice as well. For this reason, I often tell students that if they only gain the insights of the First Noble Truth and never go farther on the path, their lives will still be immeasurably improved.

FEELING THE THREE KINDS OF SUFFERING

As I described in Chapter 4, the Buddha identified three kinds of suffering that we should seek to bring into our awareness through direct experience. They are: the dukkha of physical and mental pain (*dukkha-dukkha*); the dukkha of constant change (*viparinama-dukkha*); and the dukkha of life's compositional nature (*sankhara-dukkha*).

No doubt you know dukkha-dukkha well, for it represents the vast collection of physical and emotional hurts that everyone undergoes in life, from sickness and injury to failure, abuse, and basic everyday anxiety. Included in this category of distress are all the aversions you feel to others, to yourself, and to your circumstances, as well as the disappointment you feel when you do not get something you want.

In order to directly experience this type of dukkha, you must walk consciously into the fire by opening your heart to all of life's pain. If your back is hurting, for instance, place your awareness on that experience. Go to where the "ouch" is and observe how agitated your mind becomes or how it wants to distract itself from the awareness. It is in this way that you come to know that "back pain is like this."

When pain is present, you first turn bare attention to it, as I described in the instructions on mindfulness. You don't resist that it is there; instead, you become interested in it. Then if you can relieve it, you do so. Often, though, it is not possible to relieve pain. It stays around until the circumstances that created it change. At first it may seem like the pain is constant. But in reality it isn't; your mind is creating the illusion that the pain is constant. Actually, what's happening is your mind keeps jumping back to the pain and then becomes reactive to it. You can't *fully receive* and explore the experience of the pain because the reactive mind keeps jumping around. There is no *penetration* of the pain, only resistance to it.

The practice of the second insight is to be with what's difficult without being reactive, and this takes time and patience. So you examine the pain for a while, then, rather than exhausting the nervous system by constantly being with what's difficult, you move your attention to other experiences that you are having in your body or your mind. After giving the nervous system a rest, you return your attention to what's causing your discomfort.

You also practice penetrating the dukkha of a painful emotional experience just as though it were a physical pain. You will quickly discover that all emotional pain is reflected in the body. The next time you become angry because a stranger is rude to you, or you get into an argument with your partner, or your teenage daughter misses her curfew, pay close attention to the emotions and sensations that arise in your mind and body. Experience what it actually means for your "hackles to rise." Feel how the skin on your arms prickles as the hairs stand on end. Observe how your pulse quickens and your breathing becomes more rapid. Notice the blood rushing to your face. In the end, you'll have a felt sense of the entire experience of anger, from its very beginnings at the edges of your awareness to your manifestation of it. You gain the authority of knowing your suffering by actively staying with your dukkha in this way.

The second type of suffering the Buddha described is

viparinama-dukkha, the dukkha that arises from *anicca*, or life's constantly changing nature. As you well know, there is never a moment when you can claim, "Now that's fixed forever; I do not have to worry about that anymore." Everything is in a perpetual state of flux. Therefore you're always guarding against things going wrong, fixing what has already gone awry, and trying to minimize how much things veer off course in the future. Modern philosophers from Sartre to Kierkegaard have described this as an existential dilemma, literally the fearfulness of existence. What they failed to understand was the solution that the Buddha offered.

The never-ending arising and passing of pleasant and unpleasant moments is so pervasive that it is easy to get so habituated to it that you do not notice the stress and dissatisfaction it evokes in your mind. Therefore you may experience this dukkha only as underlying anxiety. Or you may have a general feeling of frustration and inadequacy that spoils what should be a happy or peaceful time. Or else you may try to deny the truth that all things change; this resistance steadily drains your life energy and you suffer from fatigue or ennui.

The truth of the dukkha of change goes against the ethos of modern Western culture, which promotes an unrealistic expectation that you can manage your life to be secure against unwanted change. This false promise that you can maintain control creates an expectation that is a cause of suffering in itself, for you are bound to fail in this endeavor. Of course, you should act as wisely as possible to manage change in your life— to do otherwise would be folly. But the difference lies in your attitude and expectations. Can you be at ease with its unpredictable, uncontrollable nature?

It is undeniably true that the circumstances that bring you the greatest joy also cause you the greatest pain when you lose them or they come to an end. Oftentimes, when a tragedy occurs, the happiness you had magnifies the agony of your loss. Worse still, anticipation of a possible loss lingers in your mind at all times, recognized or not. It creates worry, anxiety, a feeling of incompletion or of not enough, or that something more needs to be done. Therefore, any time you experience joy, you also experience an accompanying feeling of its temporariness.

The third type of suffering, sankhara-dukkha, is by far the subtlest and hardest to recognize. It arises because all things in this life are of a conditional, ephemeral nature. Each moment of experience is composed of five components—contact, feeling, perception, mental formations, and consciousness—which the Buddha referred to as "sankharas," meaning "collections" or "aggregates." These components combine so quickly that you ordinarily never notice it's happening; however, it registers in the nervous system as effort or tension. These phenomena of experience arise and pass in less than an instant one after another in a constant stream, which you perceive as a solid event but which is not.

The compositional nature of life can result in even the most pleasant moments having a subtle undertone of oppressiveness, an unexplainable feeling that existence itself is burdensome. Sometimes people describe feeling as though just being alive takes effort. Since each moment of experience is an aggregation, there is tension inherently holding it together, which the unliberated mind perceives as stressful. For instance, you may have had moments when you've felt fatigue at having to brush your teeth one more time, or of having to eat once again, or of doing something that is ordinarily one of your favorite activities. In certain meditative states of deep absorption, the mind becomes so still and subtle that you can feel this stress arise with each moment of experience, which can be quite disillusioning when you first notice it.

I sometimes refer to sankhara-dukkha as being *"bittersweet"* because although it is present in difficult moments, it also pervades even those moments that are most dear. Without naming it, poets and philosophers have long lamented this type of dukkha and how it can undermine feelings of happiness and joy. Often the stress or dissatisfaction with life that is caused by sankhara-dukkha is not recognized, but the lack of awareness makes it no less disquieting to the mind. Sankhara-dukkha blunts the edge of joy such that you can't fully open to it.

When you first open to the direct experience of dukkha, it may seem that life is worthless; you may start to feel unease, hopelessness, or even bitterness in your life. But this is not what the Buddha intended; he often talked about "happiness here and now." Feeling the Truth of Dukkha is not about denouncing life, but rather finding a way to consciously dance with life.

Opening to Your Own Dukkha

The challenge of knowing dukkha can be separated into two steps. The first is to embrace the personal distress and unease that arise from the difficulties you face in your own life. A second step is to confront the overwhelming anguish that humans and other living beings everywhere undergo and the cruelty they exert against one another. You discover in this second step that the universal nature of suffering is a major cause of your own pattern of dread, denial, and avoidance of suffering.

Let's start with a meditation inquiry into your own dukkha. Like many people, you may be reluctant to acknowledge your own problems and difficulties as suffering, preferring to claim, "I have some challenges, but I'm not like those other people. My

life is pretty good. All this 'fire of suffering' business is for the
less fortunate." You thereby seek to maintain false pride and
avoid feeling branded as a loser. Or perhaps you seek to ignore
your suffering by adopting the attitude, "Life's tough, now let's
get on with it." Or perhaps you attempt to defend yourself from
the truth of suffering by telling yourself, "This teaching about
confronting dukkha sounds too much like psychobabble to me,"
or "It represents negative thinking."

If any of these scenarios hold true for you, then you have yet
to comprehend the Buddha's point about the inevitability of
suffering, and you may be feeling resistance to his prescription
that you open yourself to the dukkha in your own life. I understand your reservations. But keep in mind, no one—not me, nor
the Buddha—is asking you to emotionally collapse into your
suffering, or to act like a victim, or to spend all your time ana-
lyzing everything that happens to you. You're only being asked
to show up for your life in a new, more complete manner. If the
Buddha's way does not prove valuable to you, you can always
revert to your old style of being. But if it is of service, then
think of how much you stand to gain in finding freedom from
your suffering.

Alternatively, you might honestly feel that you are not enti-
tled to claim your mental anguish as suffering—it is not sufficiently severe when viewed in the context of the extreme
examples of suffering that exist in the world. The Buddha is
very clear that attempting to make such comparisons represents
unskillful thinking. "One should not look to be the same as,
better than, or worse than," he said. Forget about trying to
measure your own struggles on a scale of universal magnitude.
Simply stay in the present moment, and see what actually
holds true in your experience. Remember, with the second
insight you are not being asked to intellectually consider the

unsatisfactoriness and distress of life, but rather to notice how it *feels* in your body and mind.

OPENING TO THE DUKKHA OF OTHERS

Now, still staying attuned to your body sensations, shift your attention to contemplating the dukkha of others. Start by confronting the pain, disappointment, and uncertainty experienced by those you love and those with whom you are in regular contact. You witness their discomfort in close proximity and often feel it as your own. This empathetic anguish can prove quite exhausting, in part because you are usually helpless to do anything to relieve their suffering. This dukkha alone would seemingly ruin any sense of individual happiness you might have found if you really opened to it.

Then there is the suffering of those you do not know but witness in your daily life or hear about through the news media—homeless and mentally ill people living on the streets, millions of people dying every day because of AIDS, war, terrorism, homicide, and brutal dictatorships. The sheer quantity as well as the diversity and extremity of human suffering can overwhelm you. When you open yourself to such horrors, it is natural to feel unsafe, to lose any belief in goodness, to let go of the zest you have for life. Seeing only widespread suffering, you may be tempted to view the world as a ghastly place.

Alternatively, it may seem that your only choice is to shut it all out and become numb to the misery that surrounds you. Therefore, you may try to distort your view so that you see only the pleasant aspects of life.

However, neither drowning in the world's suffering nor denying the reality of it offers a viable long-term solution.

Nor does either course, while legitimate, excuse you from the task of opening to the dukkha of all beings. The Buddha tells us that universal suffering, even in all its horrific quantity and variety, must be felt, and fully received. Why is this so? Why do you need to put yourself through all this? First of all, because it is only when you have seen for yourself the truth that dukkha is everywhere and therefore unavoidable that you are able to realize that depending upon life going according to your wishes and plans is not a reliable path to happiness. Joy and pain are opposite sides of a single coin that represents the duality of the human experience. The Buddha knew how easily your mind finds ways to resist, rationalize, and outright lie to itself about the dissatisfactory nature of life in order to justify avoiding the difficult work of true liberation. However, once it comes face-to-face with suffering on a global and individual scale, the rational mind cannot deny the reality of dukkha.

Secondly, the Buddha taught that most of the boundaries between yourself and others are illusionary. Take, for example, a child whom you love. When that child is sick or in danger, do you not suffer as though you were the child? Experiencing the suffering of others encourages you to see how linked we all are. Therefore, you will choose not to harm others and to contribute when and where you can to relieving others' pain.

I am not suggesting that you constantly look for suffering in the world or immerse yourself in the pain of life. Nor must you always keep the suffering of others in mind. Acting in that manner will only serve to make you dispirited and bitter. Moreover, the Buddha taught that dukkha always occurs within each person's mind and body so that there is no one person who experiences all the suffering in the world. What you are trying to do is to see the truth of the ubiquitous nature of suffering.

Life is stressful and uneasy for all people everywhere; there is no way to escape pain and loss or be exempt from it. The practice of the second insight is to fully acknowledge your experience of this truth.

THE CRUX OF PENETRATING DUKKHA

As you become mindful of the three kinds of dukkha that you and all others must undergo, you may feel discouraged or overwhelmed at times. You may ask, "Why would I want to focus on this? It is so sobering." The answer is that you must begin where you are, not where you would like to be. Where else could you begin? How else could you penetrate suffering unless you consciously explore it? Bringing mindfulness to your life is a far better choice than having no conscious relationship to the journey of your life.

Now you can better understand Eliot's admonishment to be "redeemed from fire by fire." For being mindful of the fires of dukkha will burn up any illusion you have of achieving lasting happiness through trying to get things to be just as you want them. This is a necessary, vital insight. You first awaken to your dilemma—that life is like this—before you are able to consciously go forward with your journey. A deep understanding of suffering empowers you to see the cause of your suffering and, as you will see, once you understand the cause of suffering you can free yourself from it in both small and large ways.

Let me be perfectly clear: The practice of knowing suffering as the Buddha teaches it does not mean feeling sorry for yourself, or becoming masochistic, or negative, or pessimistic. On the contrary, it is a practice that leads to an insight that in and of itself brings you a certain measure of freedom. The insight is simple: *Life is like this*. It is foolish and harmful to deny and resist the very nature of existence. In refusing to accept the inevitable, you only give it more power. Once you have experienced the existence of dukkha directly in your own life and the lives of those around you, then you start to see how identified and entangled you are with it. And from there, you start to untangle yourself from it, to find meaning and joy in life's dance just as it is.

THE THIRD INSIGHT:

This Noble Truth has been penetrated to by fully understanding suffering.

CHAPTER 6

THE CALL TO KNOW
THAT YOU KNOW

KNOWING THAT YOU KNOW
THE FIRST NOBLE TRUTH

Ajahn Sumedho refers to the Third Insight as the call to "know that you know." He is saying that you must allow yourself to be consciously reshaped by what you have learned through your practice of the preceding insights. You embrace what you realized in the first two insights such that the Truth of Dukkha becomes your new reality and you develop the ability to live more wisely right now. Your entire perspective on life shifts as you reach this level of verified truth. You are altered in a manner that is obvious to the knowing eye of your teachers and those preceding you on the path, as well as to yourself. Without the integration called for in the Third Insight, the insight you realize in one moment is lost in the next, and there is no sustained benefit to your life.

THE SHADOWY SHORTCOMINGS
OF COMPARTMENTALIZATION

Why is the integration of the insights you've attained so challenging? It all has to do with the way the mind works. The human mind, among its many wondrous capacities, has a remarkable ability to compartmentalize. One benefit of compartmentalization is that it enables you to cope with traumatic experiences by filing them away rather than generalizing them to the rest of your life. For instance, you may have been injured in a terrifying car wreck, had an unpleasant relationship with a significant other, or been the victim of an unjust situation at work. Yet you are able to let each of these experiences stand on its own and appreciate it as a unique occurrence. You do not become afraid to drive or have a serious relationship ever again, nor do you become bitter toward all bosses.

Likewise, in order to be successful in your job, you sometimes may have to behave in a more cool, impersonal manner toward others than you would prefer. But you are able to compartmentalize this adaptation of your behavior. You manage to limit it to the office, while remaining personal and open with friends and family at home. These are just two examples of the innumerable benefits of the ability to compartmentalize.

However, compartmentalization also has its shadowy shortcomings. It can lead you to become so good at separating yourself from your emotions that you no longer know what you feel. And it can serve as an excuse for inappropriate behavior. You may feel indignant when others act irresponsibly yet forgive yourself for acting irresponsibly in a similar situation because you compartmentalize your moral judgments. You hold yourself to a different standard. For example, you get upset when you find out that friends have gossiped about you, but if you look carefully you're likely to discover that under the guise of "sharing news" about your friends you're actually gossiping.

An especially dramatic pitfall of compartmentalization is

that you can learn a huge lesson about yourself in a particular situation or part of your life, but find that you are unable to generalize what you've learned. What happens to you in one situation does not get applied to the rest of your life.

This inability to integrate your hard-won insights and understandings can severely limit your psychological and spiritual development. For instance, you may be trapped in a lie and think, "I'm glad I learned that lesson. I must remember to tell the truth." But then you turn around and tell a lie again six weeks later. Or have you ever experienced a moment of deep understanding about what really matters to you, only to be shocked months later when you reexperience the very same insight and realize that you haven't once referenced it in your life in the meantime? Humbly, you have to acknowledge the fact that despite how much impact the insight seemed to have, it was not enough of an impact to change your mental habits or your behaviors.

What this means is that you can only begin to feel as though you have fully realized an insight when it becomes firmly rooted in your mind and heart. Being rooted means that you have constant access to it—the insight becomes part of the framework you use to interpret whatever arises in the body and mind. It means avoiding compartmentalization and consciously seeking to integrate the insight into your life as a whole.

The Buddha understood this phenomenon of the human mind and its consequences. And he realized that in order for the Four Noble Truths to be valuable, your realization of them must be perpetually awake and readily available. Hence the Buddha's third insight for each Noble Truth, as described in the *Samyutta Nikaya*, is the realization that "this Noble Truth has been penetrated by full understanding" or "knowing that you know."

THE THREE EMPOWERMENTS THAT COME FROM KNOWING THAT YOU KNOW

The realization of the third insight empowers you in three ways. First, only by knowing that you know will you have a base of insight that will allow you to realize the remaining insights. Otherwise you will get stuck in your thoughts and emotions. While you may mentally understand the Buddha's teachings about suffering, its causes, and its cures, you will struggle to fully realize the teachings in your life. Thus, the understanding provided by the third insight serves as preparation for a further unfolding of your dance with life.

Second, by enabling you to integrate the insights into your daily existence, knowing that you know allows the dharma to make a substantial transformation in how you live your life right now. In this way, the understanding provided by the third insight serves as a skill for living wisely in the present moment.

Finally, knowing that you know is an end in itself. Ajahn Sumedho describes this state as "Buddha knows the dharma," when your true nature is in touch with itself. The result is what I call an "embodied presence": You become a person who walks your talk because you're consciously willing to bear your suffering. With the integration of each truth, your wisdom grows and this sense of embodied presence becomes stronger and stronger.

INTEGRATING THE FIRST NOBLE TRUTH

Now that you have some context for understanding the role that the third insight plays in each of the Noble Truths, let's return to our work with the First Noble Truth—your life is inseparable from suffering. You gained the first insight by examining your personal experience and verifying that the teaching holds true in your own life: You are, in fact, constantly confronting dukkha. You have felt the physical pain of sickness as well as the emotional pain of neglect or abuse; you've experienced the stress that arises from the way life constantly changes; you have suffered from losing someone dear to you, either through physical or psychological separation.

Next, despite feeling lost and clueless much of the time, you sat with your pain rather than running away from it, practicing mindfulness until you finally felt as though you penetrated dukkha. You attained the second insight: You really have experienced suffering. You have personally seen it from all sides in the gross and subtle aspects of your life and the lives of others. You can feel exactly what the Buddha meant when he said, "Life is dukkha." You got it! You can't wait to apply the First Noble Truth in your own life. You see yourself becoming perhaps not free from suffering, but certainly less caught up in it, more able to respond rather than react to it. You imagine a new feeling of spaciousness in your daily existence.

Yet somehow it doesn't work out that way. You turn out to be the same old you, with the same anxieties, unease, and uncertainty. You wonder why your experience of the second insight didn't impact your life as you thought it would—that is, if you're even aware of the fact that you experienced it. On those fleeting occasions when you do remember the Truth of Suffering, it feels like a distant memory. It's just a concept; there is no felt sense of it.

"What happened?" you ask yourself. "I really had it, or at least I think I did." It may seem confusing or mysterious, but the answer to your question is quite simple: You forgot an entire practice. You failed to complete the integration of the First Noble Truth.

Without the third insight, you aren't present to remember to apply your knowledge of the Truth. Your great understanding of the Truth of Suffering will be filed away in the mental compartment labeled "Spiritual and Psychological Development" as opposed to being interwoven into the thousands of moments that compose your daily life.

So how do you fully integrate the third insight of the First Noble Truth and ground yourself in the reality of suffering in a lasting way? You start by finding your beginner's mind.

CULTIVATING BEGINNER'S MIND

The first time you hear the Third Insight it doesn't sound very encouraging as a practice, does it? Nor should it. "The way is difficult and uncertain," warned the sages of old. There is no magic pill you can swallow that will give you an immediate and lasting understanding of suffering. It takes work. Ridding yourself of the fantasy that spiritual liberation can or should be fast and easy allows real movement to happen.

It is necessary to start your inner journey with humility. You must acknowledge the fact that you do not know how much you'll be able to achieve, or even how well you understand the task at hand. T. S. Eliot described it in *Four Quartets* this way:

> In order to arrive at what you do not know
> You must go by a way which is the way of ignorance . . .
> And what you do not know is the only thing you know . . .

If you already knew how to live more harmoniously, you would do so. But you don't, so you open to the possibility of finding freedom from suffering while still in a state of ignorance. You might think, "I am too uncomfortable," or "I do not know what to do next, therefore I should just quit." But the opposite is true: You are at your beginning. You are starting with what you do *not* know.

Therefore, in meditation and in daily life, you practice moving into the state described by the Zen master Suzuki Roshi as "beginner's mind," and called "don't know mind" in the Theravada tradition. Beginner's or don't know mind is empty of preconceived notions about what it is supposed to be and expectations as to what it can achieve. To achieve beginner's mind, the ego has to give up the idea of its omnipotence.[7] It must accept its own defeat, thus enabling the "don't know mind" to arise. Only when your ego surrenders can you move forward in your pursuit of the truth and gain access to the more subtle understandings. It may seem like a paradox, but it is easy to verify for yourself: Simply notice how the ego insists on getting in the way of your attempts to learn, change, and grow.

The next step in establishing beginner's mind requires you to forsake your desires and ideas about what you will accomplish. The promises of achieving the third insight—preparation for further unfolding, the ability to live wisely right now, an embodied awareness of suffering—all sound exciting and worthy of your diligence, do they not? These empowerments may elicit zeal and inspire you to practice, which are critical factors on your inner journey. Yet just as the beginner's mind is empty of preconceived ideas, it also surrenders any fixed concepts about the future. The Buddha cautioned: "The future is always other than you imagined it." He repeatedly stated that you must not start living as though this moment's main worth lies only in some future benefit.

---

7   I use the word "ego" to refer to the complex within the mind that serves the management function in daily life. It uses the language of "me" and "mine" in order to operate in the relative world. In an unliberated mind, the ego suffers from the delusion that its existence has permanence. *With the realization of the First Noble Truth, you are at the beginning of a journey in which the ego ultimately ceases being identified with itself and starts to serve your Buddha nature.*

Spiritual development requires that you remain oriented to the time that we know as "now." The Buddha said: "Do not pursue the past. Do not lose yourself in the future . . . Looking deeply at life as it is in the very here and now, the practitioner dwells in stability and freedom." Likewise, in *Four Quartets*, T. S. Eliot repeatedly pointed to the paradox that the eternal is outside of time, yet it is only in time that the fruits of spiritual liberation can manifest. Repeatedly, he stressed the importance of living in the now. "Quick now, here, now, always!" he exclaimed. Then he lamented as to how we usually live: "Ridiculous the waste sad time/ Stretching before and after."

So it is with your own inner journey. Look to those far lofty peaks of enlightenment, heaven, or paradise for inspiration, but live in the *now*. For in this moment, you are either creating suffering for yourself and others or you are not.

Practicing Knowing That You Know

Once you have established the beginner's mind, you are ready to start practicing knowing that you know. The problem, however, is that you cannot really practice this insight. It arises when the proper causes and conditions are present like fruit that ripens and falls from a tree. All you can do is practice mindfulness, so that you create propitious conditions that will encourage the insight to arise. Reflection plays a role as well: You can use inquiry to clarify what you perceive.

Using mindfulness in working with the Third Insight means that you practice consciously shifting your awareness, both on the meditation cushion and in daily life. For instance, if you experience pain in your back during sitting meditation, concentrate your attention not on the physical stimulus or even your experience of the pain itself, but rather on your awareness of the pain. If you become fearful upon hearing some bad news at work, shift your focus away from the bad news toward recognition of the anxiety it provoked in you. In other words, instead of just being aware that the mind is experiencing suffering around an event, notice that the knowing of it is independent from the experience itself.

One of my meditation students became quite skillful at utilizing this technique. In the past, he would often get angry at work. But as his meditation practice deepened he found that he was able to shift his focus from the situation itself to the emotions the situation elicited. One day he found himself getting frustrated during a meeting. Instead of doggedly arguing his point and alienating his colleagues, as he usually would, he noticed that he was starting to get angry and excused himself from the room. He knew that he could control his response rather than react to it. After breathing deeply for several minutes, he walked back into the meeting and calmly resolved the issue with his co-workers.

So when you start to feel something unpleasant and out of habit begin to make up a story about why this feeling has arisen, stop and say to yourself, "Oh, I recognize this. This is dukkha (the First Insight). Back pain (or fear or anxiety, etc.) feels like this" (the Second Insight). Then place your attention on the awareness that knows this is dukkha (the Third Insight). You will quickly notice that this awareness is untouched by what it is aware of, regardless of whether it is pleasant or unpleasant. It is simply there, knowing that it knows. Note, however, that this knowing is not removed from or indifferent to the experience; rather, it offers you an expanded perspective on the experience. It opens you to the awareness of the awareness itself. The Buddha was very clear on this point: Every experience is to be known from within the experience, not as a removed, outside observer.

Eventually, a felt sense of knowing that you know arises. It is ineffable, fleeting at first, and often you lose your sense of it. Sometimes you don't even remember that it is a possibility. But with persistence, the awareness returns and so lights up this very moment.

I encourage you to let loose of any specific ideas you have about how you might experience this knowing. You must experience it for yourself in your own unique manner. You may feel it as a sigh of relief, or as a weight being lifted in the midst of having a difficult time. You may feel it as a sense of heightened awareness, particularly if it is a joyful moment, and you can really feel the preciousness of that moment as wonderful yet transient. Or you may feel it as a general sense of connectedness, or a sense of presence, that you are showing up for your own life. But one thing is for sure: When you know that you know, you know it!

CHAPTER 7

THE OPPOSITE OF SUFFERING IS NOT HAPPINESS

THE WISDOM OF THE FIRST NOBLE TRUTH

Let's review the steps you have taken on your journey thus far. You have seen that there are three kinds of suffering: first, the physical and emotional pain that are intrinsic to human existence; second, the anxiety and angst that arise from constant, uncontrollable change; and, finally, the bittersweet dukkha that even your happiness has in it the *seeds* of suffering. This means that no matter how fortunate you are, if your mind is not free, feelings of stress, unreliability, dissatisfaction, and unease are inevitable. When the mind is caught in dukkha, it is alienated and reactive to the uncertainty, difficulty, and loss that are inherent in life. And it is unable to fully participate in the joy of life.

Moreover, you have seen that there is a practice that can help you develop a *new relationship* with suffering that is characterized by ease and spaciousness of mind. This practice of being mindful of the arising of dukkha in life is what I call *penetrating dukkha*. Once you penetrate dukkha with understanding and are willing to bear life just as it is, you regain your innate dignity and free yourself from fear. Experiencing the insights in the First Noble Truth is the beginning of a new noble possibility to be in direct relationship with life that allows you to *respond* to rather than *react* to the dukkha in your life. This freeing of the mind begins to manifest even while you are still caught in suffering.

You have also seen that your untrained mind with its endless stream of reactionary thoughts is unreliable. There is a reliable ground on which to stand to meet life that is your own awareness knowing itself. *It is this ground of "knowing you know" that creates the steady, nonreactive state of mind that allows you to just be with life as it is.*

A deep acceptance of life "just as it is" allows you to be more fully present in your life moment by moment, no matter how difficult or how sweet it is, and it empowers you to act more from your deepest values. Regardless of the circumstances of your life at any given time, your experience is richer, more alive. What's more, being with the dukkha opens you to an ever-deepening exploration of the inner life, eventually leading to what the Buddha calls "the deathless," which we will explore in the Third Noble Truth.

Finally, you have learned that just thinking about freedom from suffering without actually feeling the "ouch" of suffering doesn't lead to penetration of dukkha. Instead, it leads you to have false ideas of your progress, which then cause you to become discouraged when reality sets in. Even dedicated meditation students who go off to sit long retreats often skip ahead to focus on the Second Noble Truth, underestimating the importance of the First Noble Truth. Although they may return to their daily lives with some intellectual understanding, all their old patterns of stress, dissatisfaction, and endless wanting quickly return because they are not actually free from the causes of suffering.

This lack of integration of the insights into daily life is symptomatic of not following the Buddha's instructions to practice in order to penetrate dukkha. The students don't realize that their suffering is an opportunity for practice and not a sign of failure, so they mistakenly conclude that something is wrong with the practice or that they cannot do the practice. Their interpretation of their experience is being controlled by the delusion that the opposite of suffering is happiness. If you practice mindfulness in order to realize the insights of the First Noble Truth, this will not happen to you.

Inspiration for Stepping into the Fire

If you found it challenging to practice the first three insights, I offer two reflections that may inspire you to practice. First is the acknowledgment that *you have the possibility for an enriched inner life*. This is a profound realization because you may well be harboring a hidden belief that there is nothing much that you can do to bring about your inner experience. Choosing to bear your suffering takes an act of courage, but once you do, you have initiated the process of inner transformation. It is as real and genuine as making change in your outer life. You do not have to first become a new and improved version of yourself.

The second reflection grows out of the first. If in fact your own experience tells you the Buddha's teachings truly offer a noble possibility for a richer, more peaceful inner life, then why wouldn't you seize it? You are not being asked to adopt a set of beliefs or to forsake your life, so why are you resistant? Why wouldn't you choose a more meaningful and empowering relationship to your own life if it were available? The answer may be that you, like most people, have little clarity regarding the nature of your own suffering. You do not realize *it is possible to separate the arising of suffering from identifying with it.*

You might also look to the Buddha for inspiration in the way in which he bore the emotional and physical pains of life without complaint or seeking escape. For 45 years after his enlightenment, he walked throughout Northern India teaching. He was homeless, afflicted with backaches and other injuries, and experienced fatigue. Yet his mindfulness and compassion were so strong that even as he was dying of food poisoning, he insisted that a monk go to the man who had served him the contaminated food and convey that he should in no way feel guilty. The Buddha offered his existence and his understanding as inspiration for people of all classes, races, and economic status to find inner freedom.

A Psychological Perspective: Suffering Is Essential

The Jungian psychologist Helen Luke offered a stirring vision of human possibility that makes some very useful distinctions about the nature of suffering and reflects in Western psychological language the wisdom of the Buddha's First Noble Truth. Luke identified two types of suffering—one you are to bear, the other you are to abandon. The one to be borne, Luke called "essential suffering," meaning the *objective* experiences of pain and loss. The suffering you are to let go of she called "neurotic, inferior, and narcissistic suffering," that is, your *subjective* reaction to loss, anxiety, and disappointment.

Seen through Luke's framework, the Buddha's first three insights teach you to *embrace essential or objective suffering* by penetrating it. Essential suffering is the willing, conscious acceptance of the dukkha of being a human. Luke likened the ability to bear essential suffering to a wagon with the capacity to carry a load. It is the wheels of this wagon that allow you to move on with your life as you feel the load of this essential, unavoidable suffering. Essential suffering therefore is the "carriage" for your own development. It is the basis on which you build a healthy and productive life. Without judging it or labeling it as bad, Luke characterizes essential suffering as the "darkness of life." It is your willingness to carry the load of darkness that brings harmony not just to your life but to all life.

Making the radical choice to know dukkha by mindfully agreeing to bear it as your part of the burden of being human gives your life meaning, no matter how modest or challenged it is. You are *being the carriage for conscious life.* This is a stirring vision of the Buddha's instruction to "penetrate suffering." Do you not prefer this vision to the standard choice of hardening and contracting that most people take when confronted with dukkha?

According to Luke, neurotic suffering is the result of collapsing under or refusing to consciously carry the darkness of life. It is a self-centered identification with the suffering—you are the suffering and the suffering is yours. Sounding as much like a Buddhist as the dedicated Christian she was, Luke stressed that there is a spiritual call for you to consciously and willingly bear this burden of essential suffering. She did not say it is easy or fun, or something that you would prefer to do; rather, it is a spiritual necessity.

Ajahn Sumedho teaches that to *understand* dukkha you must be willing to "stand under" suffering. Similarly, Luke said you must be willing to receive suffering in the manner of "standing under a waterfall." Both of these descriptions point to the capacity of fully, consciously receiving life as it is. To voluntarily receive the distress of life and mindfully bear it with consciousness and compassion is a critical threshold for spiritual development. It is the vital first step and it empowers all further unfolding. It is both absolutely ordinary and mystically transforming. This choice gives your life meaning and, ironically, it also gives meaning to your suffering, transforming it from being senseless to being a crucial part of your liberation. This is the beauty of the insights of the First Noble Truth.

The Ego's Fear of Humiliation

When you collapse into suffering, it is because your ego sees suffering as a personal failure and feels humiliated. This sense of failure is based on the ego's mistaken idea that winning in life means no suffering. *Your ego may well be under the delusion that the opposite of suffering is happiness.* When your ego believes this, then every moment of suffering is felt as a personal defeat, insult, indignity, or proof of your inadequacy or of life being unfair. This is subjective suffering, self-centered and neurotic.

Your subjective dukkha is your ego suffering from its own ideas about how things are supposed to be. When things go wrong, your ego may feel humiliated even though you may not consciously realize it. Such suffering is your ego's narcissistic and mistaken, self-centered reaction to life's challenges. The ego collapses, becomes depressed, or grieves for itself. Or it becomes resentful and refuses to participate, or helpless and frozen with dread. Or the ego contracts into anger and lashes out. In its delusion the ego is unwilling to voluntarily carry the darkness of life. When suffering is penetrated by mindfulness and compassion, the ego dies a thousand deaths and yet ends up healthier for it. Your ego isn't bad, nor are you a bad person because you have an ego. The ego is a result of causes and conditions and, in my view, is necessary for a healthy, whole life. I tell students don't leave home without it, but don't let it drive the vehicle on your spiritual journey.

The idea of being willing to bear your suffering like a carriage carrying a heavy load is a hopeful, comforting image. *But if the opposite of your suffering isn't happiness, then what is it?* Nonsuffering is having a relaxed, composed mind that is fully present with whatever is occurring in the moment. And it is the capacity to be in relationship to whatever is arising such that you're able to respond from your deepest intentions. And it is a feeling of relatedness in your life that is free from aversion to suffering.[8]

Do Not Demand That Your Suffering End

The idea of a dichotomy between pain and suffering, between objective and subjective suffering, between suffering and the knowing of suffering is present in Western mythology also. When Prometheus chose to steal fire from the gods in order to give it to humans, he knew he would be punished yet he consciously chose to bear this pain in order to foster the noble possibility of human existence. And punished he was. He was bound for a millennium to rocks atop a mountain, while an eagle ate his liver each day, which then grew back each evening. He acted without hesitation and accepted his suffering without collapse. You too can honor all human possibility by bearing the objective suffering that is given to you.

In my experience the First Noble Truth is truly *noble*. It

---

8   One note of caution: If you start to feel that you're a martyr, it's a sign you've gotten off the path; likewise, if you feel numb, indifferent, or resigned, you're lost. The first state represents ego inflation, the second ego destruction, and both lead to the creation of more suffering.

contains the grand vision for how you can begin to live right now with more harmony, despite whatever difficulties arise in your life. In daily life it is extraordinarily difficult to not conflate pain and suffering. But you can acquire the ability to distinguish between the two through practicing the first Three Insights. Moreover, realizing these three insights provides the necessary framework that will allow you to make the three insights of the Second Noble Truth a more authentic and less conceptual practice.

You may not like undergoing this objective suffering and you may feel your share is unfair or too much. Still, your life's difficulties are there for you to bear as best you are able. In practicing being with life just as it is, you still prefer that your suffering end and you act on that preference whenever possible. But most crucially you do not demand that your difficulties go away. Instead, you consciously and voluntarily carry your suffering, and in your acceptance of it you find meaning, what Ajahn Sumedho calls "the good of suffering." Astoundingly, when you fully accept dukkha, you also discover distance from your difficulties. *The way out of suffering is the way through.* As Sumedho says, "To let go of suffering we have to admit it into consciousness."

BOOK TWO

THE SECOND
NOBLE TRUTH

THE SECOND NOBLE TRUTH

What is the Noble Truth of the Origin of Suffering?

It is craving . . . accompanied by relish and lust, relishing this and that . . .

craving for sensual desires, craving for being, craving for non-being. . . .

This Noble Truth must be penetrated to by abandoning the origin of suffering. . . .

This Noble Truth has been penetrated to by abandoning the origin of suffering.

—Samyutta Nikaya LVI, 11

CHAPTER 8

THERE IS A CAUSE
OF YOUR SUFFERING

The Insights of the First Noble Truth are practices for becoming mindful of life's uncertainties, pain, and stress and for developing the courage and skills to stay with the mind as it reacts to suffering, or dukkha. You develop the ability to stay present with life just as it is. Practicing the Insights of the Second Noble Truth enables you to use what you have developed to gain yet another level of understanding and freedom in your life. They introduce you to practices for understanding the patterns and misperceptions that cause your mind to become reactionary in the first place. With these three insights you learn why the mind contracts into suffering and how you can release yourself from these contractions.

In the Fourth Insight the Buddha reveals that dukkha has a cause, and that cause is craving (*tanha*), meaning that you cling to and identify with what you desire (*chanda*). The Buddha then defined three broad categories of craving and how craving arises for each. I've heard numerous interpretations of what the Buddha meant by "craving," including the idea that any desire is by definition suffering. In this book, I treat desire as any movement toward or away from a person, object, thought, or experience that often but not always arises spontaneously in the unliberated mind. Thus, desire can be wholesome or unwholesome. In my experience, all unwholesome desires are a form of craving, greed, ill will, and delusion. But even when desire is wholesome, if you become attached and cling to achieving the desire, you have fallen into craving.

Grasping after desire and believing that your happiness depends on getting it is what imprisons the mind, not the desire itself. This emphasis on the untrained mind's compulsion to grasp desire is at the very heart of the Buddha's teaching, for it is through clinging that you create your mental suffering. Simply stated, all grasping equals suffering. When you understand this, you have realized the Fourth Insight.

The practice of the Fifth Insight is to realize the cause of suffering by *abandoning*, at least momentarily, the attachment to getting what you desire. By *abandoning*, the Buddha means for you to simply let go of the attachment. You cultivate the intention not to hold on to or identify with any of the endless wishes and desires that arise thousands of times throughout your day.

Then in the Sixth Insight, the practice is to acknowledge that you have seen the cause of your suffering, that you have abandoned it temporarily, and to be mindful of what it feels like to be without clinging so that you can start to integrate abandoning clinging as part of your daily life practice.

The Buddha was a great scientist of the mind, a profound psychologist, really, and he saw how the mind's reaction to stimuli created a chain of what he called "dependent origination," which leads to the mind experiencing dukkha. But he saw an opportunity that no one else had realized before; the chain of suffering could be broken by a combination of mindfulness and intention. He realized there is a distinction between the nature of mind itself and how the mind is temporarily colored by its contents. Craving creates an illusion, a misperception, a deluded mental reaction, which causes the mind to contract into stress and anxiety. If this state is avoided or released, the mind is naturally calm and luminous. The three Insights of the Second Noble Truth thus represent a revolutionary approach to spiritual development—the utilization of awareness and observation to bring freedom without reliance on beliefs or rituals of any sort.

THE FOURTH INSIGHT:

What is the Noble Truth of the Origin of Suffering?

It is craving for sensual desires, craving for being, craving for non-being.

CHAPTER 9

WHY DO YOU SUFFER?

REFLECTING ON THE SECOND NOBLE TRUTH

In the Fourth Insight, the Buddha states that *when the mind starts craving, suffering will inevitably arise.* In other words, it is how you *relate* to desire that is the cause of your suffering. Therefore you are not helpless or cursed or destined to be forever tormented with anxiety, stress, and dissatisfaction. You can do something about it: You can move toward freeing your mind.

In the first Three Insights, you learned to be with the pain and suffering of your life in a manner that has prepared you for this new level of understanding. It is precisely because you can now stay present with pain and suffering that you possess the forbearance to investigate it and to see for yourself that while pain is an unavoidable part of the human experience, the subjective suffering that usually comes with it is not. The Fourth Insight represents a *crossover understanding*—that you have the power to transform your life experience from suffering to joy.

The Buddha observed that clinging arises from a chain of cause and effect: If your mind encounters something it considers pleasant, it tends to move toward it; if your mind encounters something unpleasant, it naturally tends to move away from it.

From this simple, usually automatic reaction, desire forms in the mind. If unchecked that desire causes the mind to contract as it idealizes and clings to the imagined outcome. The mind becomes imprisoned in an obsessed state, becoming clingy, or what I call "sticky" with desire.

In Buddhist psychology identifying with and clinging to desire are said to result in your "taking birth." In other words, you have created an illusory self whose happiness and well-being depend on getting what it wants. You know the feeling of taking birth already. How many thousands of times have you gotten tense, worried, and anxious over wanting something that in retrospect did not result in a lasting sense of well-being? It might have been a small desire, such as being praised for work you did, finding the right present for someone, or finding a parking place. Or it might have been a large desire, such as getting the job you want, being able to afford to live the way you want, or being with the person you want to be with. When you contract into your desires, small or large, isn't it true that your world narrows to just wanting these outcomes? Have you not felt compulsively anxious, driven, or stressed, none of which helped you actually achieve your goal? None of these desires themselves were harmful, but rather it was the clingy mind state they created that caused you to suffer.

Desire without Craving

In my own practice I make a distinction between desire and craving. Although craving always has desire in it, in my experience not all desire contracts into craving, meaning the mind is caught in greed, aversion, or delusion. This definition is slightly different than what is often taught, which is that desire and craving are synonymous, but I have found this distinction to be very useful in working with clinging.

Desires are energetic states felt in your body and mind that arise from pleasant and unpleasant feelings associated with various thoughts and sensations which then cause the mind to move toward or away from some experience. Desire can arise and pass without contracting into craving. For instance, maybe there's a movie you really want to see and you make the effort to drive to the theater where it's playing, only to discover that it's sold out. If your desire is characterized by clinging and you have contracted into craving, you will feel discontented, restless, or annoyed because you can't see the movie. If there is no clinging, then these emotions are absent and you're able to go on with your evening without losing equanimity.

What seems to me to be the actual cause of suffering is the tendency to idealize and identify with your desires so much that you become *attached* to having them fulfilled. You start to cling to the idea of getting what you want either now or in the future as being all-important. You become irritated, disappointed, or frustrated when you don't get what you want. You are not able to simply be mindful of the desire as it arises and passes.

Ajahn Sumedho says, "Usually we equate suffering with feeling, but feeling is not suffering. It is the grasping of desire that is suffering." When you cling to desire, you become defined by that desire; you see the world through the eyes of someone who wants that particular goal or outcome. It is a distorted vision; therefore you measure your life incorrectly. You experience anxiety, stress, dissatisfaction, tension, and frustrated longing. The mind is so contracted around what it is craving that it acts as though getting this one thing would make you happy. Oftentimes the goal, even if achieved, provides only fleeting satisfaction and is quickly replaced by another, and the cycle starts over again.

Just think about the onslaught of desire that you contend with each day, including small, temporary desires, recurring desires, and patterns of desire. You are living in an unnoticed storm of desire that is the source of your suffering because you do not know how to cope with it wisely. The richness to be found in being mindful of *this* moment is often lost because you are pulled into the future or plunged into the past, and the fullness of this moment is lost, discarded, and degraded.

This overwrought attempt to get what you desire never stops. Even if you get something you desire, it is quickly replaced by yet another desire in your mind. It's true, isn't it? Just watch yourself on any given day and you can easily observe the endless cycle of arising and passing desire. You can see that the cycle, like a wheel, keeps turning regardless of whether it is a "good day" and you are getting much of what you want or a "bad day" and things are not going your way. This cycle of clinging and taking birth in one desire after another is called *samsara*, and realizing the truth of it is a step toward freedom.[9]

---

9   The Buddha described suffering as a traceable path, which he called a chain of "dependent origination." From contact with an experience, depending on whether it feels pleasant or unpleasant, you have urges about having it or avoiding it, which create desire in your mind. You start to identify with what you desire; it becomes "me or mine," and you sink into attachment. The Buddha said the first link in this chain of dependent origination is ignorance. By ignorance he meant lack of mindfulness or clear comprehension of what is suffering and what it is not. Ignorance is like a cloud or dust covering the mirrorlike quality of the mind, making it unable to reflect accurately. Thus, when you gain understanding you are able to break the links in the chain through mindfulness and nonattachment and not fall into clinging. When you develop skill in recognizing the onset of clinging, you gain the ability to follow a liberating chain of events moving from suffering to faith that you do not have to live in such a manner. You feel the joy of relief from grasping, the tranquility that pervades the mind when it is not filled with wanting, and a dispassionate ease with life.

The Three Kinds of Craving

The Pali word for craving is *tanha*, which means "thirst." The Buddha identified three distinct kinds of tanha that you repeatedly experience; they are often unnoticed, because they arise and then are quickly preempted by yet another and then another. First is your craving for the six kinds of sense desires, or *kama tanha*: craving for certain food tastes or for pleasing sounds or for silence; craving for sexual, affectionate, or comforting touch or simple physical comfort in your body; craving for attractive, pleasant, comforting, inspiring sights as well as for pleasant, refreshing smells; and finally, craving for thoughts that are confirming, useful, stimulating, and reassuring to you. Just think of how many different sense desires you have in any given moment!

The second type of craving is the desire for existence and for becoming what you are not. In Pali this is called *bhava tanha*. You may want to be wealthy, or more athletic, or sexually desirable, or a better musician. The craving to "become" can be wholesome—to be a good parent or a better friend to others, or to be more generous, healthier, or more disciplined—yet still cause suffering. Even your longing for spiritual growth can be bhava tanha! It too can create suffering in the untrained mind: Will you get there? Are you going about it the right way? And it can result in greed, uncontrolled wanting, envy, impatience, self-judgment, temptation of all sorts, and unskillful words and actions.

Bhava tanha is one of the most common causes of suffering in modern culture. You are exhorted to achieve and to accumulate to the point that you take birth as "one who does and gets." Thus what might be healthy goals decay into obsession and compulsion. A tragic example of this is a story that was widely reported in the media in which a tennis father was so desirous of his children winning their matches that he drugged the water bottles of the young people with whom they competed. The dad could not stand the possibility of his children losing; it was torturous and drove him to act unskillfully. His behavior continued until one young man had an extreme reaction and died. It is easy to say the father was just crazy, but you too can become obsessive in a manner that causes suffering, only not as extreme. When you take birth in outcome, it is so torturous to you that even if you can refrain from acting unskillfully, the mind is still tormented.

The third type of tanha arises when you are so disillusioned with something in your life and want to get rid of it or want it to cease with such intensity that you crave nonexistence. This state of mind is called *vibhava tanha*. For instance, you may be so overwhelmed by chronic back pain or a difficult emotion that you are flooded with aversion to life itself. Or you have such antipathy toward your physical appearance, aging, or disease that life seems unbearable. In each of these instances, your nervous system is overcome by the energy generated by the craving, and it seems as if your whole being is rejecting existence. Vibhava tanha is annihilation. If you have ever felt suicidal, even briefly, then you have had flashes of vibhava tanha in the extreme. In its milder manifestations, vibhava tanha is part of everyday life. For example, you can feel so humiliated when you make a big mistake in front of others that for a brief moment your mind is filled with this craving.

Often students discover that before starting a vipassana practice they had been aware of cravings associated with sense desires but much less aware of suffering coming from the other two tanhas. One meditation student told me that upon hearing about the types of craving he quickly realized that he was organized around bhava tanha—always judging himself on the basis of wanting to be someone he was not. He could see that it had caused him endless, needless suffering which he had been aware of but had never known its source.

WHOLESOME VERSUS UNWHOLESOME DESIRE

Mindfully exploring wholesome desires is more subtle and complex than working with unwholesome ones. We all know what unwholesome desires are—and the harmful actions they lead us to—lusting after material goods, or sex, or escapist activities such as taking recreational drugs; wishing someone ill out of jealousy; hurting someone you love out of your own desire to be loved unconditionally; obsessing about altering your physical appearance to conform to our cultural definition of what's beautiful—the list is endless. Responding skillfully to unwholesome desires is relatively simple: All that's needed is mindfulness to know when they have arisen and an ongoing commitment to live according to your values, which gives you the strength to not yield to such desires. As you mature spiritually, you will begin to clearly see how suffering comes from pursuing unwholesome desires, and they gradually lose much of their appeal. The struggle to resist then becomes less strenuous. Your mind is no longer enchanted by what used to allure you, and you are no longer easily deluded by the surface experience of people and events.

Wholesome desires are those energetic feelings that arise from nongrasping love, compassion, and empathy toward others. However, even a wholesome desire can lead to unskillful acts and to all manner of suffering if it becomes an obsession, or if you start to rationalize or justify it in your mind. A wholesome desire becomes an unwholesome one if it brings about restlessness and worry because of craving or brings ill will toward those who you perceive to be thwarting the desire, or if it leads to a confused state of mind.

In my experience there are three skillful means you can practice that will prevent your wholesome desire from deteriorating into craving. First is committing to ethical behavior and renouncing being controlled by your desires. Second is cultivating wisdom through mindfulness and insight such that when desire arises you can discriminate between those thoughts, words, and actions that are skillful and those that lead to suffering. Third is surrendering to the truth that you cannot control what happens to you or those whom you care about. Some of your desires will be fulfilled and some will not, despite your best efforts. There is no way of knowing if what seems to be a wholesome desire will bring good or bad fortune or if the desire, once fulfilled, will be even temporarily satisfying.

A poignant example of "not knowing" the outcome of wholesome desire is the story of one student who desperately wanted to become a mother, so much so that she drove her husband to distraction with her obsession and put her body through numerous uncomfortable medical procedures before finally becoming pregnant. Once her child was born, she was dismayed to discover that while she totally loved her child she did not enjoy the activities of mothering. She found herself wishing for her child to be more grown up and in the meantime felt like she was just enduring motherhood. This is the mystery of manifest life; the only response is not to cling even to what seems wholesome.

THE DIFFERENCE BETWEEN PAIN AND SUFFERING

While it is true that there is pain in life, the amount of suffering arising from any particular pain varies from one moment to the next. You may have the same level of physical or emotional pain in one moment as another, yet you suffer far less during one experience than the other. Why is that?

The Buddha realized that emotional loss and physical pain are simply the result of the inner and outer senses coming into contact with consciousness. Suffering comes from how the mind interacts with pain. Because your mind is conditioned by past life events, when it encounters an experience it perceives as painful or unpleasant, there is immediate and direct suffering that is far greater than the actual discomfort of the situation. The increased discomfort happens in your mind, not in the actual experience. This means suffering has an internal cause, and you therefore have the ability to affect how much you suffer—you can dance with life and be a partner in how your life unfolds.

With mindfulness of the cause of suffering, what is unpleasant simply remains unpleasant, even though it is not your preference. On meditation retreats, it is not unusual for a student to tell me at the beginning that she has a condition that creates so much pain that she will not be able to sit, and then midway through the retreat report that her sitting is almost pain free. What is the difference? As she ceases to resist her condition, ceases clinging to having it be other than it is, the nervous system relaxes and there is less pain.

This same principle holds true for pleasant moments. The mind can suffer even when something pleasant is arising if it falls into habitual thinking or is in a certain state. For instance, you may be afraid when you are happy in a relationship or a job because your mind immediately starts to worry about losing the relationship or the job. If you're a parent, you may worry about the child you love so much getting sick or not doing well in school. Your worry doesn't benefit the child since you are already doing all you can for your child's welfare, and it may even cause the child to suffer. In each of these examples, your happiness is precipitating suffering because your mind's internal, reactive process is inducing stress and worry. With mindfulness of the cause of suffering, the arising of all forms of pleasant moments, including the most joyous, remains your preference, but there is no attachment or clinging to it.

The Distinction between Clinging and Nonclinging to Desire

Unfortunately, the Buddha's Fourth Insight is sometimes misinterpreted to mean that all desire should be stamped out. Such a view only increases the sense of separateness that creates desire in the first place. This misunderstanding leads to unwholesome states in which you pretend not to have desires or feel like a failure when desire arises, or try to numb yourself to desire by imitating being an ascetic. Remember Ajahn Sumedho's definition, "Desire is a natural energy of this realm." In my view, to have aversion to or fear of desire is to reject life as it is, and this is a form of nihilism, which the Buddha rejected. The proper response to desire is wisdom, which is why you practice the Twelve Insights. The Buddha admonished, "He who understands clinging and nonclinging understands all the dharma." Let those words of advice steer you in making the distinction between desire and suffering.

It is easy to see why desire itself is not necessarily bad. If you're sick, why wouldn't you want to get well? If you are a parent, why wouldn't you want your children to be safe, nourished, and healthy? Problems arise, however, when you become attached to your desire and cling to a certain outcome. Of course, you desire the best outcome for the child and do whatever you can to alleviate what's wrong. But if you cling to outcome, you and the child miss the joy of life that is here now.

When you are attached to your desire, life becomes unacceptable. You start living a *hidden demand that life be other than it is*, and then you suffer and cause others to suffer. The present moment isn't acceptable because you aren't getting what you want, or you are not who you want to be, or there is something you wish to get rid of. Even if it is a pleasant moment, you worry about the future and wanting to have still more pleasant moments, so you are still being defined by attachment. You are not willing to accept what the future may be, so you suffer in this moment over what is really only a concept. But the future is not here now. It may turn out the way you want it to, or you may change your mind about what you want. What you believe will be awful if it happens may turn out to not be so bad or to lead to some unanticipated good alternative.

Do you see how delusional it is to take birth and suffer over something that is not even here? I'm not saying that you shouldn't have goals for the future, only that you should not be attached to the outcome of your goals. Clinging to the present moment being other than it is or to the future turning out a certain way is pointless. But desire clouds the mind, and once you have taken birth, wisdom disappears, so you do not see how your mind is deluded. As the *Tao Te Ching* states:

Free from desire, you realize the mystery.

Caught in desire, you see only the manifestation.

If not the future, it may be the past you are clinging to, wanting it to be other than it was. Maybe you had an unhappy childhood, or there was an event in your life that if only it hadn't happened your life would be different, or you caused harm to yourself or others, or you missed your chance for love or fortune.

Outrage, a sense of injustice or cruelty, or a feeling of helplessness may fuel your suffering. In each of these instances, you are filled with the desire that things had been different. Can you see how hopeless and pointless this is?

One of the great gifts of the dharma is that it frees you from these obsessions. You learn to be with this moment the way it is, and that includes the past being the way it was and the future being unknown. Dharma means "truth." "This moment is like this" is the truth, and the truth will indeed set you free.

A prime example of the benefits of realizing this insight is Eve, a student in the Sunday meditation group I lead, who had a challenging set of health problems and was obsessed with "fixing" herself. As a result of clinging to her very worthy goal of getting well, she had taken a series of ever-more-dramatic medical steps, such that by the time she started studying with me her entire nervous system was in disarray. She was at the point of giving up on life. Even small aches were acutely painful, she could only eat a bland diet, and she had to pay attention to almost all aspects of her environment. Although Eve was successful and had an excellent education, her mind had narrowed so much that she lived in a world that held only pain and longing. She repeatedly exhausted herself by regretting the past while judging herself for it and imagining the worst in the future. She was also convinced that she was toxic and repelled others. In fact, the toxicity she felt was her own clinging to anger at life and self-loathing because she could not get life to be the way she wanted it.

In many ways Eve was a perfect example of how the mind creates suffering through clinging because she was reactive to every situation and was constantly clinging to one false hope after another. When Eve first started practicing being mindful of her discomfort, she complained that it was making her feel worse. Then she realized that the pain wasn't actually worse, but because she wasn't distracting herself from it, it felt like she was torturing herself. With my encouragement Eve persisted, until eventually she came to see that clinging to her desire that the pain leave greatly amplified the pain. It took more than a year of practicing mindfulness for Eve to learn to just be with her difficulties, then almost another year for her to learn to view her illnesses as coming from impersonal conditions. Slowly, Eve began to orient her attention to her present life, limited though it was. Although her health challenges did not disappear, they are no longer the focus of her attention. Once Eve released her attachment to fixing them, it allowed her to experience joy and wonder once again.

I know how horrible it can feel when you start to release clinging to your desires—as if the world is coming to an end and you will have no way of organizing yourself. But this is merely delusion. Once the release is complete, both you and the world are different. It takes a leap of faith to cease clinging; the realization of the Fourth Insight provides that faith.

SUFFERING EQUALS YOUR PAIN MULTIPLIED BY YOUR RESISTANCE

There is an analogy for the difference between pain and suffering that, while not completely accurate, gives you a feel for its impact in your life. Imagine that you have a sore shoulder, so sore that you can't comfortably lift your arm. It is hurting right now. Let's say the amount of discomfort is five units of pain. Now imagine that you begin to resent the discomfort, become irritated by the limitation it's causing, and you start thinking it's going to ruin your vacation at the beach next month. You've just added seven units of resistance to the pain, only suffering doesn't equal the five units of pain *plus* the seven units of resistance; it is a multiple of the two, meaning you're now experiencing 35 units of suffering. At 12 units of pain, you could go on with your life just fine, but 24 units of suffering starts to affect your attitude.

Now imagine that you have 15 units of pain and your resistance is 20 units; now you are coping with 300 units of suffering! Your mind becomes obsessed and you see the world as an awful place. You can understand why it is that some people you know suffer so much more than would seem appropriate for their problems. Their pain may not be that great, but their resistance is huge, 50 or 100 units for instance. They have so much suffering, yet it is so unnecessary.

Although not as precisely mathematical as this example, there is a multiplying effect in the mind between discomfort of the moment and resistance to the moment, and it greatly increases suffering, as you can observe for yourself. Feelings of listlessness, despair, frustration, and collapse are often indications of the amount of resistance, rather than the actual pain of the moment. Surrounding conditions such as lack of support in your life or overwhelming responsibilities then add more internal anguish and elicit even more resistance in you. It is this interplay of desire and resistance with surrounding conditions that accounts for why you sink into suffering in one situation and don't in another. It is also true that joy multiplied by clinging equals suffering.

Being Free from the Stickiness of Attachment

You do not have to be someone who has a helpless reactive mind that contracts into stress and worry, desperately trying to hold on to what is pleasant and avoid the unpleasant. You, just as you are, can meet life on its own terms, taking delight in that which is enjoyable without clinging to it while also living with what is difficult and unpleasant without contracting into resistance to it. To dance with life is to meet life on its terms to be at ease, even enjoy the ever-changing interplay without clinging.

Ajahn Sumedho has for the last 25 years headed a large monastery in England. But starting at the age of 31, he lived for 10 years at a monastery in Northern Thailand with his teacher, the Venerable Ajahn Chah, one of the most respected monks of the last century. He tells the story of the time when a group of Thai doctors and nurses came to visit Ajahn Chah. One nurse was very beautiful. After the visitors left, Ajahn Chah asked Sumedho what he had thought of the pretty nurse. Sumedho replied in Thai, "I like, but I do not want." Ajahn Chah nodded approvingly and said, "Not bad, Sumedho, not bad." This story poignantly illustrates the Buddha's teaching of nonclinging, of being at ease with life as it is. You do not have to crave simply because you like something—your mind can rest easy in the presence of what is attractive.

The Dalai Lama also exhibits this naturalness and ease with life. Once he attended an interfaith conference at the Catholic monastery Gethsemane in Kentucky where the monk Thomas Merton once lived and wrote his many books. The monks took the Dalai Lama around the monastery and showed him how they support themselves by making cheese and fruitcake. When the Dalai Lama later described his tour during a talk at the conference, he said, "They kept giving me cheese, when what I really wanted was the fruitcake," then he laughed and laughed. Can you see that he has no fear of his desire because desire has no control over him?

I call this ease with feelings of desire being free of the stickiness of attachment. Imagine that you want to ask someone out on a date; you can ask without being attached to that person saying yes and without needing it to be a great date—you will have a much better time without the clinging! Likewise, there are times in life, although not nearly as many as you think, when it is appropriate to ask for the fruitcake rather than the cheese. Freedom, dancing with life, is being at ease even when it turns out that you still only get the cheese. It is okay to prefer the fruitcake, but suffering arises when you are attached to getting your preference.

Desire is a critical link in the chain that leads to clinging, then suffering. For this reason, as you mature in your inner life, desire loses much of its luster and ability to captivate your mind. This can seem strange at first, as though you are going to feel less alive. In fact, you have less of a feeling that your life is a soap opera. You may be more addicted to this ersatz drama than you realize. But as your insight unfolds, your sense of well-being increases significantly and the soap opera is revealed for the superficial, ever-changing chimera that it is. You discover your genuine "Buddha nature"—the innate ability to relate to all of life. T. S. Eliot accurately reflects the feeling of Buddha nature in this line from *Four Quartets*:

Love is most nearly itself
When here and now cease to matter.

In more prosaic words, when you are not attached to what you desire in the moment, you are available to respond to what is arising with unselfish, unconditioned love. As you become less focused on fulfilling your desires moment by moment, you are able to taste your true Buddha nature. This may sound mystical and, in the sense of it being outside of your usual life experience, it is. It is not "magical," however; rather it brings clarity to the mind that yields a more accurate picture of how things are. These lines from Eliot point to the fruit of realization, and they can serve as inspiration to do the hard work involved in practice.

THE FIFTH INSIGHT:

This noble truth must be penetrated by abandoning the origin of suffering.

CHAPTER 10

IMPRISONED BY DESIRE

Directly Experiencing the Second Noble Truth

In the first four insights, the Buddha emphasized staying with your experiences, investigating them, and knowing them fully. He had you build your mindfulness to a point such that you are now ready to take action. With the Fifth Insight, the Buddha instructs you *to abandon attachment to getting what you desire.* When you mindfully let go of clinging, you spontaneously gain insight into the cause of your suffering.

The Buddha isn't telling you to discard your desires out of aversion to them. Letting go of attachment isn't about rejecting your wants in the sense of getting rid of the trash or throwing cold water on a fire. A more accurate image is allowing your tea to cool rather than drinking it from an overly hot cup and burning your lips and mouth. Think of it as *releasing* the energetic hold your desires have on your mind. Release arises spontaneously from mindful observation and wise reflection.

Nor is the Buddha telling you to stop caring about things that of course you care about. Rather he is directing you to a new relationship to caring. With this instruction the Buddha is addressing the paradox of the opposites—that good and bad, gain and loss, pain and pleasure, praise and blame, life and death, and health and sickness are always conjoined. Of course you prefer that you and those you love (and as you mature, all people) enjoy gain, health, and admiration; but the reality is that each of these desirable experiences comes with the potential of its opposite. Therefore, you are challenged to find a healthy relationship between seeking what is wholesome while at the same time acknowledging the inevitability of loss, disappointment, and failure.

The Buddha said that the way to resolve the paradox of the opposites is by releasing the clinging. T. S. Eliot captured the essence of the Buddha's instruction in these lines from the poem "Ash Wednesday":

> Teach us to care and not to care
> Teach us to sit still . . .

In other words, the ability to both care and not care is attained through finding inner stillness. It is the only way these paradoxical feelings can be resolved.

The truth of this can be seen in the story of Jason, who attended a four-week silent meditation retreat that I was co-teaching. Jason admitted in his first interview with me that he had not been a good father or husband. For several years now his ex-wife had refused to speak to him and his children wanted little to do with him, and this made him completely miserable. Jason was dedicated to finding relief from his suffering, but was repeatedly flummoxed by the practice of abandoning attachment to his desire.

Time after time, Jason would come into his interview with me and report essentially the same sequence of arising mind states in his meditation experiences. First, after a period of restlessness, his mind would become calm and collected as he followed his breath, then he would start to become profoundly aware of a constantly changing flow of experiences in his mind. Next, he would notice that all his thoughts fluctuated so much there was no reason to react to them. He would begin to feel very spacious and at ease with himself in a manner he was unaccustomed to. For a while he would feel great, as if he had finally arrived at what he had been looking for his entire adult life. But he would inevitably find himself thinking about his family, and his mind would go into sudden and jarring contraction. Jason described it as being jerked back into judgmental thinking. He would be assaulted with guilt, shame, and regret, and his mind would become flooded with his long-held desire for reconciliation with his ex-wife and children. Why were they not open to his repeated attempts to take responsibility for his past actions? Why would they not give him a chance to make amends?

Often Jason would begin our interviews being confrontational. He wondered how it could possibly be wrong to cling to his desire for reconciliation. He was trying to be responsible about his past, and his motives were good—he wanted an ongoing relationship with his children, now young adults, and he wanted to be there for them as they matured. Why should he abandon such a desire? Why shouldn't he cling to it? It was his only hope for salvation! "This 'stuff' about attachment is just wrong," he would say. "Sometimes clinging is absolutely the right thing!" Then after his outburst, which might go on for five minutes, he would usually go into a collapsed state, declaring that he couldn't do the practice, his life was a failure because he hadn't been a good father, and he had no future. Often he would end up in tears and then feel uncomfortable about crying.

We began to meet every day, and I instructed Jason over and over again to be mindful of his attachment to what was certainly a worthy desire. Did his wanting it and demanding that it happen actually help bring about contact with his children, I asked. Moreover, what was true right now—was he suffering or not suffering? Wasn't his suffering burdening those with whom he wanted to atone for having caused them suffering in the past? After our interviews I would send Jason back to his meditation cushion to practice being mindful of the aspects of his attachment. The time he spent sitting with his obsessing mind would be crucial for letting go.

Finally the time came when Jason was ready to work on learning to discern between the wholesomeness of his desire and the unwholesomeness of clinging to it. First, I had him tell me how his desire to make amends felt in his body. He described the pain he felt when memories of his past actions arose and he was flooded with the desire to end the present estrangement. By being mindful in this manner, he came to see that his desire for reconciliation itself was primarily motivated by love and compassion. It felt wholesome to him, not contrived, and not motivated primarily by his guilt.

Then I asked Jason to focus on the energy and emotions surrounding his attachment to reconciling with his family. He described the clinging as manifesting as tension in his heart and jaw and said that it sometimes felt like he was being held in a vise. At other times it felt like he was mired in a swamp up to his chest, and there was a feeling of "yuckiness" that he wanted to wash off. Jason could feel that shame, guilt, and embarrassment made his mind obsess about getting his desire met. It became painfully obvious to him that his clinging to reconciliation was fueled by not wanting to be a person who had done wrong and the dread of living with the consequences of his past actions. He had never before made this distinction, and I was encouraged that he had achieved this level of mental clarity.

Eventually Jason was able to say that yes, it was true—there was a distinct difference between his desire and his obsession with it. His clinging was composed of impatience, restlessness, and wanting to make things right, as he defined "right." He was so attached to this outcome because he was worried that he would never find peace of mind unless his family forgave him; at the same time, he had doubts about being worthy of being forgiven.

At first Jason was shocked to see that his lofty goal was caught up in an overwhelming desire to gain his children's acceptance. When he heard his own contrasting descriptions of his worthy desire and his clinging, he could feel the suffering of clinging and it would spontaneously release, at least for a while. Often at the end of an interview session, he would state that he felt better and that maybe he was past his obsession.

I never commented on Jason's own assessment of his situation. I would simply send him back to his mindfulness practice with the instruction to just meditate and when his obsessive thought patterns started up again to move his attention from the breath and focus it on his emotions. I did not ask him to do something about his attachments, only to be mindful of them, to witness their impact as suffering and not suffering, and to discover his motivation for clinging.

After a couple of weeks of this intense mindfulness practice, Jason reported that he had begun to see that every obsession is just an obsession, whether it is for money, approval, or even the worthy goal of seeking forgiveness and reconciliation. He now understood that clinging to any desire creates a driven mind state in which you are tormented by the demons of self-judgment, incessant wanting, repetitive thoughts, and compulsive fantasizing. He could see without my help that his clinging to a certain outcome did not have the same wholesome qualities as his desire to make amends.

For a day or so after experiencing an insight like this, Jason would be fine. But then he would totally forget his insight and lose any connection to his understanding as if he had never had it. He would be swept away all over again by his earnest feeling that he must make amends, they had to give him the chance! Thus the process would start over. Oftentimes he would say the very same words he had said many times before with no awareness that he was repeating himself. Usually he would go through the same emotional cycle as before.

I never objected to this process of starting over. It did not make me impatient or cause me to think that I was wasting my time as a teacher or that he was not getting anywhere. As I said in the instructions on meditation, a genuine commitment to starting over is a key element of practice. You gain insight by repeatedly connecting to your intention to stop suffering and being willing to just start over no matter how many times you lose your direction.

THE BLACK HOLE OF CLINGING

Can you see why Jason kept losing his hard-won insight and how it happens to you as well? The untrained mind has a habit of idealizing and exaggerating an imagined gain; it is its nature to cling. The mind becomes narrow and contracted when a strong desire arises, and it starts to believe that having what it wants or getting rid of what it does not want will bring eternal happiness or relief. It is like being caught in an eddy in a stream—the mind swirls round and round. Of course your mind is engaged in other activities during the course of your daily life, but you have already taken birth as one who suffers. Your mind returns over and over again to clinging to this one desire that you want more than anything else and you become completely immersed in it. So you suffer mentally, emotionally, and physically and oftentimes drag others into your suffering as well!

Now, consider that this scenario is happening to you over and over throughout your day, not just in reaction to one but to many desires, both large and small with constantly changing intensity. This is the ocean of never-ending desire in which you swim. One desire replaces another as victory and defeat merge in an endless cycle of wanting and clinging.

Clinging to what you want is like being caught in the gravitational grip of a black hole, or as Jason reported, in a vise or a swamp. The only way to know the state of your mind when it is not caught in this cycle is to *remove yourself from the gravitational pull of attachment.* Thus, the Buddha tells you to penetrate desire by abandoning your attachment to it. If you have lived your whole life caught in the cycle of desire, how else can you know what it feels like to be free of its gravitational pull? No wonder the Buddha said, "He who knows clinging and nonclinging knows all the dharma."

The Fruits of Nonclinging

For Jason a genuine experience of abandoning the cause of suffering came near the end of the retreat. He showed up for an interview smiling softly, and even before he spoke I knew something had shifted. "I get it," he said. "It's just the way it is with my family right now. It really hurts, but I can't change it. Maybe in the future they will give me another chance, but I can't control that either. You are right—I am making myself miserable, and it doesn't help me reach my goal. If anything, I'm so uptight in my attempts to get them to let me back in their lives that it's actually driving them away. Clinging is suffering!"

It was such a relief for him that his eyes teared with joy. He had at least temporarily abandoned his incessant desire—yes, he still wanted to make amends with his family more than anything else, but he was no longer demanding that life be the way he would have it. He had learned "to care and not to care."

Jason had been clinging to some future that did not exist in the present moment, while his true salvation lay in the present moment. His peace of mind was independent of how life danced with him, but only if he realized it was independent, which is why he had to practice in order to gain this insight. He had realized that it was his *unattached* love and his willingness to consciously bear his genuine regret that gave his life purpose. In the future this insight would enable him to respond to his family's actions skillfully, without fear of his own actions being misperceived.

The benefits of nonclinging to the three kinds of desires are the same for you as they were for Jason. When you are not clinging to what you want, life becomes much easier. Although the events of your life may be painful to bear at times, you accept the pain without adding suffering. Rather than demanding that things turn out the way you want them to, you surrender to life even though it often fails to deliver what you would hope. As a result you are at peace with yourself in the present moment, and you can move toward your goals without contraction.

The Buddha's instruction to abandon clinging translates into *caring without demanding, loving without imposing conditions, and moving toward your goals without attachment to outcome.* Approaching your goals with this attitude or state of mind allows you to care, to interact and take action in your job, in your relationships, and in the greater world and still have a calm, clear mind and a peaceful, loving heart. To whatever extent you can act with this spiritual maturity, you have *crossed over.* Your life is based on *being in the moment rather than on the outcome of that moment.* Being fully present in the moment becomes your most essential value and your orientation in life, and it allows you to be in the world of goals and actions without being defined by it. It is a major step toward liberating the mind. I do not present this as a theoretical teaching but as a way for you to live, starting right now. But to do so you must understand why the mind clings and how you go about abandoning that clinging.

WHY YOUR MIND CLINGS

Why did Jason have such a hard time integrating his insights about clinging to desire? He was smart, energetic, and had the support of the mindfulness training, yet his mind was repeatedly swept away by his desire. Jason was struggling with what is known as a "hindrance attack." The Buddha described five hindrances, or *nivarana*, that cloud the mind and prevent us from knowing the cause of our suffering. The first hindrance is sensual desire, or *kamacchanda*, which is the mind simply wanting something pleasurable. The second is ill will, or *vyapada*, in which the mind is filled with dislike. The third, *thina-middha*, is sloth and torpor, in which the mind is either too sleepy or too apathetic to see clearly. The fourth, restlessness and worry, or *uddhacca-kukkucca*, is when the mind is too anxious to be able to stay steady. The fifth and most difficult hindrance is skeptical doubt, or *vickiccha*, in which you lack the faith in yourself to stay mindful of what is really true and to act skillfully. I call doubt the "mother of all hindrances" because it stops you from ever beginning to let loose of clinging. Doubt freezes the mind and undercuts your ability to cope with all the other hindrances.

Jason was experiencing multiple hindrances. His mind was

clouded by desire, restlessness and worry about the future, and self-doubt. He was also troubled with aversion to his past behavior. The only hindrance that did not torment Jason was sleepiness—he was too miserable to be sleepy!

The Buddha taught that, like Jason's, your mind is usually clouded with one or more of the hindrances, but because this is such a "normal" experience, you hardly notice it. He also said that the mind's natural state is clear, luminous, and free of any hindrances.[10] Mindfulness practice returns the mind to this free state. When the mind isn't obscured by hindrances, attachment doesn't arise, and your mind is willing to just be with what is. You are not caught in wanting anything, wanting to become anything, or wanting to get rid of anything. You have undoubtedly experienced this free state numerous times in your life already, but if you are not mindful when it is occurring, the impact is minimal. Through mindfulness you feel its wholesomeness and you are drawn to do those things that encourage its arising more often.

In those moments in which your mind is free from hindrances, you are not in a reactive state. You see things more clearly, and you have access to intuitive wisdom. Although the three types of desire will still arise, you are not drawn into them. They do not define your existence—they are merely characteristics of your mind state, ever changing as they arise and pass. (This is just as true for worthy desires as it is for

---

[10] Luminous mind is referred to in the *Anguttara Nikaya* I, vi, 1–2 and has been a point of debate for centuries among Buddhist scholars. As a practitioner rather than a scholar, my view is that the Buddha is describing the nature of mind when full realization has occurred. The possibility of realizing this state of mind is one of the great motivations for practice, and having moments of foreshadowing of this luminosity in practice serves as a source of faith. You practice the Noble Eightfold Path in order to realize this state of mind, with the path being both a purification process and a developmental process of being able to clearly know the truth. For excellent scholarly commentary on luminous mind, please see the work of Bhikkhu Boddhi, *Numerical Discourses of the Buddha*, p. 36, and Thanisarro Bhikkhu, http://www.accesstoinsight.org/tipitaka/an /ano1/ano1.049.than.html.

unworthy ones, otherwise you become obsessed with them just as Jason was.)

Eventually, however, the mind loses its clarity and insight, and you once again find yourself caught in the web of desire. But as you repeat this process over a period of years, all three types of desire gradually have less impact on your sense of well-being. You become less and less defined by your desires—they simply come and go. Some desires you respond to. Those desires you don't respond to may persist as a presence in your mind, but they don't take over your mind, pull you into contraction, put you in a bad mood, or spoil your attitude toward life. You learn an entirely new method for dancing with life.

JASON'S TRANSFORMATION

I wish I could report that Jason stayed free after his breakthrough on the meditation retreat and that he was reunited with his family. But when I saw him a few months later at another retreat, he had fallen back into his struggle. Jason told me that a few days after he left the first retreat he had an interaction with his children in which they were far more responsive than they had previously been. This raised his hopes that everything was going to work out the way he wanted it to now that he was more liberated. Of course, his excitement boomeranged, and he was soon lost in desire again. Moreover, his children did something he found hurtful, which only made him want peace with them even more. But this time he knew that he was lost in attachment, and he could observe it. By the time he came to the second retreat, he had already gained some perspective on how he had gotten caught, and within just a few days he rediscovered the state of not clinging to outcome.

Despite reestablishing himself in nonattachment, Jason was suddenly overcome with an attack of self-doubt. For several days he spiraled downward and took birth as a worthless person who had nothing to contribute in life. He felt miserable. But I was excited for him. I felt his suffering represented a kind of cleansing or purifying of secret, long-held, self-negating beliefs that had led to his unskillful behavior toward his family in the first place. Eventually Jason found release from this view of himself; or rather he stopped clinging to it.

After Jason left the second retreat, he changed his career to one focused on service in the nonprofit sector. He now faces life with a new sense of confidence grounded in humility, which keeps him from falling into the kind of grandiosity that characterized his previous suffering. He has subsequently managed the ups and downs of his campaign to reconcile with his family with much more dignity and grace. His children are still mostly standoffish with him, but his other relationships with co-workers and friends have improved immensely. He reports amazement at his mind's ease although he still struggles at times, and he has taken his spiritual exploration to a deeper level.

Does this mean that Jason is liberated? Not at all. But it does indicate that he gained a measure of peace and freedom in his life and that he is poised for further spiritual development. His spiritual motivation is grounded in his life, not in running away from his life through magical thinking. He is comfortable in his own skin and he knows that the inner experience has meaning for him. He still seeks to have his situation with his children improve, but his happiness and unhappiness are not dependent on their actions. Although Jason's story doesn't have a "happily ever after" ending, it is a good example of how the dharma manifests in daily life and how it can prepare you to dance with life.

What Is Meant by Abandoning

Because letting go of clinging is a paradoxical practice, it is easy to misunderstand what it means. Ajahn Sumedho says, "Letting go is leaving things as they are. It does not mean that you annihilate them or throw them away." He goes on to explain how abandoning works: "If we *contemplate* desires and *listen* to them, we are actually no longer attaching to them." He likens clinging to holding a clock in your hand for a long period of time until it becomes heavy and your arm begins to ache. If he tells you to let go of the clock to relieve your discomfort, he is not telling you to throw it away—it is a perfectly good clock, one that is easy to travel with and keeps good time. Therefore, the clock is not the problem; your grasping is. Putting the clock down will relieve your arm from cramping, free up your hand, give you more energy for other things, but it wasn't the clock itself that was causing your suffering, only that you did not know to put it down.

Do you understand the distinction Sumedho is making? For many students it is a hard distinction to sustain; therefore, visualizing a commonplace image like the clock can be helpful when you are being assaulted by clinging. In life you will inevitably have many goals, and they will determine how you spend your time. But there is a distinction between acting according to what you value and being attached to the outcome of that action. You don't diminish your commitment to the goal by letting go of grasping to the outcome. Test this for yourself with something you really care about.

Of course there are unwholesome desires, which the Buddha said are like "holding a hot coal" that you would immediately drop. Wishing someone ill out of jealousy or wanting to harm another person because you want revenge are examples of such a hot coal. In my experience students are often well aware of when they are clinging to hot coals and are able to work with releasing them. But students have a much more difficult time abandoning their clinging to wholesome desires, such as wanting good health, that bring suffering when the mind is caught in obsession, fear, or compulsion, as often happens around illness or injury.

How to Practice Abandoning

Students often complain that even when they get the idea of abandoning clinging and are inspired to do so, they don't have a clue as to how to practice it. There are many teachings about how to let go of clinging, but I recommend using mindfulness to clearly see what is true for you right now, just as Jason did. The first step is to separate your desire from your attachment to it. Then examine the desire itself and see how it is related to the arising of pleasant or unpleasant feelings. Observe whether the desire is based in the present, or if it is linked to the future or the past. Be interested in the energy of the desire and how it propels the mind in various directions. Notice whether any images or words accompany the desire. Is there a little movie running in your head about the outcome? Is the desire an end in itself, a way to entertain yourself or the result of wanting something to want so that you can be the star of the soap opera that's your life?

Now start to look for signs indicating that you are caught in clinging. Usually it manifests as tension in the body, or as a general feeling of urgency or anxiety, nausea, or hypertension. Examine the story that accompanies your clinging to outcome and the drama it creates in your mind. Observe how narrow your mind becomes when it is clinging. Be interested in any obsessive and repetitive thought patterns and notice how they drain your energy. Ask yourself if this clinging is suffering or not suffering. Can you separate the desire itself from the clinging to having the desire fulfilled? Keep working with it until you can do so.

Once your mind has made these distinctions, begin to note that your awareness of the clinging is separate from the actual clinging. Once you can begin to make this distinction with some ease, you can start to invite the mind to let loose of clinging. Be careful not to fall into aversion by condemning the clinging. Without judging, just silently observe that the clinging is burning the mind and body, and invite the mind to let loose of it. You can imagine the letting go as a physical act, like putting down the hot teacup. Imagine ease filling your mind when the clinging is gone. Smile at your resistance to letting go of the clinging and be very sympathetic to feeling the need to cling.

In no way are you supposed to substitute clinging-to-abandonment for clinging-to-desire. It is skillful to want the mind to be free—such a passion is connecting you to your deepest intention to not cause suffering by clinging. But if you start to have aversion to clinging and start to grasp for nonattachment you are falling back into the trap of demanding that this moment be other than it is.

Why Compassion and Loving-Kindness Are Essential

In Chapter 2, I emphasized the importance of learning to fully receive the moment just as it is if you wish to be mindful in your life. Fully receiving the moment can be quite difficult when what's arising is irritating, threatening, confusing, disappointing, or boring. For instance, when you read Jason's story you saw how hard it was for him to stay in the moment. He would repeatedly be swept away by his desire to reconcile with his family because he was so attached to it. The two techniques I told Jason to practice in order to build up his ability to stay with the grasping experience were compassion (*karuna*) and loving-kindness (*metta*).

In the Buddhist tradition, the terms loving-kindness and compassion refer both to qualities of the mind and heart and to specific meditation practices that help you develop these qualities. As you learn to practice loving-kindness and compassion, you will experience these mind-heart qualities on a temporary basis. Then as your spiritual practice deepens, they occur with increasing frequency and last for longer periods of time. You will discover that they greatly refresh the mind. These two qualities, along with feeling *sympathetic joy* for the happiness of others and having *equanimity* no matter what is happening, compose the *brahma-vihara*, or "heavenly abodes," which are said to be the only mind states that arise when you are totally liberated.

Both compassion and loving-kindness are concentration meditations in which the mind is focused ever more firmly on the repetition of a few key phrases that help incline the heart to the emotional quality that you are cultivating. Learning how to develop these heart qualities is part of spiritual development. When they start spontaneously blossoming on their own it is a sign of spiritual maturation. As one of my teachers, Sharon Salzberg, says in her book *Lovingkindness: The Revolutionary Art of Happiness*, the purpose of these practices is to cultivate the intention to embrace all parts of yourself and to overcome feelings of separation from yourself and from others. Thus, you learn to receive and work with your faults as sources of needless suffering, and spontaneously move toward change in order to relieve that suffering. As these practices mature there is an actual felt-sense of warmth, good intention, and deep sympathy toward yourself and others.

Compassion is a responsive movement of the heart; in the Buddhist tradition it is described as "the heart's quiver in response to suffering." Compassion lies at the heart of what it means to be fully human, and it is what allows you to be at peace in the midst of pain and turmoil. Compassion is an energetic response, not a mental idea. It is what you feel when you see a small child fall and scrape a knee. Your natural response is to pick the child up, not because your embrace can make the scrape go away, but because it provides a kind of comfort that is healing to the spirit of the child. It is in this same energetic spirit that you hold yourself when you are fully accepting the truth of your own past experiences, just as I asked Jason to do. The task is to find the humility and the courage to open to yourself in this manner, and it is not easy. If you work with intent, persistence, and patience, you can build your capacity for compassion. To establish these feelings a kind of prayer or mantra is often taught that you say over and over silently to yourself. The mantra can be quite short or quite long. A compassion practice mantra that I sometimes use goes like this:

I can feel this suffering, may this suffering cease.

May the light of love and understanding penetrate
   the darkness of this sorrow and regret.

May this suffering cease, may this suffering cease.

You will eventually experience your expanding compassion in the body as warmth and well-being.

Loving-kindness is the intention of goodwill toward yourself and others. As with compassion it is not about striving toward some critical amount of loving-kindness; rather it is about building the intention and holding it as a core value. There are certain classic phrases that are taught for practicing loving-kindness, such as:

May you be well.

May you be safe.

May you be happy.

May you have a life of ease.

Energetically, loving-kindness is more proactive than compassion, meaning it does not come about because of pain and sorrow; it is always there. It is like seeing a child happily playing and spontaneously feeling loving-kindness just for the existence of that life, rather than responding to pain or fear. Loving-kindness and compassion greatly enhance your ability to stay mindful in both meditation practice and daily life.

I instructed Jason to practice compassion and loving-kindness at the beginning of his meditation sessions in order to build his tolerance to the turmoil created by his grasping. I also told him to switch to one of these two practices if his mind became overwhelmed with longing during meditation. I have found these practices to be essential to truly knowing the felt sense that "this moment is like this." Otherwise the mind becomes beset with the grief, frustration, impatience, self-loathing, or even the physical pain that motivated the clinging in the first place.

A New Possibility for Dancing with Life

Various spiritual traditions offer differing views about how desire should be understood. Some practice cultivating desire;

others promise its fulfillment in an afterlife while denying it has any value in this life, while others condemn it outright. But if you accept the view that desire is a natural energy of this realm, as Ajahn Sumedho says, then a *fourth possibility* becomes available to you—using desire as a tool for your transformation and liberation. T. S. Eliot beautifully describes this potential in *Four Quartets*. Eliot uses the word "memory" instead of "mindfulness," which is one of connotations of *satipatthana*:

> . . . This is the use of memory:
> For liberation—not less of love but expanding
> Of love beyond desire, and so liberation
> From the future as well as the past.

Notice that Eliot is not condemning desire when he says "Not less of love." Instead he is saying that spiritual development through mindfulness allows you to expand, or transform, desire into love. This is liberation: freedom from suffering around your desire that the past be different than it was and that the future turn out a certain way. If you are fully present in the sacred now, suffering is transformed into joy.

THE SIXTH INSIGHT:

*This Noble Truth has been penetrated to by abandoning
the origin of suffering.*

CHAPTER 11

YOU'RE NO LONGER A VICTIM

KNOWING THAT YOU KNOW THE SECOND NOBLE TRUTH

The Sixth Insight calls for you to cultivate *knowing* when you have let go of clinging. The direct knowing that *abandoning has been accomplished* allows the wisdom and benefits of nonclinging to be integrated into how you actually live your life. If you fail to be mindful that clinging has been abandoned, you do not receive the realization of release and it won't significantly impact your life. But when you reach the stage of knowing that you have released clinging in some aspect of your life, the impact is tremendous, as Pacco, one of the students in my Sunday meditation class, discovered.

Pacco is a bright "computer jock" type. For his entire adult life he had experienced alienation and dissatisfaction in almost all of his interpersonal interactions, both at work and in his private life. Pacco is quiet and nonaggressive, so he didn't get into confrontations with others, but his internal experience was so filled with judgment and irritation that a low-grade feeling of dukkha was almost always present, even during times when he felt good. After a period of practicing mindfulness and studying the dharma, he realized that he was clinging to his views about everyone and everything that he encountered in his daily life, and this was how he defended himself from what he perceived as an assault by the world. During one particular meditation he suddenly saw that he did not have to cling to this way of meeting the world—it was just an old habit and a cause of suffering. Immediately he felt a new sense of connectedness to others and it stayed with him. Pacco had this insight two years ago and he reports that it is true—knowing when he has let loose of clinging to his views makes his life better. It has affected his marriage and his work relationships, but most of all it has given him a sense of internal ease for which he expresses continual gratitude.

A second, quite dramatic example of the impact of realizing the Sixth Insight is Joan, a woman in her early thirties who attended a meditation retreat I was co-teaching. This was Joan's first retreat experience. One afternoon I was teaching loving-kindness meditation, and I started off with a special meditation for forgiveness. At the 6:00 a.m. meditation the next morning, Joan approached me and asked to have an interview immediately. As soon as she sat down, I knew what she was going to tell me. As a young girl she had been repeatedly abused by a family member and had never told anyone, not even her husband. As a result she had felt both ashamed that it had happened and guilty for hiding it. But she had clung to the belief that no one must ever know and consequently had paid a high price in terms of intimacy and ease with others. During the forgiveness practice she found that she could not even think of forgiving the person who had abused her, and she saw for the first time that she could not develop spiritually if she clung to her secrecy and her feelings of hatred. She needed me to witness her letting go of clinging, and it was an honor to see her go through her self-revelation and then let go of clinging. Amazingly, she did not have to repeat this process. Once it was done she knew that it had been abandoned, and she was totally committed to not falling back into the clinging mind state around her trauma. Although I guided her in how to tell her husband, who was also a meditator, and provided some support, it was the confidence she had gained from knowing that she had abandoned her feelings of hatred and aversion that carried her through.

Joan's breakthrough could be looked at in psychological terms, and she certainly experienced major psychological growth, but transformation always happens when you let loose of clinging. It was true for Pacco as well, and for every other individual whose story I have presented in this book. But Joan was not focused on a psychological solution; she was focused on freeing her heart. Her insight that clinging to her old wound was preventing her from finding freedom provided the structure for her amazing transformation that four years later is still unfolding.

How Do You Know That You Know?

So how do you know when you've abandoned clinging? One student in the Sunday evening meditation group I lead asked the question this way, "I have a difficult situation with a member of my family. It's very painful and not likely to improve. I have worked hard to let go of the clinging to my desire for things to be different, just like you tell us to do." He paused and then continued, "It seems to me that I have let loose of clinging. I feel more peaceful than I have in years. But then a little voice of doubt inside me asks, 'How do I know that I am not just in denial of my clinging and fooling myself?'"

This student was asking a very insightful question. I often encounter individuals who have fallen into hopelessness or numbness because they have suppressed a difficult desire and believed that this was nonclinging. So how do you know if you are falling into that trap? First of all, when clinging has been released, you experience a distinct felt sense of spaciousness, well-being, and lightness. Depending on your nature, you will feel it more strongly in either your body or your mind. Secondly, you have a felt sense that something is over and that something new awaits you. A third sign is that when you reflect back, you can see how your clinging was making a bad situation worse. Each of these signs is quite distinct; when they are present you should trust these feelings.

In the previous chapter you witnessed Jason's struggle with this Sixth Insight of knowing abandonment has occurred. He definitely had moments when he was not clinging to wanting his past to be different, but initially he could not integrate the wisdom of the Second Noble Truth such that he wouldn't get caught in clinging once he left the retreat. While on meditation retreat, he would experience *temporary release* from his strong wanting and he would feel relief, but he could not integrate it as *realized wisdom*. For a long time, there was no shift in his perception, which is the indicator that this insight has been realized. But as Jason went through the process of becoming mindful of his clinging over and over again during the retreats, his sense of knowing that he could abandon the clinging around his family eventually became sufficiently integrated and he started to change his life.

The One Who Knows Suffering and Nonsuffering

Knowing that you know clinging has been *abandoned* allows you to reconfigure your perceptions, mental habits, and goals to reflect your new understanding that *you are the knower of suffering and nonsuffering, the knower of clinging and nonclinging.* You are prepared for *the challenge to be fully present in the sacred now of each moment of your life.* As one who knows, you can now recognize clinging to desire, you know for yourself this is suffering, and, motivated by this knowing, you release your attachment. You have this capability right now, despite all of your imperfections. You can't always do it, but sometimes you can, particularly in relation to small or petty things in your life. For instance you may cling to little ego needs around status at work, or to a point of view in your relationship that creates constant friction, or to an agenda for a friend that is creating distance. Start letting loose of these less-charged areas of clinging in your life as best you can. With practice your ability to abandon clinging will greatly expand and you will be ready to take on the big issues of your life in which you really get caught.

Once you realize the Sixth Insight, you know deep in your bones that you can always "just start over" by letting go whenever you are caught in clinging to what you want. This knowing that you can start over is a mindfulness practice in itself and is very important if you tend to be a goal-driven person because it is so easy to get discouraged initially by how often and how intensely you cling to what you want. What you learn is that it doesn't matter how long you have been lost in clinging, once you become mindful of what you are doing, you simply start over with letting loose because you have the confidence that you can do so. *You let loose of clinging in this moment even if in the very next moment you contract all over again.*

Keep in mind that realization of the Sixth Insight can only occur once you have actually abandoned clinging. It can't be integrated by merely intellectually understanding the cause of suffering as outlined in the practice of the Fourth Insight. Why? Because the intuitive knowing of abandoning clinging comes only from the direct experience of letting go of it. You can't think integration, you must feel it—and that is what makes conscious knowing of abandoning so life changing for you.

THE DILEMMA OF DENYING DESIRE

As you begin to practice the Sixth Insight, you will quickly discover the felt difference between letting loose of clinging for just a moment and having truly abandoned it. These short, temporary releases, which I call "tastes of release," are quite important in realizing the Sixth Insight. Each time you let go of clinging (no matter how minor the clinging) and are fully aware that you have done so, you are retraining your nervous system to abandon its tendency to cling. The habit of clinging seems to be stored throughout the nervous system and is often embedded in your unconscious, so each moment of nonclinging interrupts your conditioning. In Buddhist terms you are creating healthier karma that will blossom in the future. Also, each moment you let go of clinging brings *momentary relief* from your suffering; having mindfulness of that relief reinforces your practice.

However, a taste of release does not bring the felt sense of spaciousness, freshness, and sustained relief that qualifies as knowing that suffering has been abandoned. Do not be discouraged when you discover that you are clinging to some want that you were sure you had outgrown—perhaps it's for recognition, or for acknowledgment for being right, or for wanting to have something go your way. It is quite common to find yourself temporarily or episodically caught in such a manner. Likewise, you must beware of becoming attached to your moments of feeling spacious and free—that's clinging to nonclinging!

Denying your suffering while telling yourself you have abandoned clinging can take many forms. Sheila, a very bright and well-trained meditation student who attended a retreat I taught, claimed that her mind stayed in the nonattachment that comes from knowing the emptiness of all experience. She was quite articulate and very aggressive about her view when pressed. Yet I felt that she was actually numb to her own expe-

rience. After much dialogue and doing various reflective practices that I suggested, Sheila had a life-changing insight: She
was in fact resisting being present in the moment because it
brought attachment with it—she was disassociating from her
own emotional life. Sheila had been unwilling to trust that she
could be with life just as it is, and not fall into clinging, and
going numb was her solution. Sheila quickly came to see that
being numb to life disguised the cynicism, suppression, bitterness, defeatism, and apathy she had been feeling in recent years.
She came to see that all these were deadened states of mind.
Without meaning to she had flattened her world—she was no
longer seeing that life is mysterious, ever changing, and suf-
fused with possibilities for joy. What an insight it was for her!
Since that time she has grown increasingly happier and more
engaged in her spiritual development.

THE RICHNESS OF LIFE LIES BEYOND DESIRE

When you are not clinging to desire, you feel more alive, not
less. Your mind is open to simultaneous realizations that the
world is both manifest and an illusion, that suffering is endless
and that you wish to end suffering. This paradoxical perspective softens and strengthens your heart such that it is able to
respond to suffering, and it enables you to clearly see what's the
most skillful response in any moment. And you realize that you
certainly don't want to contribute more suffering! These states
I am describing are real and available to you. Initially they may
not last very long, but they grow over time, and you become
someone who clings less and less to outcome.

In *Four Quartets* T. S. Eliot describes the distinction between
the aliveness of nonattachment and the deadness of nihilism
this way:

> There are three conditions which often look alike
> Yet differ completely, flourish in the same hedgerow:
> Attachment to self and to things and to persons, detachment
> From self and from things and from persons; and, growing
>   between them, indifference
> Which resembles the others as death resembles life,
> Being between two lives—unflowering . . .

The indifference Eliot is pointing to is attachment to not caring or nihilism and ultimately, to death. In contrast, the detachment of nonclinging creates vitality and openness to life. Ironically, because attachment has life energy in it, it actually comes closer to liberation than indifference.

I am always troubled when students report a belief that they should not care about anything since everything is always changing and that if they care they must be clinging. Such a view cultivates indifference and moves you further from the Buddha's dharma, not closer to liberation. How sad it is when your life takes this form; it is a waste of a precious human birth.

REDEMPTION FROM REGRET

There is one form of attachment or clinging that is particularly insidious, often unseen, and can be the source of much misery in your life. This is clinging to the desire that your past be other than it was. Maybe your childhood contained a terrible experience, or you committed some self-destructive acts in your past, or you caused harm to others in a way that is now hard to bear. Or maybe your life so far, or parts of it, hasn't been what you had hoped for. Perhaps you made some bad career or relationship choices. The list is seemingly endless. Most people carry around an invisible bag of regrets, even though they deny it when it's first pointed out to them. When you see that the past was hurtful and feel sorry that it was so, this is compassion, not clinging. But when you stay locked in anger or grief, or demand that life be other than it was, you are adding additional suffering to what is already suffering.

Your willingness to fully accept all your life, including the pain it has contained, presents benevolent possibilities for your life, no matter if the opportunities aren't in the form you would have preferred. You have the opportunity right now to benefit yourself and others by embracing the life you have had and garnering the wisdom of nonclinging from it.

In the book *The Art of Happiness*, the Dalai Lama was asked whether he had any regrets. He replied yes and then told the story of a senior monk who sought his advice about a particular practice. The Dalai Lama told the monk that the practice he was inquiring about was best started as a young man and suggested that he might want to forgo it. To the Dalai Lama's dismay, the monk later killed himself in order to be reborn so that he could do the practice. When the Dalai Lama was asked how he had abandoned his regret over the incident, he replied, "I didn't get rid of it. It's still there. But even though that feeling of regret is still there, it isn't associated with a feeling of heaviness or a quality of pulling me back. It would not be helpful to anyone if I let that feeling of regret weigh me down, be simply a source of discouragement and depression, or interfere with going on with my life to the best of my ability."

This is a poignant example of how your actions in the present give redemptive meaning to your past actions. Are you willing to be present in this manner?

IF LIFE ISN'T ABOUT MEETING YOUR DESIRES, WHAT IS IT ABOUT?

One form of resistance to practicing nonclinging to outcome that I often encounter comes in the guise of a question: "If I let go of desire, what do I have to live for?" Students ask this question because they are confused about the difference between goals and attachment to goals. I remind them that in abandoning the cause of suffering they are not ceasing to have desires and creating goals from those desires, instead *they are changing their relationship to desires and goals*. They are ceasing to be attached to getting what they desire, and this includes spiritual goals.

The Buddha got it right—your life has no permanency, therefore fulfilling your immediate and ever-changing desires does not result in a sense of well-being; instead it simply leads you to having more desires. Likewise, despite what your mind tells you at the time, not getting what you desire does not result in everlasting misery. Instead, your mind becomes filled with new desires or goals that you will not accomplish or if you do achieve them, they will become unfulfilling, so you need still more desires!

In my experience, what makes life worthwhile is living from your deepest or core values. You may be wondering, "But how do I know what my core values are?" This is a good question, and the answer only reveals itself through your exploration. You would not be reading this book if you did not already have values that are compatible with those reflected here—knowing the truth; finding freedom; not causing harm to yourself or others; being of service to others; meeting the world with compassion and kindness; having the qualities of gratitude, patience, persistence, generosity, curiosity, and humor; and continuing to learn and grow psychologically and spiritually. The more you practice mindfulness of suffering, its cause, and the path to ending suffering, the more your core values will be revealed to you. Does this mean you will always be able to act from your core values or that you will always know how they apply in every situation? No. Beware of measuring yourself against ideas of perfection. This is a gradual path; not until you are fully liberated will you always manifest your core values. But the more insights you have through practice, the deeper your connection to your core values will be and the less likely you will be to get caught in craving. Witnessing the truth of this evolution in your mind gives you inspiration to keep doing the hard work of practice; the very possibility of your maturing in this manner is motivation for you to begin.

Your core values and the qualities associated with them serve you no matter what the conditions of your life are in any particular moment. In a time of happiness, you are able to appreciate your good fortune and enjoy it without becoming identified with it. You do not compromise yourself in order to get what you want or keep what you have. Likewise, in times of distress or disappointment, you don't act out in a manner that causes harm, and you don't become lost in your suffering. Thus you don't physically or mentally collapse, or resort to destructive behavior, or fixate on what is difficult.

A casual observation of your life reveals just how temporary and fragile the conditions you hold most dear are—from your health to the well-being of those you love to physical and economic security. It just takes an auto accident, an illness, or an economic downturn to radically alter these conditions. Yet so many people will not allow themselves to know the truth of this fragility and persist in grasping after desires, despite the fact that their life experiences prove that this is not a successful strategy. Through the practice of mindfulness and letting go of clinging, you discover that living from your deepest values moment by moment is by far the most successful strategy for attaining purpose and meaning in your life, for feeling related to others, and for achieving a sense of ease and well-being.

The approach I'm recommending doesn't mean that you have to reject or deny your desires. But rather than contracting around getting your desires met, your life becomes centered on mindfully and skillfully moving toward your goals. However, in order to establish this new relationship with your desires such that you can abandon clinging to them, you will need to learn the practice of renunciation in your daily life.

THE NEED FOR RENUNCIATION

When you cling to desire, your ego identity (that aspect of the mind that regards itself as "me" and "mine") becomes organized around fulfilling desire and starts to measure how well it is doing by how many of your desires are met. If you genuinely want to be less caught in clinging and suffering, you need to develop some form of renunciation practice that interrupts this pattern and disengages from the ego's drive to have what it wants. If you don't, your ego desires will continue to rule your life, set your priorities, and allocate your time. Renunciation is not about killing your ego or developing aversion to it; rather, it is about forming a new relationship with your ego such that it reflects your deeper values rather than its immediate wants.

Practicing renunciation means that you consciously give up certain attitudes, views, behaviors, and goals because they lead you to clinging and suffering. You don't cease being motivated by your ego; after all, it is a source of interest and energy. Think of the ego as a puppy—it likes to play, chase after things, wants attention, and creates messes, but it is still lovable and a source of warmth in your life. And it can be trained and developed to serve your deeper values.

Students often feel dread when I bring up the topic of renunciation. But their fear is unfounded, because renunciation enhances rather than diminishes your life. Many people associate renunciation only with celibacy, dieting, or acts of modesty, but it has much greater applications. I once saw a sign in a restaurant men's room in Alaska that read, "Celibacy is not an inherited trait." Indeed it's not! Nor is any other act of renunciation, for each is a behavioral trait that you develop through repetition.

It's true that monks and nuns take a number of vows of austerity, which can include giving up almost all material goods and living by certain precepts that greatly restrict their behavior. For this reason, it is said that they have "gone forth." They are choosing these limitations and to live in a community of like-minded seekers in order to create a strong container of support for their spiritual aspiration and to live a lifestyle that reflects their values.

The Buddha often gave talks on renunciation addressed only to those who had gone forth; therefore it is misleading for laypeople to assume that such teachings are meant for them. But even in the talks he gave to lay followers, he still called for renunciation. So what did he have in mind for you?

The most basic type of renunciation is keeping precepts. These are training principles to live by which lead you to develop ethical behavior and help you avoid causing suffering for yourself and others. Examples of the precepts the Buddha prescribed are not killing, not taking what has not been freely given, practicing nonharmful speech and sexuality, and not intoxicating the mind with drugs and alcohol so that you don't lose your ability to think clearly. On a more challenging level, there are lifestyle renunciations that enable you to live according to your values. Examples would be not taking a certain job because it doesn't allow you to manifest your values; or accepting less income in order to have more time for spiritual practice; or living modestly in order to have a simpler life that doesn't cloud your mind.

THREE EGO-RENUNCIATION PRACTICES

In addition to taking the precepts and practicing the lifestyle constraints that the Buddha suggested, there is another category of renunciation techniques that I have found to be helpful to modern practitioners. These are renunciation practices that directly challenge your ego's desire to always be in charge.

After some years of experimentation, I discovered three ego-renunciation practices that loosen the ego's grasp on the mind but don't require you to make any outward changes in your life. The first is *renouncing your attachment to being right*. Most of us cling to the need to be right, and making this renunciation can dramatically affect both how you interact with others and how you interpret events. When the renunciation starts to be real, you have a much easier time making decisions and have less of a need to position yourself with others or in your own mind. Giving up always being right doesn't mean you forsake your opinions or your right to seek social justice, but you are not defensive, judgmental, or self-righteous in your approach to life. You mindfully live with the fact that even when you're wrong, it's okay because you are coming from your deepest intention. Also, you learn from being wrong (or right), therefore you become a more effective person.

The second ego-renunciation practice is committing to *no longer measuring the success of your life by how many of your wants are met*. This renunciation allows you to still have desires, but they're not at the center of your life. You fulfill those wants that can be fulfilled while living from your deepest values, and you slowly abandon the rest. This means that your sexual desires are constrained by nonharming, material gains are limited by ethical and generous behavior, and your ego need for achievement and attention is less of a priority than living according to your core values. Of course you still have to fulfill your basic needs and live up to your responsibilities as best you can, but you renounce measuring success by what you have or what you have achieved. You may be surprised to discover how much you have been judging your life by this standard. It is so common that it is almost entirely unconscious, and it is devastating to inner growth because the ego can always distract you with yet another want.

The third ego renunciation is *giving up being the star of your own movie*. The unfolding of events that make up your life is like a movie, is it not? And you interpret every scene or event from the vantage point of being the star of your movie—is it good or bad for you, do you like it or not, and so on. Once you renounce being the star of your own movie, you begin to see the unfolding of each scene and the movie as a whole from multiple perspectives. You don't forsake your role in the movie, but once you cease making it be all about you, the movie creates less anxiety and you are more able to live from your core values.

Beware: Clinging That Has Been Abandoned Will Arise Again

As your renunciation practice begins to show results (you start to feel better about yourself and your life), beware of your ego seizing any opportunity to reassert itself and usurping your hard efforts of letting go for its own glorification. For instance, one student, Michael, who had been a successful executive but felt miserable as a person, retired from the business world to pursue his inner development. Despite having more than enough money to support himself the rest of his life, on the very first meditation retreat he attended Michael conceived of an idea to build a chain of health centers based on the inner life. He was immediately hooked on the concept and started planning. It made no difference to Michael that the constant tension of business activity was what had lead him to become miserable in the first place. He wanted me to give him reasons for not starting the new business, while I wanted him to view this as opportunity for renunciation practice, so I would frustrate Michael by saying, "You know, it really is a good idea, and you could probably pull it off. Despite that being true, let it go!" It took Michael two years to finally release his fixation on this idea.

Another student, Bonnie, a journalist who dropped out of the marketplace to be with her family and spend time developing her inner life, had an idea to create a new book series. Her ego seduced her into believing that the series would be "hot" in the marketplace and she would finally get the recognition she felt she had never achieved in her twenties and thirties. Of course this meant once again limiting her time with her children and spouse and for meditation retreats and pushing her somewhat health-challenged body. Bonnie's ego would say, "Just one more time, go for it!" So I asked Bonnie if the process of creating the book would be more rewarding than spending time with her family and in meditation, and she said, "No." Then I asked her if she would have a better life if she wrote the books and they were successful than if she took care of her inner and outer life during these next four years. Again she replied, "No." Finally Bonnie got that her mind had been captured by her old ego need for glory. She realized that she was not that person any longer and professional success was not her priority anymore. For a long time, though, not doing the book series felt like renunciation practice to Bonnie.

In both of these examples, the individuals were being drawn back into old patterns of seeking ego fulfillment that had not worked for them. Although their ideas were perfectly fine, their egos were driving their decisions and diverting them from the next step in their inner journeys. In order to realize their higher aspirations, the ego was going to play a less important role in their lives and it fought back. You can imagine how unhappy they were with me initially when I suggested that they were falling prey to their egos' endless wants and recommended that they pause and reflect for some weeks before making a decision. Each of them reported that they felt I wasn't supporting them, and their egos acted out against me. Eventually, though, they thanked me for holding the possibility of their liberation from clinging.

Ironically, the less often you fall prey to clinging, the easier it is for you to meet your ego's needs in a healthier manner. If you reach this point in your practice and are able to let go of clinging but are still primarily committed to the outer life of accomplishment, you are not doing anything wrong. What matters is that you consciously choose to find the balance between your outer and inner life and not be helplessly addicted to your ever-shifting stream of desires. If you keep practicing, the time will come when your spiritual development becomes the most important thing in your life.

Once you cease to be a slave to your ego's endless wants, it may take a while for a new sense of well-being to arise. At first you may feel worse because you are frustrating the way you used to be, but you have not established a new way of being yet. This is a time of "wandering in the desert," and it can feel terrible and disorienting. To get through this period, you have to remind yourself each day of why you chose the course you did and of your intention behind the decision. Ego renunciation is a hard road to travel, so be gentle with yourself and restrained in how much change you make in your priorities at one time.

CHAPTER 12

THE PARADOX
OF DESIRE

THE WISDOM OF THE SECOND NOBLE TRUTH

In this chapter we will be delving into deeper and more challenging reflections about the role of desire in your life, but first let's take stock of what you have encountered in the Second Noble Truth thus far. You have learned through reflecting on the Fourth Insight that suffering is a mind state that manifests when you fall into craving for what your senses desire, or for what you desire for the future, or for what you want to cease. It isn't desire, but rather the craving it elicits, that is the problem.

Having realized the Fourth Insight, you then began to utilize the Fifth Insight to switch the manner in which you measure the success of your life from getting all of your desires met to answering the question: *How do I wish to meet life, regardless of whether it is pleasant or unpleasant?* You also learned that by letting go of your attachment to outcome, you experience abandoning as a realization and get at least a taste of release from suffering.

With the Sixth Insight you gained confidence in your relationship to desire because now "you know that you know" what it means to abandon clinging. When you are not clinging to outcome, you are able to be in the moment just as it is, and you are temporarily free of suffering. When you are able to accept things being just as they are without collapsing, withdrawing, or losing your passion for the highest good, you turn defeat into joy. You are dancing with life.

Freedom from attachment to outcome allows you to connect to your intention in each moment. When you are living and doing what is right in this moment as an end in itself regardless of the outcome, you are able to bring your deepest values into your life. And when you are able to be fully present in the moment while aligned with your deepest intention, you live a vital and wise life, regardless of the challenges you may face. Being present and staying with your intention are skills that come from learning to abandon clinging. Thus, abandoning clinging as the cause of suffering is both a *result* of practice and the *means* of practice. Your goal is to be free of clinging, but your practice and your intention are to release clinging right now!

Having reached an understanding of clinging and nonclinging, you are now ready to reflect on the proper role of desire in your life. I suspect you will discover that it is a more subtle and mysterious undertaking than you've ever imagined.

AN IDENTITY OF DESIRE

No doubt you are aware of the consequences of obsessing about various desires, but it is less likely that you have spent much time reflecting on the nature of desire itself. It is easy to not notice desire. For instance, when you flip through a catalog not because you need something but because you *want to want* something, you are feeding an identity of desire. But do you notice it? If you become immediately discontent with whatever level of worldly achievement you attain and feel you have to have more, you are feeding an addiction of desire. If you view your significant relationship mostly through the eyes of what it lacks, you are falling prey to an identity of being someone who wants. Leaving the relationship because it doesn't work is one thing, but choosing to be in a constant state of wanting is something else. Is this how you want to condition your mind around desire?

I left *Esquire* thinking that 40 percent of the time I would feel longing and regret for all that I had given up while the rest of the time I would feel as though I had made the right decision. To my surprise I didn't feel regret for what I had left behind, but there was a problem I hadn't counted on—the person who woke up each morning was accustomed to having goals. He liked difficult, seemingly impossible goals. He didn't mind delayed gratification and could flourish without reinforcement, but he did need a goal. It was how he organized himself for meeting the world. Yet the very practice I had chosen was to be goalless, to simply sit and wait for inner understanding to emerge through meditation and reflection. I did not even have a specific spiritual goal.

What was I to do with that person who awakened each morning ready to achieve some desired goal? It was very disorienting. In my more confused moments, I would start looking around for something to want just so I could have a goal. I made a number of poor decisions that I called "falling off the wagon" (since I had been something of a workaholic for the previous 20 years) in which I took on a project just to have a goal. But gradually my identity loosened. The day finally came after some years of "wandering in the desert" when the person who woke up in the morning was not a goal achiever, yet he wasn't apathetic either. I still knew how to achieve goals but was no longer addicted to them. *I knew that I knew* that an entire pattern of clinging had been released, and it gave me the faith to continue on in my practice. I had made a crossover. I had become someone whose primary orientation was to live from his intention. This inner change marked a turning point in my relationship to desire that is still unfolding to this day. I also know that I know my exploration is far from over.

One Who Has No Expectations Is Never Disappointed

There is an amusing cartoon greeting card titled "the Dalai Lama's Birthday," in which he is shown wearing his trademark sunglasses and holding a present while three of his monks stand off to one side beaming. The box is open, revealing that there is no gift inside, and the Dalai Lama exclaims, "Nothing. Just what I always wanted!"

This card reflects the message, which is often conveyed in Buddhist circles, that those who desire nothing are never unhappy. This view of desire has certain merits, but at the same time it is misleading. Without clarification it can easily lead you to believe that your life and your practice are at odds with one another.

On the positive side, it is true that if you have no desires, then by definition you are not fearful of disappointment and you can be more spontaneous in the moment with whatever situation arises. Desiring nothing does not, at least theoretically, preclude your being delighted when something pleasant arises. In fact, you've probably experienced doing something simply because it was the right thing to do or needed doing, and were surprised to find that it was a lot of fun or felt truly rewarding.

However, living without desire can easily be misunderstood as not caring for others. For most people the goal of the spiritual path is not to cease desiring good things for the people they love but rather to increase their love so that they desire good things for everyone. Do you for one moment think that the Dalai Lama doesn't care about his people and their shared culture? The Buddha taught precisely because he cared. This type of caring is benevolent love, not self-referential love, but it doesn't ignore the self, either.

Also, to never be unhappy is a suspect goal in the first place, because not being unhappy does not necessarily mean that you have a satisfying existence. You can drug yourself and not be consciously unhappy, or you can cultivate an attitude that provides a feeling of not being unhappy although it is also true that you do not feel particularly fulfilled. Furthermore, as you saw in Chapter 7, the opposite of suffering is not happiness, but rather it is nonsuffering and having a peaceful, meaningful relatedness and sense of well-being in all of your life, even in difficult times. When you get down to actually living your daily life as practice, it quickly becomes obvious that developing ethical behavior, deep understanding, and strong mindfulness actually requires desire—*a lot of desire.*

Rather than fixating on how you desire too much, which can easily deteriorate into self-judgment and condemnation, you are better off mindfully practicing letting go of expectations about having your desires met, even your spiritual desires. So instead of accepting the view that "one who desires nothing is never unhappy," I prefer the perspective that "one who has no expectations is never disappointed." Do you see the benefits of this instruction? It allows you to desire what is wholesome without being disappointed if it doesn't come to pass. You are responsible for living out your intentions—this is wholesome desire—but what comes of those intentions is not within your control, and clinging and expectations are simply foolish endeavors. Of course I don't mean to imply that you should forsake common-sense expectations, such as if you eat too much you can expect to have a stomachache, and forms of contractual trust, like expecting the auto mechanic to repair your car's brakes.

I have found that the fewer expectations you have, the less addicted you are to desire creation in the first place. The wisdom that arises from this insight is that *you don't strive to get rid of your desires; they simply become less interesting once you cease to be organized around your expectations.* I realize that you may find this unlikely initially, but why not open to the possibility that this is so?

Constantly Seeking Fulfillment of Desire Is a Hell Realm

Alan, a student with whom I worked for several years, was always getting caught in expectations, some positive and some negative, and therefore was plagued with the hindrance of restlessness and worry. He was quite bright and accomplished in the world, but he was never satisfied. As soon as he accomplished something or received recognition, he was immediately plagued by a new desire and feelings of discontent about not being good enough or not receiving the full amount of credit he was due. Because of this discontent, Alan lived in a hell realm, a miserable existence camouflaged by what seemed outwardly to be a glamorous, enviable life. He frequently changed jobs and was obsessed with getting peer and public recognition. Through both public comments and mood displays, he constantly broadcast his relentless desires and resentments to colleagues and friends. As a result, a reservoir of ill will and impatience built up toward him both at work and in his home life. When confronted by those who cared about him, Alan's standard defense was, "I just want to live up to my potential and to receive what is my due in terms of compensation and recognition."

Then, as a result of an incident in which he caused a colleague much suffering, Alan received widespread public criticism from his peers. In his misery, Alan finally was able to realize that he was caught in clinging to expectations about himself and how others should treat him. During one key interview with me, he blurted out, "This is suffering!" He was referring to how insidiously his expectations had become entwined with his sense of self-worth and resentment that he still felt from childhood neglect. Although it was slow going, Alan began to separate his emotions of insecurity, ambition, and anxiety from the future story that his expectations represented. Once he could make this distinction, he realized that his mental pattern was to be reactive to his own story making around expectations. He was so possessed by his clinging that his sleep was often disturbed and he would engage in self-medicating behavior that was potentially very harmful.

Eventually, Alan came to see that taking birth in expectations was truly delusional. He learned to be aware of his desires as they arose and let loose of the story making that solidified his expectations. After a couple of years of mindfully working in this manner, he reported that not only did his life improve but also a lot of his old desires disappeared without his noticing it. Alan had reached a true beginning in his practice where he could start to understand clinging and nonclinging.

Notice that it took years, not days or weeks, for Alan's insight to bear fruit, and in the meantime he had more conscious misery than previously when he had avoided facing his clinging. It may well be the same for you. So many earnest, well-meaning students give up on their mindful exploration because they are disappointed when this initial insight doesn't bring instantaneous relief. Alan's many months of facing the consequences of his clinging represented "grinding up" the conditioning that had accumulated in the preceding years of his life. There was no skipping ahead for him, and that was fortunate, not unfortunate. So do not be discouraged if an initial sense of freedom from clinging is followed by a prolonged time of discomfort as you see the consequences of your actions more clearly. Just remember to be gentle with yourself.

Deconstructing Desire

Like Alan, you need to delve into self-exploration around desire at some point in your practice in order to understand its place in your life. This is accomplished by deconstructing desire such that you can see its origins and its component parts. Most people have never done this; consequently they have little knowledge of themselves in relationship to desire. To begin your self-inquiry, first reflect on what Ajahn Sumedho means when he says, "Desire is the energy of the realm in which you live." To me this means that desire cannot simply be ignored or treated as loathsome because it is a naturally occurring energetic state in nature. Instead, it is essential that you develop a way of relating to desire such that it does not imprison you, yet allows you to be responsive to it naturally arising in your life. All caring, all kindness, all love is fueled by desire; how you perceive and relate to desire when it arises determines whether or not it leads to suffering for yourself and others.

From the study of child development, we know that desire plays a critical role in the human development process, especially the brain's maturation, and that a child who isn't cuddled and stimulated suffers from what is called "withering disease." Therefore, it is healthy that as a child you had desires and needed stimulation. Beginning at birth you felt those desires that are associated with basic survival instincts—to be fed, to be physically comfortable, and to be safe. Then early in infancy you started to realize your separateness from others. You began to identify with the emerging stream of sensations and thoughts in your field of awareness as "me." Such identification is inevitable and healthy, although it is an incomplete view of your life. Next, you began to develop an ego, meaning an energetic complex of memories, associations, concerns, and goals, in order to manage your feeling of separateness. Over time you became more and more identified with your ego, and you learned to choose and fulfill its desires so as to protect it, please it, and make it more secure and powerful in its own reflection. The strength or weakness of the ego complex is a result of your genetic inheritance and whether or not you were sufficiently nurtured, and it is not independent of the conditions that formed it. The ego complex is inextricably bound to fulfilling desire. In a sense, that is its purpose, which is why Ajahn Sumedho says, "Your personality never gets enlightened."

As you spiritually mature you come to see that your desires just naturally arise as a reaction to causes and conditions. They are not independent or constant, nor are they based on something that is solid and unchanging. Desires are simply your ego's way of helping you thrive in life. And you begin to realize that there is a more profound manner for you to relate to life than pursuing your desires. In searching for this more satisfying way of living, you use your heart as well as your mind to discern your deeper values, in contrast to your reactionary desires, and you realize that living in alignment with these values brings more well-being and freedom than chasing after desires.

In Jungian psychology, which is the closest of all Western psychological approaches to Buddhist psychology, this maturation is referred to as "individuation"—the process of separating from your cultural conditioning and beginning to utilize the capacity of the ego to serve something greater than the desires of the ego self. According to Buddhist psychology you begin to realize that *the ego complex or ego mind is not your true nature*. With this wisdom as a guide, you abandon clinging to desire in order to be able to live from your true nature, your Buddha nature.

What makes this process of finding freedom challenging is that early on the ego complex is presented with an incredibly confounding realization—that it and the body it identifies with are vulnerable to all sorts of harm and that its ability to protect itself is limited. The ego reacts to its real and imagined limitations by falling into worry and lamentation. To compensate for its inadequacy, the ego develops the ability to deny threats, distract itself from the truth, or project its uncertainty onto others. To whatever degree your ego is wounded, it develops various forms of grandiosity, such as judging and comparing mind, to compensate. This uncertainty and lack of control makes your mind quite anxious. In trying to manage all of these feelings, the ego becomes overwhelmed because it can never find stability, and so the mind clings to any and all possibilities of happiness of any duration it can find.

Can you see how difficult and challenging it is for your ego when you start to accept that dukkha is an unavoidable part of life? Imagine how hard it is for the ego to accept the uncertainty and instability of moment-to-moment existence. Is it any wonder that the ego would try to ignore and deny its constantly changing nature or that it would start to succumb to all kinds of desire and start grasping and clinging to objects that seem to promise happiness? I tell students to regard the ego with compassion and appreciate the difficult situation it is in.

Death Is Your Ego's Ultimate Dilemma

Worse than the day-to-day uncertainty is the ego's realization that its existence is time based and that there is a time in which it will not exist—it is going to die! It is daunting to have this capacity to know the certainty of your own end, without knowing when, where, or how, and that there is nothing you can do about it. All three kinds of desire or tanha can be seen in your reaction to your mortality. First, there is kama tanha, your tendency to escape into sensual desire, which includes the ego pleasures of being right and feeling important. Next there is bhava tanha, or the desire to become something that the ego desires, such as being famous, or having perfect health, or even having a child in order to ensure its continuation through genetic extension. For the same reason the ego has a natural tendency to embrace belief systems that guarantee future life. Then there is vibhava tanha, or the desire not to exist, in which the ego just wants to end the stress, pain, and uncertainty, so it desires nonexistence in that moment or even death itself. None of these reactions is horrible; they are just ill informed and incomplete.

As you spiritually mature, you directly realize the true nature of the physical realm of existence—that you are incarnated in a composite of matter that is located in space and time, therefore all things including yourself are subject to constant change. At first such a direct knowing (not your intellectual knowing but the gut-wrenching felt experience of it) is disconcerting and disheartening. But after more compassionate mindfulness practice, you cease reacting and grasping after a solution to the dilemma of your mortality, and *you accept that life is like this in this realm*. Sometimes great temporary states of well-being arise when clinging is abandoned. For instance, you may realize that everything is perfect just as it is or that everything is interdependent, and you lose any sense of separateness. Or everything may seem illuminated, as though you are really seeing it for the first time.

Temporarily, the ego is not your central reference point, and you get at least a small taste of your Buddha nature. But most importantly, something new is now possible: You can experience the arising of a desire and not have that desire be contaminated by your ego's anxiety that it must have what it wants. Likewise, you do not expect desire and its fulfillment to relieve you from the existential dilemma of your mortality. You are not just in a temporary state of freedom; you know that you know you have abandoned clinging to desire. The mind has equanimity around the desire and you have freedom in how you choose to respond to it.

Desire as Movement

By being in this physical realm, you are undeniably involved with the energy of desire, just as Ajahn Sumedho suggests. Therefore, feelings, even wholesome ones such as caring and compassion, are an impersonal form of desire. This, then, is the paradox of desire—it leads to suffering when grasped after, yet without it there is no movement to tend to your child's needs or to help your sick neighbor, or to free yourself from suffering. Thus, your challenge is not to rid yourself of desire, but rather to choose your desires wisely and respond skillfully. There is a Native American story that beautifully captures how to hold this paradox in your life. According to the story, a grandfather tells his two grandchildren that each of us has two wolves inside—one is filled with wanting and anger and thinks only of itself, while the other is caring and protective of others—and the two are engaged in a fight to the death. One of the children asks, "But grandfather, which one will win?" The grandfather pauses, smiles, and then says, "The one you feed is the one who will prevail. You determine the winner."

Desire always involves movement—either *toward* something pleasant, or *away* from something unpleasant. There is movement in desire whether you are reacting to something that is happening right now, thinking about the future, or even remembering the past. The frozen states of apathy, helplessness, cynicism, and depression have little movement and, therefore, little life. They are hindrances to freedom and well-being. Such wounded states of mind point to the necessity of movement for healthy life. They also reveal that you need healthy desire to provide the energy (*viriya*) you need to seek liberation.

To understand the relationship between movement and your desires, there are two refinements that I suggest you reflect upon. The first is to make the movement of your desire the object of your mindful attention. By focusing on the energetic movement, you can quickly determine if what you are being drawn toward or repulsed from is in line with your deeper values. By directly feeling the energy of the desire in your body, you gain separation from it and you are not so identified with it, such that if following that energy is going to lead to suffering, you halt the impulse. The Buddha called this "right effort." Combining awareness of the movement of desire with right effort allows you to trust yourself and not be rigid in meeting life.

One yogi, Mark, who was distressed over how he often unintentionally spoke or acted in ways that were not skillful, started focusing on the energetic feelings of desire in his body. He quickly discovered that he often had no conscious awareness of having been "activated" by desire, so he was not catching himself before speaking or acting. Awareness of the felt experience of this energy in his body provided Mark with an early warning system and the chance to pause and reflect on his choices before responding. It was a few years before Mark developed an understanding of the psychological dynamics that triggered many of his unconscious impulses, but that was okay because he felt he was no longer "out of control."

A second refinement for working with the energy of desire is to explore the great mystery of stillness. Stillness is not apathy or collapse; it is vibrant, fully alive energy. In stillness the movement is neither away from nor toward any object. In *Four Quartets*, T. S. Eliot describes stillness this way:

> Neither from nor towards; at the still point, there the dance is,
> But neither arrest nor movement. And do not call it fixity,
> Where past and future are gathered. Neither movement from nor towards,
> Neither ascent nor decline. Except for the point, the still point,
> There would be no dance, and there is only the dance.

By becoming aware of the moments of stillness in yourself (and you do have them!) you gain the ability to clearly see your desire as movement. You see how desire arises naturally from causes and conditions and aren't beguiled by it. You know that clinging to desire is not the freedom of stillness. You understand that in order to be free your challenge is to come to terms with desire and to cease to be attached to it. When this insight is present, clinging is spontaneously abandoned and there is certainty in knowing that this has occurred.

Desire Itself Is Not Desirable, Except . . .

By now you can see how finding the right relationship with desire is essential for dancing with life. But you are probably wondering how to let go of clinging while living a life in which you want to care because caring is what gives your life meaning. This question will most likely remain a paradox throughout your practice. T. S. Eliot captures this dilemma more beautifully than I could ever hope to when he writes in *Four Quartets*:

> Desire itself is movement
> Not in itself desirable;
> Love is itself unmoving,
> Only the cause and end of movement . . .

Eliot is making two points that are important to your understanding of the role of desire in your life. The first is the difference between desire and love. Desire is characterized by wanting, so it always involves the movement of energy toward or away from something. This inherent movement makes desire vulnerable to grasping for security from past unease and future uncertainty, which causes the mind to collapse into clinging to outcome. Therefore desire does not seem to be desirable, as Eliot says. The love he is referring to is pure love, not sense-driven love. Pure love is unmoving, not desirous of anything, and does not manifest as energy or movement toward or away from something. It is not involved in the world of change, hence not vulnerable to contraction or clinging. Pure love has benign energy that is not corrupted by desire, therefore it simply *is*; such energy has no wanting or aversion.

You may feel pure love as a wonderful state of receptive stillness in the mind and heart or as a sensation of being connected to all things. Or you may experience it as a state of emptiness in which all objects of the mind arise and disappear. Or it may manifest as the realization that everything is beautiful and perfect just as it is, or that everything lacks permanence, or that life is dreamlike and there's no self who experiences it. Feelings of relatedness, responsiveness, and meaningfulness are intrinsically present with pure love, and you know that clinging to them would be pointless. There is nobody to cling and nothing to cling to. This is a liberated state of mind in which there is no suffering. But Eliot acknowledges the paradox of your life. While pure love is desireless, it can be the motivator or cause of movement; that is, love itself generates desire. The realization of this paradox is what I believe inspired the Buddha to teach the dharma. It is the mystery contained in all acts of kindness in which there is no self-reference or, as in the Buddha's case, there is not even a sense of a self.

BOOK THREE

THE THIRD
NOBLE TRUTH

THE THIRD NOBLE TRUTH

WHAT IS THE NOBLE TRUTH OF THE CESSATION OF SUFFERING?

IT IS THE REMAINDERLESS FADING AND CESSATION OF THAT SAME CRAVING; THE REJECTING, RELINQUISHING, LEAVING, AND RENOUNCING OF IT. . . .

THIS NOBLE TRUTH MUST BE PENETRATED TO BY REALIZING THE CESSATION OF SUFFERING. . . .

THIS NOBLE TRUTH HAS BEEN PENETRATED TO BY REALIZING THE CESSATION OF SUFFERING.

—SAMYUTTA NIKAYA LVI, 11

CHAPTER 13

YOU CAN END
YOUR SUFFERING

As you begin to explore the three insights of the Noble Truth of Cessation, your practice advances to a new level of subtlety. Therefore, it is important that you remember your first taste of freedom, which you experienced with the Second Noble Truth when you learned to abandon clinging to your desire (the Fourth Insight). You then repeatedly practiced abandoning clinging and by doing so you realized the truth of how craving controls your mind, and at that point your mind was temporarily free (the Fifth Insight). And finally you practiced being aware of your mind being free (the Sixth Insight). One result of attaining these six insights is that you repeatedly experience at least brief periods of choiceless awareness in which your mind does not favor or lean toward any particular experience. It is quite literally content with whatever it happens to be experiencing. These periods of calm and equanimity condition the mind to receive the dramatically more profound experiences that come with realizing the insights of the Third Noble Truth. Having done these previous insight practices equips you to explore an even deeper level of knowing cessation and to realize a stage of consciousness in which your mind is no longer reactive, despite external and internal conditions. This is the architectural brilliance of the Twelve Insights—practicing each one prepares you for the next.

Now, through the three insights of the Third Noble Truth, the Buddha introduces you to a new reality. He is telling you that it is possible for you to move from the "taste" of the mind being free of clinging to the *direct knowing of pure awareness, in which there is no object of awareness, no observer, and no awareness of awareness.* All that exists is awareness itself. By repeatedly going in and out of this altered state of pure awareness, you experience *cessation*; you no longer identify with or are defined by the ever-changing moment-to-moment stream of ordinary awareness. When you have reached total cessation, your mind is relaxed and nongrasping without any special effort on your part, and all delusion has stopped. The mind is completely unperturbed by any conditions that arise in your body, in your life, or in the lives of others. No matter how difficult those conditions or how desirable, no clinging arises.

With the Third Noble Truth, the Buddha is asking you to take a *quantum leap in your perception* of human potential. Total cessation entails moving beyond your ego such that you cease being defined by your ego, and you become ever more your true Buddha nature. You are challenged to let loose of old beliefs you may have about yourself and the ultimate nature of awareness. This is not an easy task because so much of your sense of self is based on familiar, habitual, and regularly occurring mind states and your ego's reaction to them. However, the longing for cessation is innate to the human experience. And just as water flows from the mountain to the sea, so your mind feels an impulse to return to its true nature whenever it encounters the various kinds of dukkha that are an inimical part of life.

Your aspiration for cessation is an *intuitive response* to the feeling of being on a treadmill that is created by the constant presence of stress and the lack of any lasting satisfaction in your life. Although you know that living like a marionette and being jerked around by the ever-changing strings of desire is not the ultimate meaning of life, you are not sure what to replace it with because you care about life and you do not want to reject caring. In fact, you deeply appreciate the blessing of life.

So you start to reflect on the possibility of there being a more wholesome, fulfilling way of relating to life that is not defined by endless stress, judgment, and wanting, and you seek a path that will lead to *cessation of being identified with the treadmill*. You discover that your aspiration for total cessation is not separate from your intuition that there may be an *unseen order or priority* that if realized and lived will bring ease to your mind and give your life its richest and fullest expression. *Your path to cessation starts from the sprouting of these small seeds of intuitive knowing.*

THE SEVENTH INSIGHT:

The Noble Truth of Cessation is the abandoning of all craving.

CHAPTER 14

TASTING THE HIDDEN JOY OF LIFE'S IMPERMANENCE

Reflecting on the Third Noble Truth

Imagine your mind totally free of craving, ill will, and delusion. It is clear, alert, and unaffected by external and internal conditions, whether pleasant or unpleasant. This liberated mind state is what comes with the realization of the Third Noble Truth. In the Seventh Insight the Buddha is asking you to reflect on the possibility that freedom through cessation of grasping is achievable. Then in the Eighth Insight he asks you to practice the direct realization of it. The fruit of realizing cessation is *nibbana*, in which you are no longer affected by dukkha.[11] Nibbana literally means "cooled" and is analogous to a fire that's no longer burning. Thus, when there is cessation, *your mind no longer burns in response to the arising of pleasant and unpleasant in your life*; it isn't reactive or controlled by what you like or dislike. In

[11] I deliberately use the phrase "no longer affected by dukkha" here to characterize what is often described as the "end of suffering," which can leave the impression that the Buddha became some kind of superhuman such that he didn't even feel physical pain. Although I certainly respect this view, to me full cessation means that there is no longer any resistance in the mind around any conditions. Said another way, dukkha arises but there is nowhere for it to establish itself in the mind.

daily reality your mind exists in a constant *state of choiceless awareness* when this *stage of complete realization of cessation* is attained. Your mind is willing to be with what is true in the moment and isn't disturbed by it. From this place of nonattachment, you are free to respond to the moment in a manner that is aligned with your values and reflects your deepest wisdom.

Choiceless awareness stemming from the cessation of all clinging is not the same as indifferent or noncaring awareness. *You still care, you still love, but you cease to take caring so personally.* Choiceless awareness is a genuine, realizable stage of attainment, not some imagined concept. You will have many foretastes of it on your inner journey in which your mind will be in a temporary state of nonclinging, and you will know that this is so. But when you reach the stage of total cessation, choiceless awareness is no longer just a temporary state; it becomes the essence of your being. You are not controlled by any external conditions nor does your mind create unwholesome states, not even brief ones. You are unaffected by threats or loss to your well-being and mortality. *You are living the deathless; you are no longer defined by, living from, or identified with whatever is arising and passing.*

This does not mean that your body no longer gets sick or hurt—life in this physical realm of space and time remains coherent and consistent, in other words, the conditions that create dukkha still exist. The difference is that *the mind is unperturbed by the perturbations of life*; it has broken through the conditioning that causes attachment and reactive mind. Furthermore, the Buddha says, even the seeds from which greed, ill will, and delusion could potentially arise in the future have been uprooted. Can you envision a future in which there would not even be a possibility of your mind contracting around anything that happens to you or those you care for?

Cessation and its resulting freedom of mind are referred to by many names other than nibbana (*nirvana* in Sanskrit), including the unconditioned, nonsuffering, the deathless, the absolute, luminous mind, *satori*, awakening, pure awareness, emptiness, nonattachment, nonclinging, Buddha mind, and that elusive term, enlightenment. Enlightenment is not a word I use very often because it has so many meanings and because so many people seem to think that there is an "I" who gets enlightened when in fact one of the fruits of cessation is the recognition that there is no permanent self.

In the Theravada tradition a person who has realized nibbana is referred to as an *arahant*, someone who is free of the darkness of ignorance that leads to clinging and suffering. It is said that an arahant no longer accumulates karma or future consequences from his actions, although he must still live out the consequences of past karma, including inhabiting a body that gets sick, ages, and dies.

From the perspective of this book, *such a person no longer dances with life*, but rather has *gone far beyond* the need for or interest in dancing with life. A fully enlightened person has moved into an entirely different stage than those who have transformed themselves in the many beneficial ways that are described in earlier chapters of this book.

Within the Buddhist teaching community there are differing opinions about what cessation is exactly. When cessation has been realized, some Buddhist teachers say, you spontaneously see the interdependent, co-arising nature of the world and directly experience the essentially empty nature of all conditioned phenomena. You have perfect knowledge of what is suffering and not suffering and are no longer subject to reactivity in the mind. However, others say it means that the mind has literally stopped all activity, either briefly or for several days; this is what's known as fully realized cessation, or *nirodha*. Still others say cessation is any time you fully and profoundly let go of all grasping even for the briefest moment. I recommend that you not rush to take a stance on what you believe cessation to be, but rather reflect on the question, "What does cessation mean to me?"

Ajahn Sumedho advises, "Do not feel as though you have to embrace any particular teacher's interpretation of total cessation, or even that you have to quickly come to your own understanding of cessation. Instead, let it be an open question, a mystery, and live the question: What is possible in the way of freedom for me, right now, in this very moment, just as I am?"

REMEMBER THAT YOU DO NOT KNOW

Not being someone who has achieved fully realized cessation, I can't speak from firsthand experience about how life feels once you are fully free with no possibility of falling back into clinging. I am someone who still has to live each moment knowing that his actions create the seeds of karma. *The only thing I know for sure is that I do not know that which can only be known from full realization.* This realization of *knowing that I do not know* has served as a guide during the many years I have practiced with the insights of cessation. It has helped me avoid clinging to various exalted mind states that have arisen, it has guided me to just stay with the practice during periods of discouragement, and it has kept me humble and attentive in my daily life as I learn to create less suffering for myself and others. And it has helped me avoid clinging to concepts, views, and interpretations of the dharma that inevitably arise.

Your actions also have consequences, and at this point in your practice, you too will benefit from cultivating the realization of not knowing. It is easy to become attached to your opinions or to beliefs presented by others whom you admire. But only through an attitude of humility and don't know mind can you open to directly experiencing the insights of cessation which at times are frightening and discouraging to your ego self. It is ironic that you must cultivate a *not-knowing* attitude in order to *know* the realization of cessation, but it is true.

This truth is exemplified in a renowned Zen story in which a very learned Buddhist scholar approaches an elder meditation master and smugly announces that, having taught so many people about enlightenment, he is now ready to learn meditation in order to become enlightened himself. The elder responds by offering the scholar some tea. The scholar accepts and holds out his teacup as the elder pours, and pours, and pours, until the cup is overflowing. After overcoming his embarrassment for the elder's seeming absentmindedness, the scholar says to him, "Do you not realize that my cup is already full and all that you are pouring is overflowing?" The elder replies, "So it is with your mind, how can I teach you when it is so overflowing with all that you know?"

I have sometimes encountered this "I know all about it" attitude in practitioners. So often their false confidence comes from believing what they have been told by others, not from their own experience! The Buddha taught that you are deluded when you do not realize that you do not know when you cling to views, including rituals and beliefs, and mistake your views as knowing. In modern terms, when your ego is so caught in what it thinks it knows or when you cling to beliefs without direct experience, your mind, like the scholar's cup, is overflowing and you lose access to beginner's mind, which is crucial for realizing cessation.

Dancing with Life While Cultivating Cessation

To cultivate cessation, I consciously live with the question, how do I find freedom of mind right now, even in my state of ignorance? Over and over again, I inquire and reflect: *Is this thought, word, or action suffering or not suffering?* Sometimes cessation happens spontaneously from this inquiry, but other times my attachment is so strong that I have to engage in right effort (which I describe in more detail in Chapter 20). If cessation still does not come about, then I simply continue inviting cessation to occur, and either the grasping releases or it doesn't. If I start making judgments about myself, such thoughts only get in the way of release happening.

This process of mindful inquiry that I am describing arises out of the ground of my intention to not cause harm to myself or others. It is not dependent on my perfection or even my ability to know for sure if a given act is skillful or not. Likewise, the practice of clear intention to not cause harm forms the foundation for you to cultivate wisdom and compassion and it utilizes all your experiences—both your wise and foolish choices—for you to grow deeper and more profound in your understanding.

Having practiced many years with a not-knowing attitude, I can tell you how it is to continue dancing with life as one moves along the path of realizing cessation. I have both my own experience and the teachings of those who have guided me thus far as resources to offer you. Like the scholar with the overflowing teacup discovered, an intuitive feel for cessation will serve you best, not some intellectual definition or some very specific experience that you grasp and begin to crave.

Ajahn Sumedho teaches that the path of cessation comes through being mindful and reflective of your immediate life experience and utilizing inquiry and reflection to go beneath the surface appearance of things: "People rarely realize cessation because it takes a special kind of willingness in order to ponder and investigate and get beyond the gross and the obvious. It takes a willingness to actually look at your own reactions, to be able to see the attachments and to contemplate: 'What does attachment feel like?'" Sumedho's words echo the wisdom of his teacher, Ajahn Chah, who said, "As you proceed with your practice you must be willing to examine every experience."[12]

---

[12]   Ajahn Sumedho. *The Four Noble Truths.* Amaravati Publications, 1992, p. 39.

Sumedho goes on to say, "In my practice, I have seen that attachment to my desires is suffering. Attachment is to be understood and contemplated; then the insight into nonattachment [cessation] arises. This is not an intellectual stand or a command from your brain saying that you should not be attached; it is just a naturally arising insight into nonattachment or nonsuffering." Then he explains how this reflection on attachment brings the insights of cessation: "We reflect as we see the nature of desire; as we recognize that attachment to desire is suffering. Then we have the insight of allowing desire to go and the realization of nonsuffering, that is the cessation of suffering. These insights can only come through *reflection*—through really contemplating and pondering these truths, *they cannot come through belief.*"[13]

LIFE IS YOUR TEACHER AND YOUR ARENA FOR PRACTICING CESSATION

In daily life you've no doubt experienced many moments of cessation when your mind was finally free from stress and contraction after a period of suffering: There were the arguments in which you were attached to being right, but winning them suddenly no longer mattered; there were your old desires of receiving recognition or acceptance, or getting some material object, but now you realize you no longer care about them; or there was the time you were rejected by someone you were in love with and it hurt for a long time, but now there is no pain. The stress you felt about all of those things that you thought you had to have just disappeared.

The late Thai meditation teacher the Venerable Ajahn Buddhadasa says that each of these ordinary moments in which

---

[13] Ibid., p. 40.

the mind is no longer grasping is a moment of nibbana, a little sampling of the mind being free from clinging. He teaches that if you did not have many of these small, brief moments of cessation each day you would literally go crazy from the tension and stress that arise from clinging. There are hundreds, even thousands of moments each day when your mind is not grasping at anything. Your mind is temporarily, albeit briefly, content with how things are, and it is not stressed.

If you reflect on all the times your mind has been filled with anxiety or dread about the future, or blind with lust, or overwhelmed with grief such that you thought you couldn't bear to live another moment, you will realize that each of these mind states underwent a cessation that allowed you to go on living and functioning. Paying attention to these brief moments of release gives you a feeling for the greater stages of cessation.

In the Tibetan Buddhist tradition these brief moments of freedom are referred to as "symbolic" or "temporary" cessation because they can be reversed by the next moment's experience. This teaching of the temporary cessation of reactive mind may seem obvious and unimportant, but it is one way that you open your mind to the subtle, refined shift that is the full realization of cessation. The Buddha knew this teaching was subtle. Liberation from the stressful, reactive, and grasping conceptual mind is itself a concept, yet you cannot learn this truth with the conceptual capacity of your mind. This is why he taught mindfulness meditation and why he most often used negative or "what cessation is not" language.

THE ULTIMATE GOAL OF PRACTICE: TOTAL CESSATION

Cessation can happen to you gradually as the result of years of practice, or it may occur instantaneously after you are exposed to a teaching, or while you are sitting in meditation, or after you experience a "lightning-bolt" moment of spontaneous liberating insight in daily life. For instance, Kondanna, one of the Buddha's five friends to whom he first taught the Four Noble Truths, had an "all at once" awakening upon hearing the Buddha's sermon on cessation. In response to Kondanna's realization, the Buddha said, "Kondanna gets it," and proclaimed him, "Anna Kondanna." Anna means "profound knowing," therefore, Anna Kondanna is "the Kondanna who knows."

In describing Kondanna's enlightenment, Sumedho asks, "What did Kondanna know? What was his insight that the Buddha praised at the very end of the sermon? It was: 'All that is arising is subject to ceasing.' Now this may not sound like any great knowledge, but what it implies is a universal pattern: Whatever is subject to arising is subject to ceasing; it is impermanent, not self. Rather than just thinking about it, really contemplate: 'All that is subject to arising is subject to ceasing.' Apply it to life in general, to your own experience. If you profoundly understand and know that all that is subject to arising is subject to ceasing, then you will realize the ultimate reality, the deathless, immortal truths. This is a skillful means to that ultimate realization."[14]

THE GRADUAL PATH TO CESSATION

Since you do not yet have the profound knowing of Anna Kondanna, you will find yourself grasping and causing suffering. Therefore, your life's practice is to let go of whatever grasping has arisen and *to invite cessation in this very moment*. Each little moment of cessation, no matter how brief, brings well-being, even though it may be replaced so quickly by yet another moment of grasping that you do not notice them in your practice for

---

[14] Ibid., p. 41.

some time. Have faith in the gradual approach: By creating brief moments of cessation you will develop insight and skillful habits that will lead to more frequent and longer-lasting moments of nonclinging, which will continue to expand until your mind is ready to realize full cessation.

In following the gradual path, you may sometimes experience *dramatic altered states with intense feelings of cessation*, particularly if your disposition is such that you gravitate to lightning-bolt moments. On the other hand, your disposition may be such that you experience *hard-to-notice subtle shifts of consciousness*, such that profound wisdom and feelings of well-being arise over time. The methods you use to practice will make a difference in how many big moments you have, that is, whether you do long silent meditation retreats, sit for long intervals of time such as two or three hours, include absorption or concentration practices, and engage in intense controlled breath work that helps induce altered states.

Neither the dramatic altered states nor the subtle shift in consciousness is superior to the other. It isn't the amount of fireworks you feel, but rather how much actual lessening of grasping and arising of insight you experience and the amount of time that the mind is at ease even in difficult situations that indicates your progress toward liberation.

You may already have had a major insight of cessation, either through meditation or spontaneously, and may well spend the rest of your life understanding the importance of that insight and working to integrate it into your life. Whether you experience dramatic moments of oneness with great realizations of emptiness and interdependence or you experience a gradual deepening of understanding that releases you from the compulsion of your grasping, the endpoint of your journey is the same: To reach spiritual maturation where the mind is less and less controlled and driven by your desire, greed, ill will, anger, envy, confusion, doubt, and delusion. Having a fixed idea about what your liberation will look and feel like is more likely to hinder your spiritual maturation than to help it. Clinging to ideas about cessation will cause you to attempt to create some experience of cessation that matches your concept of *what it is*, rather than just open to *what is*.

Taking this flexible, nondefining view of cessation allows you to utilize both your meditation time and your time in daily activity as opportunities to practice creating the conditions that allow you to experience a taste of cessation. You simultaneously get the blessing of being more skillful at dancing with life.

THE CROSSOVER MOMENT OF FULLY REALIZED NIRODHA

It is taught in the Theravada tradition that there are stages of sustained cessation beginning with stream-enterer, followed by once-returner, then nonreturner, and culminating with arahant. *Fully realized cessation* occurs during a *crossover moment* at which point your mind is so fully transformed that there is not even a seed from which greed, hatred, and delusion can arise now or in the future. At this point you have become an arahant, the fourth stage of realization, in which you are permanently free. This crossover moment happens only after many cycles of first experiencing, then losing, and gradually rediscovering varying degrees of realization. All the moments of mindful cessation in which you let go of grasping and realize "this moment is like this" help bring you to this crossover moment. For most people this means that liberation is gradual—beginning with your ego structure becoming more purified, compassionate, and wiser and culminating in a total transformation of the self that transcends ego and goes even beyond transcendence.

Ego structure in this context means the central organizing aspect of the mind that recognizes your separateness as a functioning entity in ordinary reality and takes on the task of protecting and developing the body, the emotions, and the mind. It tends to think it is permanent, despite the fact that it is constantly changing. Through the process of spiritual development, the ego becomes healthier and wiser, although it ultimately ceases to be the central organizer and interpreter of perception. One caution: If you are *only* intent on achieving total cessation, your ego will not mature and any experience of cessation you may have will be just a *singular* experience that doesn't manifest throughout your life. This means that a genuine moment of cessation may recede into various types of delusion in which your ego self thinks you are partially or wholly enlightened.

The Buddha compared the tendency of the mind to repeatedly organize and mistakenly become identified with the ego to a house builder. Your ego constructs a self in order to shelter itself from the anxiety and stress of the truth of suffering. You then spend your time and effort on furnishing the house and repairing damage to it. Thus you seek status, material goods, a guarantee of physical and emotional safety, and insurance against all the uncertainties of life. But through the realization of cessation, you cease to believe the delusion of your separateness and your permanence and cease to compulsively build a shelter for your ego. Here is how the Buddha described his own cessation:

> House builder you have now been seen;
> you shall not build the house again.
> Your rafters have been broken down;
> Your ridge pole is shattered.
> My mind has attained the peace of nirvana
> And reached the end of every kind of craving.[15]

---

15   Kornfield, Jack, ed., with Gil Fronsdal. *Teachings of the Buddha*. Shambhala, 1996, p. 25.

The Buddha is describing cessation of craving and unskillful mind states—clinging, reacting, contracting, and all the compensatory behaviors of avoidance, fear, worry, and stress. There is no longer any compulsion to build a structure in the mind in order to handle life; the mind and heart are free. Can you feel this possibility for yourself? Just a stirring of this freedom in your heart can inspire you strongly.

Cessation Is a Path of Practice, Not a Demand of Yourself

Regardless of the degree of your spiritual maturity, the humility of your attitude, the diligence of your practice, and the passion of your goal, you do not get to choose to have total cessation in this lifetime. It arises of its own accord when conditions are appropriate. There are simply too many conditions that are beyond your control. Still, it may happen. For certain, you can move down the path toward total cessation and experience many individual moments of cessation as well as the extinction of all sorts of patterns of suffering. All of the opinions and ideas you have about what it might look and feel like are just concepts. As I have urged repeatedly in this book, just show up for your deepest intentions, as best you can, and then allow the dharma, the truth of awakened presence, to do the work.

The ego maturity that comes from practicing mindfulness alone is worth all your effort because of the ease and well-being that it brings to your life. I have consistently pointed out these ego benefits throughout the first six insights because they are so tangible, and they help keep you motivated to practice. But make no mistake about what the Buddha meant by the Seventh Insight: *that cessation entails movement far beyond ego.* You cease being defined by your ego, and instead you become free.

THE EIGHTH INSIGHT:

This Noble Truth must be penetrated to by realizing the Cessation of Suffering.

CHAPTER 15

WHEN THE DANCE ENDS, FREEDOM BEGINS

DIRECTLY EXPERIENCING THE THIRD NOBLE TRUTH

As we begin to explore the Eighth Insight, let's first pause to acknowledge that practicing cessation is not as straightforward as working with the first six insights. You will discover that noticing cessation calls for a more subtle level of mindfulness than the practices that have preceded it, and this can take time to develop. Also, you may find it psychologically challenging to cope with the insubstantial and unappealing aspects of life that surface at certain points in the practice. Moreover, even if you have an established mindfulness practice, working with this insight may not yet be your primary focus. However, none of these reasons should deter you from investigating cessation as described in this chapter. Even if you never develop any major interest in realizing cessation, you will gain essential wisdom from practicing this insight that will serve your life *right now*.

Just as you practiced *understanding* dukkha in the First Noble Truth and it empowered you to be *more present and to live from your heart* no matter how difficult your life is, and just as you practiced *abandoning* clinging in the Second Noble Truth and it empowered you to *live from your deepest values* no matter how much wanting or aversion was present in your mind, so too when you practice *realizing* cessation you will be empowered to *face loss and to be far less defined by your ego*, regardless of your responsibilities and cares. Thus, you continue to cultivate the art of dancing with life just as it is even as you open to this eighth realization that takes you far beyond your ego-centered life.

Remembering Your Practice Is Your First Step toward Cessation

To investigate cessation requires that your mind be concentrated and steadfast in the face of difficulty and that you be dispassionate and detached when rapture and altered states arise. Fortunately, you have spent time working with the previous insights and are well prepared to practice cessation. For instance, when you practiced direct knowing of dukkha (the Second Insight), you began to develop a noble heart (courage), which enables you to maintain steady awareness and investigation in the face of any discomfort, fear, and longing that arises as you explore cessation.

Similarly, to realize abandoning of clinging (the Fifth Insight), you practiced investigating or knowing all kinds of sensory and mental experiences by letting loose of grasping of each of them; thus, you cultivated nonattachment. Nonattachment is critical for realizing cessation because when your mind becomes more still and concentrated you will sometimes experience altered mind states, including rapture, euphoria, and a sense of peace. These states can be so wonderful that you get attached to them and strive to re-create them rather than going on in your practice.

ACHIEVING CESSATION
THROUGH DAILY LIFE OBSERVATION

You can explore cessation through a variety of practices, including noticing it in daily life, inquiring into and reflecting upon it, and devoting your attention exclusively to working with it in intense silent meditation practice. More than likely you don't have much time for meditation retreats, so daily life is where you have the most opportunity for observing and working with cessation. Do not be discouraged from practicing cessation if this is your situation. Ajahn Chah used to say, "We focus on the here and now dharma. This is where we can let go of things and resolve our difficulties. We look at the present and see continuous arising and ceasing. When the mind starts to realize that all things without exception are by their very nature uncertain, the problems of grasping and attachment start to decrease and wither away. I keep saying this but people do not take it to heart."[16]

Ajahn Chah was not so interested in utilizing intense absorption (jhana) meditation practices to induce a crossover moment. He did not separate daily life from extraordinary experience. Instead he urged his students to just be continually aware throughout their day. In his style of practice, you notice when clinging is present and when it is not, and you notice the effects of wanting mind, aversion, and conceptual thinking. You notice when suffering is present and when it is not. He taught meditation and he instructed his students to do a lot of sitting and walking practice, but he was not promoting striving or the idea of achieving or becoming, or even the idea of enlightenment. His instruction was to simply inquire: How can you bring about cessation of clinging at this moment?

To practice Ajahn Chah's style of moment-to-moment awareness in daily life, when your mind is not engaged in a specific

---

[16]   Ajahn Chah, *Everything Arises, Everything Falls Away*. Shambhala, 2005, p. 37.

task, you train it to automatically rest in awareness of breath and body sensations. Eventually breath and body awareness will become the "default" position for your attention. Once you develop this ease of attention on the breath and body, you begin to note that every breath and every sensation ceases. At first, practicing noticing these endings may feel mechanical, but gradually a realization of wonder emerges: *It is really true—everything that arises disappears!* Such a moment of wonder is the *direct experience* of cessation. If you only develop one practice for cessation, this is the one I recommend.

A second and more challenging daily life practice that I have found valuable in learning cessation involves applying more subtle mindfulness when you are engaged in daily activities. In this method you automatically *note the arising and passing* of pleasant and unpleasant feelings in whatever task you are doing. This may seem daunting at first, but you can train your mind so that for many moments of your day you will, without much effort, register whether what is happening has a pleasant or unpleasant tone. Next, you start to become aware of *how the pleasant- or unpleasant-feeling tone in the moment is affecting your mind and body.* Then you note that each of these pleasant or unpleasant feelings also disappears. Eventually you have the realization that like a puppet on a string your mind reacts to pleasant and unpleasant feelings, even though they quickly cease to be! You directly know that being reactive to such feelings is a waste of time.

In a still more subtle daily practice of cessation that I find useful, you learn to note pleasant and unpleasant arising in the minds of others and observe how they too are controlled by these feelings. You start to directly experience that other people's moments of pleasant and unpleasant are also always ceasing and see that they too are being controlled by these fleeting moments, which brings forth compassion and clear seeing in you when disagreements arise. In these moments you are able to experience a temporary cessation of your own reactive mind to the words and actions of others. Even though it is momentary, you realize that you do not want to habitually be in a reactive mode to either your own or someone else's pleasant or unpleasant feelings, and you are motivated to explore cessation more deeply.

Oftentimes cessation of clinging happens spontaneously with just your recognition of it. Therefore, another effective technique is to *notice whether there is clinging or nonclinging in this moment and to observe what happens when you bring awareness to it.* After many years of practicing this way, my mind knows without a doubt that clinging to desire is suffering, and I know that I do not want to cling. Repeating this process of noticing clinging and releasing it thousands of times is how you create new mental habits.

In very trying circumstances remembering your intention to not cause suffering and remembering your "don't know mind" can lead to cessation of suffering. The first step in this process is to ask yourself, "Is this suffering or not suffering?" whenever you are having thoughts about saying something or taking an action. If there is suffering, then invite in the possibility of the cessation of suffering. For example, if you are getting irritated at someone and start to have a flood of negative thoughts, ask yourself if what is going on is suffering, then invite cessation to arise and notice what happens. Those times when you feel a definite release, pay attention to the felt sense of the moment, but beware of grasping after the ability to evoke cessation at will!

ACHIEVING CESSATION THROUGH REFLECTION PRACTICE

Cessation can also be cultivated by making it an object of your attention—what Ajahn Sumedho called, ". . . observing the continuing, ever-changing flow of arising and passing." Specifically, you begin to reflect on the truth that all things end. You reflect on how all things in the physical realm cease to be, even mountains, suns, and solar systems. Through inquiry you realize that every want you ever had faded away. Likewise, anything that arises in the mind also disappears. You note that each minute, each hour, and each day ends. When you are riding in a car (not driving, please!), you start to see how each moment is like a scene in a movie that quickly arises and passes. Pretty soon you start to notice that in the same way, each moment you spend in a meeting at work ceases, independent of how pleasant or unpleasant it was. Likewise, all the good moments in your personal life just disappear; they cannot be summoned to reappear.

As you continue your inquiry into what happens with each rising and passing moment, you discover that they are so short that it is actually hard to catch and experience most of them. You only have time to register the tail end of most moments. Focusing your inquiry on the unpleasant moments, you notice that they too are arising and passing rapidly and are not as constant as you once thought. That pulled muscle or headache doesn't stay constant in your mind; it just arises and disappears and reappears so rapidly that it seems constant. When you start seeing that it really is true that everything arises and passes, it changes your perception and orientation.

Achieving Cessation through Meditation Practice

An extended period of silent meditation practice, particularly a residential retreat in which you withdraw temporarily from your worldly identity and duties, is ideal for practicing cessation. In such an environment there is little disruption to your

observing your mind, which allows you to develop strong concentration, maybe even to the point of full absorption. You then
turn your concentrated mind toward observing the cessation of
all phenomena. You investigate your emotions, body, mental
processes, other physical objects, the nature of time, hindrances
to your clarity, and fetters to your own maturity that lead you
to clinging. You carefully and repeatedly note that all these
objects of the mind are characterized by cessation.

One student, Marie, who attended a three-month silent
meditation retreat, was practicing in just this manner when she
had what she believed to be a direct experience of cessation.
Through the many weeks of practice, her mind had become
very still and clear. She could see that anything that arose in her
mind disappeared, and it did so very quickly. She observed that
the mind registers what is seen, heard, and felt in the body so
rapidly that in an ordinary state of consciousness they appear to
be continuous, but in fact they are simply reregistering over and
over again, giving the illusion of lasting for some duration when
they don't even last for a second!

Marie was quite skilled at staying with the breath. Previously
she had thought of a single inhale as one experience, but now
she realized that it was actually many experiences. One day
while working with this observation, she suddenly experienced
what she called a "blink." It was as if she had been asleep,
although she knew she had not been. It didn't last long, but she
felt different afterward, calm and clear. Then two weeks later
Marie had another blink moment, and when coming out of this
one, she felt as though she had "pierced the veil," meaning she
had penetrated the illusion of an unchanging reality in which
she existed as a separate being. For her this experience was cessation, and she has never looked at the world in the same way
since. She feels as though she is constantly aware that our ordinary world is made up of passing phenomena and this insight

dispels any temptation to cling to things that will cause her to suffer. The result is that she feels significantly happier and more peaceful, although she knows her journey is far from over.

Another student, Kim, reports that he did not experience a period of blankness while noticing cessation; instead his mind moved into total abandonment of all objects. For an extended period of time he was resting in pure awareness. No thoughts, body sensations, or any other sense experiences arose, although he was totally awake and alert. Nor did he have any sense of himself as a subject or any *awareness of awareness*. He was literally not separate. It was only in coming out of this state that he was aware of having been in it. Like Marie, Kim has not sought to label or evaluate this experience. He does not feel any need to have any thoughts about it. He feels the loosening of grasping and the growth of equanimity, and for him this cessation of dukkha is enough. Both Marie's and Kim's experiences are examples of ever-deepening insight into cessation.

DISENCHANTMENT IS NECESSARY AND NATURAL

Some Buddhist teachers, particularly in Burma and Sri Lanka, teach a systematic approach to gaining insights regarding cessation based on an ancient text called the *Visuddhimagga*. Using nomenclature such as the "Seven Contemplations of Insight" or the "Progress of Insight," these teachers lay out a series of "knowledges" or "perceptions" that lead to total cessation. These systems describe passing through various phases of less-than-total cessation along the way, including one in which you experience disenchantment and disinterest in the world, which can be very disheartening and disorienting if you do not have a teacher to help you through it.

I was on a multimonth meditation retreat when disenchantment first arose in me, and it lasted for several days without letting up. The effect was that even my favorite things—my breakfast cereal, which I could prepare just the way I liked; my daily walk through the nearby forest; and the splendid sunsets—were all just dukkha. Mentally, I remembered that the cereal still tasted good, that the forest still soothed my mind, and that the sunset was still beautiful, but my predominant experience was of their temporary, composite nature. They held no attraction; I was indifferent to and unmoved by them. The hypnotic appeal of the pleasant and appealing aspects of life had ceased. Fortunately, this direct realization of dukkha was the beginning and not the end of the insight process for me, and it will be the same for you.

THE BUDDHA'S FIRE SERMON

The Buddha addressed the arising of this insight of dukkha and the cessation of attraction to the sense world in a teaching titled the "Fire Sermon." In it he characterizes every single aspect of your experience in daily life, whether in your body or your mind, as "burning." Reflecting on this teaching can help you know cessation because the Buddha is so literal and so specific in his descriptions:

> Everything, O monks, is burning.
> And how, O monks, is everything burning?
> The eye, O monks, is burning; visible things are burning;
> the mental impressions based on the eye are burning;
> the contact of the eye with visible things is burning;
> the sensation produced by the contact of the eye with visible
>   things,
> be it pleasant, be it painful,

be it neither pleasant nor painful,

that also is burning.[17]

Through years of contemplating this teaching and my own experiences of cessation, I have come to the realization that every step in your internal process of cognition produces a disturbance in the unliberated mind. The Buddha described this disturbance as burning, but you might also think of it as heat or friction. Literally every step in the cognitive process is characterized at the very least by low-grade stress, no matter how innocuous it may seem. Take, for instance, the process of eating: *Seeing* the food is burning, *picking up* the food is burning, *opening* the mouth is burning, *tasting* the food is burning (regardless of how good or bad it actually tastes), and *swallowing* is burning. For the food to exist means that it too is burning, as well as the container holding it, and the table it sits on!

Burning or friction is natural, and it is a necessity of life. Scientists tell us that nothing can exist in this world without movement or vibration and that all movement involves friction. So science validates the Buddha's teaching that all things are burning with friction. But the Buddha was not trying to be a scientist; he was teaching us how to liberate the mind and to bring about the cessation of this endless cycle of burning.

The Buddha used the fire analogy to reveal that dukkha is a characteristic of life—"life is like this." He wanted you to feel this burning in your life with all its difficulty, uncertainty, and stress and for you to realize that this burning is inherent and impersonal and that it applies to pleasant and unpleasant phenomena alike. He also wanted you to directly feel the truth or heat of the fire (and I don't mean intellectually comprehend it, but rather experience an "Oh, I get it!" moment).

---

[17] Kornfield, Jack, ed., with Gil Fronsdal. *The Teachings of the Buddha*. Shambhala, 1996, pp. 42.

All Movement into Aggregates Is Burning

Like a fish that doesn't know it lives in water, you live in a world that is a composite of temporary, vibrating phenomena, therefore, you may not have developed the necessary detachment (or "science of the mind" as the Dalai Lama says) to see its true nature. In the Fire Sermon the Buddha points out that this blindness to the basic conditions of this realm is the root cause of your unease with life and that *cessation* of this blindness or delusion will bring you freedom.

The Buddha used the fire analogy to help you *directly feel what he means by cessation.* In saying "The eye is burning; visible things are burning," he means that your experience of *seeing even the most neutral of objects involves stress or burning.* In order for your eye to have the capacity to see means that it is burning, and for there to be an object for you to see, like a flower, means it too must be burning, otherwise it could not manifest in space and time. As the mind starts to engage in seeing, a mental impression of the flower is formed when light hits the retina of your eye, and this too is burning. Before you have even consciously registered seeing the flower, the very act of seeing means that you are immersed in the friction of phenomena-based existence. Friction or burning is the medium in which your perceptions are taking place, in much the same way that water is the medium for the fish.

All of these components of seeing that the Buddha is describing *aggregate* into full-blown consciousness and you know, "This is a flower." This culminating mental cognition involves even more burning as the neurons in the brain fire in order for the recognition to occur. *It does not matter if the object seen registers as pleasant, unpleasant, or neutral in your mind, you are participating in a process that is burning.* There is no escaping it! But if your mind becomes reactive by wanting the flower or not wanting it, then the burning turns into a bonfire. This reactive mind state adds more fuel to the burning and binds you to the entire experience. Like the fish, you stay in the water, identify with it, and never see it clearly. However, unlike the fish, you have the possibility of knowing your world for what it is.

ALL THINGS ARE BURNING LEADS TO THE INSIGHT OF DISPASSION

In daily life, practitioners often have a strong but temporary experience of this insight that all is burning when they are facing a life-threatening illness or tragedy, such as the death of a child, or overwhelming fear about something in the future. Many times they will even go so far as to say, "Everything has turned to ashes." This feeling is not the same as depression or despair, in which nothing seems to matter. These latter two feelings are nihilistic, often stemming from a disorder of the mind; in contrast, the Eighth Insight comes from great clarity of the mind. My own first experience of disinterest in the world came from the realization that it is all burning and therefore dukkha. It seems that there is no way to avoid this step in awakening.

Initially, you may feel dismay over the realization that everything is burning, but if you take the insight as your object of meditation, it will lead you to spontaneously let go of clinging to any objects of experience because there is no attraction. In letting go of wanting the world to be attractive, you have taken a step forward on your path. As a result you may feel a sense of euphoria and well-being that is quite exhilarating. This euphoric state, which is often accompanied by various forms of rapture and bliss, can be so strong that it is often referred to as "false enlightenment." It may be characterized by a sense of illumination, or unbroken calmness, or inexhaustible energy.

Although genuine, your altered state is false enlightenment because eventually your mind state shifts and you fall back into clinging and grasping. To really find freedom from burning, you have to keep practicing, which means not getting lost in the euphoria as well as going through some more rough times on the meditation cushion before a deeper form of nonattachment arises, one that is independent of your various mind states.

In the Fire Sermon, the Buddha proceeds to describe this burning as happening at all of the sense gates and with thinking itself. Again the Buddha is very specific in his descriptions:

The ear is burning, sounds are burning, . . .
The nose is burning, odors are burning, . . .
The tongue is burning, tastes are burning, . . .
The body is burning, objects of contact are burning, . . .
The mind is burning, thoughts are burning,
All are burning with the fire of greed, of anger, and of
    ignorance.[18]

Just as a star burns energy each moment until it burns up or a lightbulb vibrates until its filament burns out, your neurochemical system is also constantly burning. The firing of neurons in your brain is stressful—the brain is literally burning with movement! Sometimes in deep meditation states, the mind becomes so subtle that you are able to directly experience this burning—you notice that even the quietest thought or most neutral smell or softest touch is burning. As your insight starts to mature, you come to realize that all objects of awareness, even those that seem neutral, create a kind of stress, and they too are burning. Only *pure awareness* has no movement and is free of burning.

---

[18] Ibid.

The Felt Experience
of Burning in Daily Life

As you practice being aware of the felt sense of seeing objects in daily life, it becomes somewhat easier to feel the burning the Buddha is describing. Applying mindfulness, you begin to observe that the associations you have with what you see and the story or interpretation you have of the visual object elicit even more burning. You also start to see how all the little physical and mental processes within the body and mind are contributing to this burning, even though you are not consciously registering them.

Your increased awareness of how the moment manifests through burning is empowering. You begin to register the visual experience as tension, movement, separation, and duality. Your visual experience becomes more "clearly seen," that is, you know that the cognitive process is characterized by insubstantiality, therefore there is no permanent place for the mind to rest while in an ordinary state of consciousness. Neurochemical signals and electrical impulses keep arising and passing, fueling the ego's need to suppress some input while binding other input together to make it cohesive. It is no wonder that your ego is so uneasy, and the mind falls into grasping!

In deep meditation experience an altered state can arise in which the mind completely breaks through the illusion of ordinary seeing and is able to see what are called *kalapas* or what seems like a stream of atomlike elements that make up all experience. Your mind is able to perceive this phenomenon and still function; it is as if the mind has gained a new capacity. When it first happens, this can be a startling experience. What you're seeing is a stream of signals that make up seeing and other sensory experience (even thinking) as they form in the brain. (I assume, but do not know for sure, that the mind has become so subtle that it is "seeing" the nerve endings fire.) It is not possible to describe this mind state with words because it so defies our conventional assumptions.

Such an altered mind state is not *fully realized cessation*. But once you know that the apparent solidity of the visual field is actually an illusion, ordinary visual experience feels more like watching a movie and loses some of its ability to create attachment. Do not think that you have to achieve this or any of the other altered states of perception I am describing as part of your examination of the Buddha's Fire Sermon. Such altered states of mind may never happen to you. They are not necessary for your own movement into a nonsuffering and meaningful relationship with life. But such states of perception do occur and can give credence and inspiration to your own exploration.

You Do Not Have to Be Defined by Burning

Although all things in this world are burning, the Buddha taught that *you have a choice to not add fuel to the fire, to not make the burning personal, and to not be identified with the burning*:

> With what fire is it burning?
> I declare unto you that it is burning with the fire of greed,
> with the fire of anger, with the fire of ignorance,
> it is burning with the anxieties of birth, decay, death,
> grief, lamentation, suffering, dejection, and despair.[19]

---

[19] Ibid.

Here the Buddha is saying that your identification with the ever-changing phenomena of the material world fuels the burning that turns it into dukkha. In each moment you have a choice to either add fuel in the form of wanting, aversion, and ignorance or not. When you let loose of wanting, aversion, and demanding that the moment be other than it is, you gain the ability to see that this moment is like this. Then the world is just burning by nature, like the water that the fish lives in is just wet. *You are in it, but not of it.* This complete freedom only comes with complete cessation.

Before realization of total cessation is possible, you first need to understand why you don't see that you can choose to not fuel the burning, which has to do with how your field of perception has been conditioned since childhood. From the time you were born, you were biologically and environmentally programmed to compose the world as you are now accustomed to seeing it—as semi-still and tangible and not the constantly changing flow of atomic particles vibrating in a quantum field that it is. The creation of this delusion was a necessary step in your development, and to some extent it remains necessary in order for you to function in the material world. Scientists inform us that the brain removes cognitive dissonance so as to create order. For example, your brain creates a stable visual field even though it receives signals that are quite different from what is actually there. Thus, you are habituated to think that you are seeing a stable object, yet science confirms the actual input experience via all of your senses is in constant movement.

The brain conducts this process of sorting out, selecting, suppressing, and ignoring input through every sense gate— touch, hearing, taste, smell, sight, and thoughts. In exactly the same manner, your ego complex imputes the illusion of stability to your emotions, desires, dislikes, and interpretations of the past and the future. The ego complex develops to perform this function.

Your ego clings to this cognizing function as a source of stability in a constantly flowing stream of ever-changing "you." Overall this selective perception is valuable because it would be impossible to function if you did not have a core of memories and associations that you organized around, but it forms an identity based on the illusion of stability. When you try to find stable happiness under such circumstances, you are taking birth in a world that is burning with constant change; therefore, dukkha is inevitable. *Cessation can be understood as being the moment when you cease to make this false identification.*

In order for you to function in the material realm, your brain creates a *subject*, you, who is experiencing an endless series of physical and emotional *objects*, and your ego complex has the job of maintaining this illusion by trying to get the desirable objects and avoiding the unpleasant ones. Of course, it falls into greed, aversion, fear, anxiety, irritation, dissatisfaction, stress, loneliness, and despair! As long as and to the extent you are identified with this delusion, you are bound to the burning of this existence! Like a not-so-funny slapstick comedian, you keep slipping on the banana peel.

If your view of life is that there is a "you," whose only meaning, happiness, or purpose in life comes from getting all the objects that "you" desire and all those objects are burning, then inevitably you will be burned. But when through practice you enter a temporary state in which you have no resistance to how things are, there is no friction and no burning in the mind. You are able to experience at least a foretaste of what comes with the full cessation of attachment. At least for that moment you are able to taste the fruit of nibbana: *The mind has cooled, even though the fire of life itself continues to burn.* You are having a direct, felt experience of the *cessation* of attachment in your body and mind.

As your practice matures, you experience more and more of these moments in ever-deepening and subtler forms. *It becomes clear to you that you no longer want to be defined by wanting things to be other than they are.* You absolutely know that such wanting only leads to suffering for yourself and others. *You still care, but you care without attachment or expectations.*

It is no wonder the Buddha emphasized the foolishness of wanting and clinging as a strategy for achieving happiness. You will inevitably experience loss and grief since all the objects you love will sooner or later burn to extinction, just as you will age and die. The opportunity for freedom lies in the realization that when you grasp after and cling to "happy objects" you imprison yourself in this burning reality. The Buddha taught that in any moment you have the choice to let go of clinging to that which is burning.

> Considering this, O monks, a disciple walking in the Noble Path, becomes
>
> weary of the eye, weary of visible things,
>
> weary of the mental impressions based on the eye,
>
> weary of the contact of the eye with visible things,
>
> weary also of the sensation produced by the contact of the eye with visible things, be it pleasant, be it painful, be it neither pleasant nor painful.
>
> He or she becomes weary of the ear, and so forth . . . down to . . . thoughts.
>
> Becoming weary of all that, one divests oneself of grasping;
>
> by absence of grasping one is made free;
>
> when one is free, one becomes aware that one is free;
>
> and one realizes that rebirth is exhausted;
>
> and that there is no further return to this world.[20]

---

[20] Ibid., p. 43.

Notice that the Buddha defines cessation as divesting your-self of grasping after the ever-changing stimuli received through all the sense gates. By "weary" he does not mean disheartened or embittered; he means that you cease to accept the illusions that the brain creates. *You no longer believe the "if only" thoughts* that your ego constantly creates in its search for stability and happiness. Your mind becomes tired of chasing after what is unsatisfying in the end, and it ceases to be enchanted by what once seemed exciting, or pleasant, or important. "No further return to this world" means that once you have realized cessa-tion you are no longer of this world, although you physically remain in the world.

Through your direct experience of the truth of burning you realize the impermanence and emptiness of all things. You should not interpret "emptiness" to mean that you aren't sup-posed to attend to your experiences or care about people and ideals in life. The awakened response to the realization that everything is burning is to act from love and with responsibility but without attachment to future outcome or to the past. To live with such nonattachment is to live outside the tyranny of ordinary time, to be liberated from the past and the future. As Ajahn Sumedho says, "You are the Buddha knowing the dharma."

THE NINTH INSIGHT:

*This Noble Truth has been penetrated to by realizing the
Cessation of Suffering.*

CHAPTER 16

IT'S NOTHING PERSONAL

KNOWING THAT YOU KNOW THE THIRD NOBLE TRUTH

When realization of full cessation occurs, you experience a *felt shift in consciousness*—you directly know that you know cessation. Before *knowing cessation*, you perceived yourself to be separate, solid, and unchanging and it caused you to be reactive, which led to your suffering. Now you know that your perception was distorted and you experience your mind being free from disturbance and reactivity. It seems to me, but of course I don't know for sure, that *if you are not altered in a manner that manifests throughout your life, then the insight of cessation has not been known.*

One way to describe realization of the Ninth Insight is that you directly know the truth of emptiness, meaning the insubstantiality and impermanence of all material phenomena. Ajahn Sumedho captures the freedom that comes with realizing full cessation beautifully when he says: "There is no Buddhist monk in the emptiness. Buddhist monk is merely a convention, appropriate to time and place, it's just *suchness* which is another way of saying 'it's like this.'"

This ineffable yet completely tangible quality of cessation is so paradoxical that the Ninth Insight is often described using metaphor or the double negative forms of unwholesome mind states. For instance, knowing full cessation is defined as knowing nongreed, nonhatred, and nondelusion. Moreover, you know that greed, hatred, and delusion will not arise in the future because the very roots from which they might arise have been uprooted. Therefore, you know nonsuffering.

When you have attained full *cessation*, you know that you have completely realized all twelve insights of the Four Noble Truths, which until this point were only partially realized. Paraphrasing the Buddha, "You have done what needed to be done." Your mind is that of the arahant, a fully enlightened one. At this *crossover moment*, you know you have experienced a *felt shift in consciousness* that cannot be captured with words. Ajahn Chah said, "Realizing the truth of original mind, we see that it is impossible to describe or give to another. There is no way to show it, nothing to compare it to . . . realization of the truth must be accomplished by each individual."

It is easy to believe that such attainment is beyond your knowing, but Ajahn Chah taught, "We are sentient beings working to become awakened beings, bodhisattvas, the truth, and whoever is awakened to that is the Buddha. . . . So the Buddha and sentient beings are not that far apart."

NEITHER FIXATE ON NOR FORGET CESSATION

There are two notes of caution to be aware of on your journey toward realizing full cessation. The first is that in modern life there is often an emphasis on immediate, practical results and the promise of "here is how to feel better about yourself right now," so the possibility of attaining full cessation is often not given sufficient attention. In my view this is unfortunate because the foundation of the practice rests on the truth of full cessation. You will most likely need some connection to the possibility and mystery of full liberation to be inspired to practice and to maintain the compassion that allows you to genuinely examine suffering in your life. Thus, despite the fact that in the weekly sitting group I lead I emphasize living the dharma in daily life, I repeatedly teach wise living in the context of liberation. Finding freedom is your organizing principle and your motivation for seeking the cessation of suffering.

The second note of caution is that it is very easy to fall into comparing mind regarding whatever level of attainment you may have achieved, to identify it as ego accomplishment, and to crave the duplication of past peak experiences. For this reason many teachers discourage fixating on full cessation. For instance, in *Zen Mind, Beginner's Mind* the great Zen master Suzuki Roshi states: "If you continue this simple practice every day, you will obtain a wonderful power. Before you attain it, it is something wonderful, but after you attain it, it is nothing special. . . . You may say 'universal nature,' or 'Buddha nature' or 'enlightenment.' You may call it by many names, but for the person who has it, it is *nothing*, and it is *something*."

What Suzuki Roshi is saying about full cessation applies to all your attainments along the way. They are nothing, really. You are still a human being living in a temporal world as best you are able, yet something has occurred that yields the definite fruits of well-being and freedom in this very life.

FINDING LIBERATION FROM SUFFERING IS NOT THE SAME AS ABANDONING THE WORLD

The knowing of cessation does not necessarily mean that you retreat from the world. The Buddha certainly didn't just sit in bliss for years after his full realization of cessation. Instead, he spent 45 years teaching and dealing with the mundane problems of living in a community, including jealousy from other teachers and accusations and resentment from the lay community. The same is true for you; you are not practicing cessation in order to be somewhere other than where you are. Just the opposite is true: Knowing cessation means that, for the first time ever, you are able to be *just where you are* in this very moment, fully available and responsive.

Ajahn Sumedho describes how you relate to the world after realizing the Ninth Insight in this manner: "In emptiness, things are just what they are. When we are aware in this way it doesn't mean we are indifferent to success or failure and that we don't bother to do anything. We can apply ourselves. We know what we can do, we know what has to be done, and we can do it in the right way. Then everything becomes Dhamma, the way it is."

In the Zen tradition, it is taught: "Before enlightenment chop wood and carry water, and after enlightenment chop wood and carry water." *Life continues to be an ever-changing stream of moments, but how you perceive and relate to the stream changes.* The difference is that because you now know the essential insights, you are able to live wisely and be in harmony with life in this realm, however it manifests. You do what needs to be done without taking it personally or being attached to results of actions. Or as Ajahn Sumedho says, "We do things because that is the right thing to be doing at this time and in this place rather than out of a sense of personal ambition or fear of failure."

A clear example of this understanding can be found in the Zen Oxherding pictures by Kakuan. This series of 10 drawings begins with a picture of a man having a sense that something is missing in his life, which is symbolized by the ox. Next he sees the footprint of the ox, which awakens inspiration in him to become his true nature. From there he searches until he finds

the ox, develops a relationship to it, and then discovers its emptiness, i.e., cessation. But the series doesn't end with emptiness.
In the last picture the man returns to the marketplace with a
beatific smile on his face, and the text says that he "returns to
the marketplace showing no sign of holiness, but if he touches
the dead trees they come into full bloom."

When you are around someone who has deep experience in
cessation, it is like the description of the ox herder returning to
the marketplace. Such a person resides in a feeling of freedom
from attachment; *they know they know,* thus they are able to
freely participate in life. You feel assured, relaxed, even a little
blessed being in their presence, as though the insight they have
realized brings out the best in you, too.

CHAPTER 17

YOU ARE NOT
YOUR SELF

The Wisdom of the Third Noble Truth

Many students suddenly switch gears in their brains when they begin their inquiry into cessation. Rather than continuing on in whatever manner they have been practicing, they seem to think that working toward cessation is totally different. For instance, one student, Andy, got very excited when he began to achieve states of strong and steady absorption. He started reading descriptions of "big" moments in meditation and asking teachers how far along the path to enlightenment they were. He announced that he only wanted to study with people of major achievement. Andy was several months into his new identity as a great meditator when he attended a concentration retreat I was teaching. He spent the first two-thirds of the retreat trying to duplicate his previous retreat experiences. It was challenging trying to help Andy rediscover his beginner's mind and realize that his ego had taken possession of his practice. He was judgmental and impatient with himself and with the practice. He refused to acknowledge that he was trying to force his experience to match his views about what constituted a great practice. It took Andy two years to return to just practicing with the present moment and relinquish his concepts. Please don't let this happen to you! If you disconnect from all your previous practice, you run the risk of losing your momentum and getting lost in your concepts and idealizations about spiritual practice.

In your very first encounter with the state of nonclinging, you experienced your first "taste" of cessation and you felt the possibility of the mind being free. Most of your journey to cessation will be similar to your first taste. As I said in Chapter 14, many people find liberation without ever having any dramatic altered states; instead they experience a slow, steady unfolding of realization. Therefore, do not measure your progress by the number or amplitude of dramatic moments you have had, but rather periodically ask yourself: Is my practice stronger? Do I suffer less? Do I cause less suffering? Do I have a clearer, calmer perspective in daily life? What matters is that you make your life your practice. Making your practice the core of your life is cessation in the sense that you cease pursuing the illusionary and you cease trying to find well-being and meaning in what can never yield freedom.

For the most part you will not know *where* you are on the path to cessation, only that you are indeed *on* the path. The rest is not your business. T. S. Eliot describes the "don't know mind" attitude that you are to cultivate concerning progress in these lines from *Four Quartets*:

> . . . These are only hints and guesses,
>
> Hints followed by guesses; and the rest
>
> Is prayer, observance, discipline, thought and action.

Can you feel the call to trust in your practice in Eliot's words? I have found this attitude to be crucial as you explore cessation. The *hints* you will encounter in your practice fall into three categories: those moments when you know you are suffering less because of your practice; those moments when you feel the wholeness or sweetness that comes with choosing to dance with life in this manner; and those moments when you know your mind is free. The *guesses* are your intuitive feelings regarding the mystery of life. They are always grounded in *don't know mind* so that you do not become deluded into thinking you know something just because you received a hint. The humble student who knows she does not know is content to practice, as Eliot says, with "prayer" (*intention*), "observance" (*mindfulness*), and "thought and action" (*the wisdom and ethical parts of the Noble Eightfold Path*).

THREE STAGES OF REALIZATION: TRANSFORMATION, TRANSCENDENCE, AND TRANSPARENCY

There are a number of systems that various teachers and traditions employ to help you envision what happens as your practice ripens and starts to bear fruit. However, I am offering an alternative concept of spiritual progress that comes from my own experience. In my first years of practice, I was often confounded when I encountered teachers who clearly had attainments but who did not seem free to me although they were proclaiming themselves to be. As I tried to understand the apparent split between "knowledge" and "being" in these teachers, and to respect and learn from them despite this split, I conceived this particular framework of development, which you may apply to whatever system of realization you may be studying.

To begin with, you may greatly facilitate your understanding of spiritual progress by making a distinction between *states of mind* and *stages of awareness*. *States of mind*, no matter how exalted, are always temporary and are not predictive of your overall behavior or indicative of your level of development. You can have temporary states of mind that are more advanced than your actual level of development. *Stages of awareness*, which can also be called *stages of being*, however, are indicators of spiritual maturation and manifest throughout your life. The confusion and conflation of these two dramatically different attainments is the source of much suffering.

There is nothing wrong in cultivating and exploring various exalted states of mind as long as you don't identify with and cling to them. Exalted states of mind can reinforce you on the path or be a source for later insight. For instance, you may have beautiful visions of Buddhas, or deities, or of the universe itself; or you may have horrific visions. You may experience great bliss states characterized by feelings of oneness and completion that lead to tears of joy; or you may be bathed in a beautiful white light. You may have extended periods of great concentration in which your mind is absolutely peaceful. You may have synesthesia, in which one sense experience shows up in another. Or you may feel an interspecies connection with wildlife and nature. Or you may have what seems like foreknowledge of the future, forms of rapture, or even moments of great insight in which you truly comprehend the dharma. Some of these experiences are simply what Zen Buddhists call *makyo*, meaning displays of the mind that are to be ignored. Others can be a foreshadowing or a genuine taste of what it is like to have a mind that is free and a heart that is open. Yet no matter how illusory or visionary these events may be, they are merely states of mind; therefore, they are temporary by nature. No matter how serene or exhilarated the mind is when it is in one of these states, its basic structure is not changed by simply being in them. These mind states are sometimes referred to as *corruptions of insight* because they can deceive you into delusion and attachment.

I have met a number of individuals who have experienced incredible states of mind at some time on their path. Unfortunately, they are often quite identified with these mind states. Witnessing them while they are in such a mind state, I have been happy for them and hoped that the experience would significantly change their lives. Yet, this seldom seems to happen. At best, some people are able to occasionally reconnect to their exalted mind state. But beyond the limited time spent in the altered mind state, neither their minds nor their lives are otherwise liberated from clinging. They continue to live most of their lives participating in samsara and creating suffering while often thinking they have become something special when in fact they are only clinging to a memory.

In contrast to states of mind, *stages of awareness or stages of being are distinctive levels in your spiritual maturation and are not dependent on being in a temporary heightened mind state.* Your inner development progresses according to *three major stages of awareness* that are beyond the *ordinary stage* of awareness where most people live their lives. In moving from ordinary awareness to the first stage, *you transform your ego structure*; in attaining the second stage, *you transcend your ego identity*; and in the full realization of the final stage, *you become transparent to ordinary reality*, which is equivalent to reaching nibbana.

With each successive stage of awareness, your mind is controlled less and less by pleasant or unpleasant conditions until you reach the final stage, in which your mind is not even affected by surrounding conditions. *Thus, at each stage of awareness you create less suffering for yourself and others, independent of your mind state in any moment.* Since authentic spiritual development comes from advancing to the next stage of spiritual maturity, you don't aspire to exalted states of mind, even though you welcome them when they arise. Rather, you practice in a manner that completes the stage of awareness you are currently working in and invites the arising of the next stage in your development.

You may often have extraordinary states of mind that presage a stage of awareness that you have not yet attained. Again, this is a blessing in and of itself, but such a foretaste can cause you confusion. There are many *degrees of attainment* within each stage and you may mistakenly think you are more fully manifested than in truth you are.

STAGE ONE: TRANSFORMING THE EGO

To get to know these stages, let's assume that you make a new commitment to your spiritual growth right now. You are beginning from the *ordinary stage of awareness*—you have your good moments, but mostly you are inclined toward clinging and contraction. We can trace how you might move from where you are now to the first advanced stage of awareness in which you have *transformed your ego structure*. Remember, you begin your journey from where you are and just as you are. Therefore, becoming mindful of yourself is your first act of practice. Slowly, you begin to see yourself more clearly and to act more skillfully and to give attention and priority to your inner life. *At first your inner changes simply mean that you are becoming psychologically or emotionally healthier.* Being emotionally healthier is good in and of itself, and it greatly facilitates your movement toward freedom. When you have a healthy ego, you are able to work more easily with the various mind states that arise. Of course, you also have an easier time dancing with life.

Now that you feel better about yourself, you have to fight off temptations to abandon your spiritual goal and fulfill your ego's wants. But you intuitively know your journey is about something larger than just creating a healthier ego; therefore, you stick to your practice. What are at first just small shifts in your thinking and behavior gradually and cumulatively amount to substantive changes in how your mind is organized, and you enter a new stage of development. You realize that *your suffering is the result of the way you are, not the way the world is.* You *know you know* this is true, not because someone told you or you read it in a book, but because you feel it in your body. This direct knowing *transforms you within your ego structure.* At this point, the world loses much of its allure, and you have much less anxiety because you know the truth of the arising and passing of phenomena.

You truly are *transformed.* You have matured spiritually, and although you remain primarily defined by your ego's view of itself and the world, you are far freer than you would be otherwise. You realize that within this transformed ego structure you have the opportunity for still more growth and you act to balance your ego's inadequacies. Thus you *advance in degrees of attainment.*

Once you reach the *ego transformation* stage of awareness, you feel a sense of ease with life and selflessness that makes you more available to others. Therefore, you choose to spend your time being a devoted family person, or dedicate your career to helping others, or become a social leader, or a great innovator, or someone who is primarily devoted to your practice. These are just roles you are playing; after all, you have to do something with your time. *You continue to be organized around your ego, but the ego's identity is transformed, therefore, much of its focus is on wholesome behavior and serving others.* There are certain areas in which your ego is not transformed, and you struggle not to fall into unskillful behavior. But these areas are limited, you know how to work with them, and you are dedicated to doing so. If you are disposed to experiencing altered states of mind, you may have a variety of them upon arriving at this stage of awareness, but now you are too wise to identify with them, cling to them, or feel special because of having them.

At this stage of spiritual maturity, *cessation means you have ceased being self-referencing.* You are much less tormented by greed, ill will, and delusions. Despite whatever flaws you may have at present, you are capable of achieving genuine ego transformation. Having a teacher affirm for you that you are capable of this transformation can serve as inspiration that allows you to do so. Your own journey may not carry you any further than this, but such a transformation is in itself an extraordinary accomplishment. It empowers you to fully dance with life.

If you are exceptionally motivated, you realize at some point that you could spend your entire life exploring and developing within the transformed ego stage and you would still not be free. Therefore, you do not lose the thread of your inspiration. You stay connected to your deeper calling—your heart's full liberation. So you persistently practice noticing clinging and nonclinging and witnessing arising and passing of phenomena. You can imagine that transcending the ego might be possible. You are not clinging to a desire for transcendence, it is a natural progression; the mind and heart spontaneously move in this direction.

Stage Two: Transcending the Ego

To reach the *transcending-the-ego stage*, you continue to practice, but now *you have your transformed ego as a foundation*, so you create less suffering, encounter less inner resistance, and

have more faith. Still, it is hard work and there are many pit-
falls and distractions, so you may regress into ego neediness
from time to time. One way that you can know you have
attained this level is that when you act unskillfully, you are
aware of it from the dharma perspective, not from your habitual mind, and you now do what needs to be done to find
release from the suffering.

Transcendence can arise either slowly and almost impercep-
tibly or suddenly and dramatically because of a lightning-bolt
awakening event. Either way, at this stage of liberation *you cease
to primarily identify with your ego sense of self.* You are not suddenly a perfect person; you still have your quirks and shortcomings, but you are no longer thinking, speaking, or acting in ways
that are likely to cause harm to yourself or others. You may be
living what looks like a very ordinary life and no one pays much
attention to you. Or you may be serving society in such a way
that draws much attention. The particulars of how your transcendence manifests do not really matter. What matters is that
you have transcended ego. Therefore, in relating to life, you
spontaneously and consistently respond to what is called for,
and you do so from a sense of being part of the mystery of the
unfolding of your life rather than from your ego. *You have not
become someone new—you have become more your true nature.*
Said another way, you have shed something that was stifling or
imprisoning you, which was your identification with the ego
self as a fixed entity. Your ego still exists, but it is no longer the
center of your being. As with the stage of transformation, there
are degrees of maturity even within this subtle, refined manner
of being. For instance, you are still attached to higher mind
states; therefore you have a sense of a subject or an "I" who has
transcended the ego.

Initially, your experience of transcendence may be sporadic
and inconsistent, and you may occasionally relapse into your

transformed ego identity, but over time the transcendence grows stronger and more consistent, and you eventually evolve into a new way of being in the moment. You have not yet realized your full Buddha nature, so your mind still occasionally contracts, but you do not add to the pain by identifying with it. You have many more moments when your mind is at ease with whatever conditions are arising, regardless of whether they are pleasant or unpleasant.

If you are fortunate, you will maintain your humility as you continue to work on the degrees of your transcendence, but there are tragic examples of great teachers who lost their way despite their attainments. In Buddhist mythology, the god Mara represents the inner voice of temptation and inflation. It is said that the Buddha continued to be visited by Mara even after full realization. Each time the Buddha was not deceived and responded by saying, "I see you, Mara."

Many people believe that transcending the ego is the highest human potential. At this stage of being, you cease to identify with the duality that arises in your mind, although there is a "knower" (the subject) and "that which is known" (the object). You are still dancing with life, but the dance is no longer a struggle; it is effortless and natural because you have stopped clinging.

Stage Three: Transparency

The third stage of awareness, *when your mind becomes transparent to ordinary reality*, represents the total realization of cessation. At this stage, you are no longer dancing with life, for you are not organized in the ordinary human realm anymore. You are resting in the absolute and have become *a direct part of the mystery that illuminates* all of ordinary reality. You have achieved the *deathless*.

When your mind has realized cessation and become transparent to ordinary reality, you experience all the moments of
your existence as equal and meet them with tranquility and
compassion. When a moment is pleasant, tender, or beautiful,
you receive it as just that; your mind has no inclination to make
it you or yours, and there is no clinging to it. The moment is
complete; there is no future and no past. Likewise, when a
challenging physical or emotional situation arises, or you are
confronted with pain and loss, your mind has no inclination to
contract; it remains open, available, and calm. What is unpleasant is just unpleasant, what else could it be? You don't object to
how it is, and you don't demand that the pain go away, or wish
for life to be other than it is. It is just unpleasant and your mind
is unperturbed in its knowing. You are free; you have experienced *the sure heart's release* that the Buddha promised.

Total cessation is directly experienced through the realization of *anatta*, or "not-self," and *sunnata*, or *emptiness*. By emptiness I mean that all your sense experiences are empty of
self-reference, that your mind in meditation is empty of grasping, and that your mind is empty of any hindrances to your
investigations. A renowned expression of this realization of
total cessation is this mantra from the Heart Sutta, a Mahayana
Buddhist teaching:

Gate, gate,

paragate,

parasamgate,

bodhi svaha[21]

---

[21] I interpret "svaha" to be an exclamation of awe at the dazzling, unexpressible mystery
of the realized mind. Balyogi Premvarni, the Indian teacher who initiated me into
using this mantra, taught that "svaha" conveys the felt sense of breaking through
conventional reality. It means, "Wake up! Let go! Right now!" Thus, "svaha" is
pronounced with an energetic, explosive quality.

A traditional English translation of this mantra is:

Gone, gone,
gone beyond,
unfathomably further than gone beyond,
into awakened mind, ahh

Within the framework of the three stages of awareness, the phrase "gone, gone" alludes to the first stage of transformation; "gone beyond" refers to the second stage of transcendence; and ". . . further than gone beyond" points to the third stage, transparency.

The full realization of cessation results in a fundamental change in consciousness to pure awareness and the realization of emptiness that transcends the ego personality. This core shift is beyond words because your being is essentially reorganized. You are transparent to the delusion of ordinary reality. You are in nibbana.

When you experience cessation, all attachments and all fetters of the mind fall away and all that is left is luminous mind. Here's how the Buddha described the mind at this stage in the *Anguttara Nikaya*: "Luminous is this mind, brightly shining, and it is free of the attachments that visit it." At another point the Buddha describes this stage as ". . . awareness without feature, without end, luminous, all around: here water, earth, fire, and wind have no footing. Here long and short, coarse and fine, fair and foul, name and form are without remnant, brought to an end."

Although this stage of transparency is beyond your personality, the luminous mind shines forth through your personality. This fully evolved stage is often described as *unborn, uncreated,* and *unmanifest*—*unborn,* because it is not defined by conventional time with its cycle of birth and death; *uncreated*, because there is nothing beyond it that originated it; and *unmanifest*, because even though it appears to be present in time, it cannot be located anywhere in space/time. It is your achievement of transparency that allows it to be seen and felt so directly. Because your mind has awakened and become transparent to this pure awareness, it is now part of that great impersonal illuminating source for all life.

BOOK FOUR

THE FOURTH
NOBLE TRUTH

THE FOURTH NOBLE TRUTH

WHAT IS THE NOBLE TRUTH OF THE WAY LEADING TO THE CESSATION OF SUFFERING?

IT IS THE NOBLE EIGHTFOLD PATH . . . RIGHT VIEW, RIGHT INTENTION, RIGHT SPEECH, RIGHT ACTION, RIGHT LIVELIHOOD, RIGHT EFFORT, RIGHT MINDFULNESS, AND RIGHT CONCENTRATION.

THIS NOBLE TRUTH MUST BE PENETRATED TO BY CULTIVATING THE PATH . . .

THIS NOBLE TRUTH HAS BEEN PENETRATED TO BY CULTIVATING THE PATH.

—SAMYUTTA NIKAYA LVI, 11

CHAPTER 18

THE WAY TO END YOUR SUFFERING

A s you have seen through practicing mindfulness, *your thoughts, words, and actions have consequences;* they condition future moments in your life that will create either suffering or nonsuffering. For this reason, to fully realize cessation of all clinging requires purification of the mind as well as training in mindful awareness. Therefore, you deliberately and repeatedly create these liberating conditions of mind utilizing the purification trainings that the Buddha describes in detail in the Fourth Noble Truth, and which he called the Noble Eightfold Path. You cultivate ethical behavior (*sila*) so that your mind is not disturbed by guilt and denial. You develop mindfulness and concentration (*samadhi*) both in meditation and life so that your mind is steady and awake during all your daily activities and so that you are present to make choices that do not create dukkha. And finally, you cultivate wisdom (*panna*) through meditation, observation, and reflection so that you develop the discernment to know what brings happiness and what causes suffering. All three—sila, samadhi, and panna—act together to purify the mind.

Purification of the mind brings the steadiness and the clarity that allows insight to arise. Both purification and insight are necessary for genuine liberation. Purification practice without insight and compassion leads to fundamentalism, a fixed view about right and wrong. It lends itself to superstition, to condemnation of others, and to imposing your will on others. Likewise, insight without purification can result in nihilism or hedonism, self-serving ignorance, and lack of accountability such that any behavior can be justified or rationalized. Even when you have profound insights they cannot be integrated into your life if your mind is unpurified. You are unable to move to a new level of consciousness, and you continue to cause suffering for yourself and others.

Most likely, your journey will consist of interplay between growing purification and deepening insight, and they will not feel as separate as I am describing them. But without a conscious awareness of the importance of balancing both, you are at risk of losing your way.

As I stated in Chapter 13, in practicing the Noble Eightfold Path, you come *to know* that you need to develop three capacities that transform your life. First, you must learn to *sustain practice* over a long period of time such that you don't become discouraged or disinterested. Second, you must be able to create and stay with *intention*, which then becomes the bedrock for peace of mind and well-being of heart in your daily life. Third, you must surrender control and trust that your innate capacities for caring and responsiveness will manifest as best they're able.

When these three capacities start to mature, you discover that there is a *state of wholeness* that evolves quite naturally from *living the spiritual life*. As you spend more and more of your time in this state of wholeness, then the mysteries of the Eightfold Path start to reveal themselves in an ever more subtle manner until full cessation has been reached and you know you have completed walking the path. The differences between your inner life and outer life are dissolved.

Unfortunately, even serious dharma students sometimes forget the Buddha's core teaching that inquiry and reflection are the essence of practice, whether one is meditating, running a business, or raising a family. Instead, they start to believe in a concept of nirvana, based on what some teacher has told them or their own views about enlightenment. I have found that when students get caught in conceptual thinking, they are less involved in the *practice of insight* and more involved in following a *belief system*, even if they do not recognize it as a belief system. By contrast, the act of skillfully dancing with life through the Noble Eightfold Path brings about the precursor moments of well-being and freedom that move you forward to full cessation.

THE TENTH INSIGHT:

*What is the Noble Truth of the Way Leading to the Cessation of Suffering?
It is this Noble Eightfold Path.*

CHAPTER 19

AN INTEGRAL APPROACH TO PRACTICE

REFLECTING ON THE FOURTH NOBLE TRUTH

Up to this point in your life, your mind has been so conditioned by years of *reacting* to arising thoughts and feelings of pleasant and unpleasant concerning the past, present, and future that you spend most of your time in a *reactive* mind state, which prevents you from creating a new and more meaningful way of dancing with life. Oh, sure, you learn from your mistakes and gain some perspective—life forces that on you. But to really establish a new *responsive* relationship to life based on your *deepest intentions* requires taking a *systematic* approach to your life. For this reason the Buddha introduced the Noble Eightfold Path as a way for you to live from a spiritual orientation and to proceed at your own pace toward greater freedom. The Eightfold Path is not a list of what to do if you want to become a good person. Rather, it is a *matrix of behavior, understanding, and practice* for finding peace of mind and meaning in your life.

In the Tenth Insight the Buddha asks you to *realize* that there is a path to finding freedom from the angst of your life and experiencing more joy. Implicit is the authentic possibility that you have the power to change your inner experience of life, and there is a specific means for you to do so. The realization of this insight evokes in you the faith to undergo the discipline, hard work, and renunciation that are called for in the Eleventh Insight. If you do not believe there is a better way to dance with life, and a path for getting there, and that you personally are capable of practicing that path, you will never commit to changing your life—why would you?

The Noble Eightfold Path reflects the gradual path to liberation, rather than the instantaneous insight of full awakening. When you begin practicing the Eightfold Path, it is important to let loose of self-judgment, your ideas about progress, and your concepts about how your inner life is supposed to unfold. At times you will be out of balance in relation to some part of the Eightfold Path and yet continue to grow. For instance, you may well realize that your means of livelihood doesn't reflect your inner values, but for various reasons you stay in your job for several more years, all the while deepening in your inner life. You may fall off the path in major areas of your life, but *the sincerity of your intention and the wise attention you bring to meeting your life provides for growth even when you stumble.*

Specifics of the Noble Eightfold Path

The eight path factors or elements are often presented as three classifications of practice: *panna* or wisdom practices, which include right view and right intention; *sila* or virtue practices, which are right speech, right action, and right livelihood; and *samadhi* or concentration practices, which include right effort, right mindfulness, and right concentration. There is a spiraling, dynamic quality to the Eightfold Path; each element enriches the others directly and indirectly.

Some students find the analogy of the "folds" very instructive because each of the eight factors "unfolds" as you practice it. For example, as you practice right intention over time, its meaning becomes increasingly more subtle and complex.

The first of the eight path factors is *right view*, which means you are to engage in observation and reflection, which in turn leads to clarity and insight about what life does and does not offer. Right view is also referred to as *wise understanding* because it empowers you to live in harmony with life just as it is. Essentially, right view means using the Four Noble Truths to understand your life.

From right view you develop your core values. These core values provide the foundation for the second path factor, *right intention*, meaning those priorities you manifest moment by moment in your life. In Buddhist terms right intention means to be mindful, to not cause suffering to yourself or another, and to respond to life with loving-kindness and compassion. Classically, right intention begins with practicing renunciation of sensual cravings. Right intention is also referred to as *wise aspiration* and *right resolve*.

The next three path factors—right speech, right action, and right livelihood—refer to behaviors that are outward manifestations of the other elements and are likely to impact others. *Right speech* is the primary way you interact with others, and it is the way in which you can most easily cause harm to another. *Right action* is the cultivation of a manner of interacting that prevents you from getting caught in your wants, emotions, judgments, and views. You practice skillful actions and abandon those that seem unskillful. Then with the factor of *right livelihood*, you practice providing for yourself in a manner that is not exploitive of others.

The last three path factors have to do with practice, both formal meditation and being mindful in daily life. *Right effort*, the sixth factor of the path, refers to how you pay attention. You cultivate and train your mind in order to shift your attention from one object or thought pattern to another. You learn how to apply effort in this manner so that when you find yourself obsessing on a thought that is not wholesome, you have the ability to shift away from it. Such a shift comes from your wise understanding and right intention, not from aversion. When your mind is focused in a wholesome manner, you have the ability to sustain your attention.

The seventh path factor, *right mindfulness*, is the clear understanding of your experience in the present moment. As you have already experienced, the practice of insight is dependent on right mindfulness. You cultivate the skill of mindfulness in daily life in order to stay present with what is happening, see it clearly, and respond appropriately. In formal meditation right mindfulness means keeping the mind alert and free from hindrances in order to see clearly what is true in the moment, particularly in regard to your mind clinging.

The last of the path factors is *right concentration*, and it applies both to meditation practice and to being concentrated and present throughout your day. In order to live your wisdom in daily life, your mind needs to be collected and unified. This state of mind allows you to stay grounded in the Eightfold Path despite the pressures and distractions that constantly bombard you. Although concentration is presented as a separate element of the Eightfold Path, in actual practice it is impossible to be mindful without a certain level of concentration, which gives you the ability to focus clearly and stay with what is happening to you in any given moment.

LIVING THE DHARMA AS AN UNFOLDING PATH

You aren't necessarily supposed to embrace the entire Eightfold Path all at once. For instance, Jeff, a man who regularly studies with me, attended his first silent meditation retreat just to get a break from the constant pressure of his thriving psychotherapy practice and his family life. He liked what he did for a living, and he loved his wife and kids. It was all good, but he felt the need for a break, and he was curious about mindfulness meditation, having experimented with other kinds of meditation in his twenties.

Jeff's first step on the path can be seen as a respite from daily life. It is not unusual for people to start practicing for this reason. The need for a break may be motivated by physical exhaustion, emotional pain, stress, boredom, or restlessness.

Jeff was surprised by how good he felt on retreat, and upon returning to his therapy practice saw that what he had learned about mindfulness was helpful in working with his clients. So a year after his first retreat, Jeff went on a longer retreat. This time Jeff's motivation was more practical and deeper—he wanted to learn more about his own mind. The desire to know yourself in this manner is a stronger and more committed motivation. Fortunately for Jeff (because it does not always unfold in this manner), he had an intense retreat with a number of personal insights.

Following his second retreat Jeff started meditating in the mornings, although not with any great discipline. If asked about the Eightfold Path, he would have endorsed it, but it held no personal meaning for him. He was simply interested in the benefits of meditation. But then during his third retreat, Jeff's insights moved from the personal to realizations about the very nature of life itself, including what causes suffering and the impersonal nature of most experience. He started to realize the profundity of the dharma and that meditation was affecting him in ways that also benefited others in his life. Slowly he started to make his whole life his practice, and he began to consciously work with the Eightfold Path. He embraced right speech and right action, put more effort into being mindful throughout the day, and took time to study and reflect on what he was doing with the brief time he is embodied on this earth.

Now Jeff tells me with confidence that he is "going for it" in this lifetime, that is, he intends to reach full liberation. Yet if you looked at his life today, the outward circumstances wouldn't appear very different from when he attended his first retreat. This is because walking the Eightfold Path is primarily an internal experience.

As Jeff discovered, the eight factors are not just developed sequentially; rather, they are an overlapping and interrelated set of practices and behaviors that lead to spontaneous deepening of insight. For instance, when your understanding of what is important for your inner peace grows, then you are more likely to practice right action. With your newfound clarity you see that it makes sense to be skillful in your actions. You are not being *moral* based on a belief system; you are being your *realized* self.

The Path Is a Living Experience, Not a Concept

In the next chapter, you will learn how to practice each of the eight path factors. But without knowing *how to practice* practice, you can easily become discouraged or confused or even quit on yourself. Therefore, it is essential that you master the art and science of practice itself. The Buddha taught the Noble Eightfold Path as a gradual path; in other words, you are going to be doing it for the rest of your life, and it will be constantly changing. For these reasons there are three skills you will need to investigate and develop: how to *sustain your practice* over your lifetime; how to *reference your practice* such that it becomes an organizing presence in your daily life; and most importantly, how to *open to the deep realizations in your practice* that lead to the fruition of the path, freedom.

Walking the Eightfold Path is a humbling undertaking. You will spend a lot of time on various plateaus where nothing seems to be happening in the way of less suffering or more insight. Sometimes, as you become more aware of your thoughts and actions, it can actually feel like you are suffering more. When you start to give up behavior that once stimulated, entertained, and distracted you, it can seem as if you've made the sacrifice for no good reason. Therefore, it is necessary that you learn to love the plateaus. I mean *really* love them. *Practicing* practice becomes the ground for your journey. Day after day, you find joy, or at least a sense of alignment, by simply practicing each of these eight factors as best you are able. You learn to laugh at the follies of your mind, to stop being self-judging, and to just get back on the path when you have wandered off.

Once at Spirit Rock Meditation Center, where I am a member of the teachers council, we hosted an international gathering of Buddhist teachers from all lineages and invited the Dalai Lama to lead us for one of the days. To show our appreciation to the student volunteers who staffed the event, we asked the Dalai Lama to meet privately with them and to answer their questions about practice while we Spirit Rock teachers listened. The meeting took place in the walking-meditation room of the Center, and it was packed with staff and their families, who had also been invited. One student raised his hand and said, "I've been practicing for many years now. I go to retreats. I have a home practice and I do the ethical precepts. At first I felt all sorts of change, but not for a long time now. It seems like I am not getting anywhere in my practice—what do I do?"

The room became totally still; everyone there had felt the

same discouragement. The Dalai Lama was quiet for some time, and then replied, "I know just what you mean. Sometimes I feel as though my practice is not progressing." You can imagine the feeling in the room; this was the Dalai Lama speaking— a man who gets up at 3:30 a.m. every day to practice—and he too feels such discouragement. He continued, "What I do is reflect over the 10, 15, 20 years of my practice, and I can see that some movement has occurred." This is an example of loving the plateaus—having faith, patience, perseverance, and most of all humility to just surrender self-judgment and the demand for a preferable outcome in order to live your intentions as best you are able.

The Noble Eightfold Path as Integral Practice

The Tenth Insight is a call for *integral* practice, meaning that you are to bring the practice of the Eightfold Path into the whole of your life, including your work, your personal and family relationships, and even your inner life. Take for example right speech, which involves saying what is not only true and useful but also timely. Each time you speak becomes an opportunity to integrate your practice with your outer life. So at work you restrict your speech, being mindful not to criticize coworkers behind their backs, or repeat gossip, or make fun of someone simply because you are bored or irritated.

This may sound simple to you, but just wait until you actually try practicing right speech! You will discover that much of the time you spend talking serves little or no purpose for you or others. It is simply your brain discharging the pressure you feel through casual, fairly random utterances or running commentary on what you are currently experiencing. You quickly discover that such speech actually drains you of energy and often creates situations that then demand more of your attention. Or you may discover that much of your speech is just a space filler to avoid silence or for the purpose of being entertaining when it is not really very interesting to you or the other person. As you gain some degree of mastery over your speech, it may well give you a new kind of confidence because when you open your mouth to talk you have a sense of purpose and integration.

An integral approach to the Eightfold Path can also mean developing a body/mind integration practice, which includes a movement practice such as yoga or qigong to complement your meditation practice. The felt sense of being present in the body while working with each of the eight factors of the path is essential to fully realizing their impact. In the Buddha's core teaching of the Four Foundations of Mindfulness, body awareness is a central feature. "There is one thing monks, that cultivated and regularly practiced, leads to a deep sense of urgency . . . to the Supreme Peace . . . to mindfulness and clear comprehension . . . to the attainment of right vision and knowledge . . . to happiness here and now . . . to realizing deliverance by wisdom and the fruition of Holiness (*arhatta-phala*): it is mindfulness of the body," he said.[22]

When I left *Esquire* to give myself over full-time to pursuing the inner life, part of my practice was to spend a number of years exploring the martial art of aikido, which I did most weeknights, and to continue my yoga practice, which I did in the early mornings after my meditation. I also trained in the Feldenkrais method for building body awareness and took workshops in dealing with body trauma. I found that my ability to stay present in my body during meditation grew significantly,

---

[22]   Thera, Nyanaponika. *The Heart of Buddhist Meditation.* Weiser Books, 1996, p. 158.

and the body awareness manifested in my daily life when I was walking down the street, sitting talking with another person, or while teaching. This integration provided me with new physical ease, stopped my energy drain that was due to body tension, and increased my awareness, particularly in pressure situations such as a difficult discussion with someone. It has also been invaluable in my teaching duties.

The Role of the Psychological in the Noble Eightfold Path

For me, integral practice has also included growth in psychological understanding. Sometimes meditation teachers are reluctant to refer to the psychological for fear it will foster attachment to an ego identity. But in my experience, if you include awareness of your psychological and emotional issues in your inquiry, your spiritual practice becomes richer and more fully integrated into your life to the benefit of yourself and others rather than reduced to the goal of creating a better self. When you apply mindfulness and right understanding to the ego complex, the hindrances are less present, meaning your emotional issues do not manifest as blockages or distortions in your mind. *The result is a healthier, more balanced ego, although that is not the goal but merely an effect of integral practice.* Psychological awareness in one sense is simply one more form of mindfulness.

When you integrate mindfulness of the psychological into your practice of the Eightfold Path in this mature manner, you become far less identified with your ego, although it will continue to make up stories and create views about your life. The difference is that you are not seduced by the contents of those views and stories; you see them clearly for what they are. Thus, there is no need to reject your ego personality, only the call to know it fully and to not be misled into clinging by its tricky manifestations.

Committing to an integral approach to liberation involves constantly asking yourself, "At this moment am I causing suffering or not causing suffering?" As soon as you start to regularly ask yourself this question, it becomes obvious that growth in psychological awareness is critical for walking the Eightfold Path, otherwise you lack the ability to read situations well enough to answer the question.

I have repeatedly observed that a student who is out of balance or undeveloped emotionally has trouble achieving, sustaining, and integrating spiritual insight. It is not unusual for me to recommend that a student do therapeutic work in order to gain some understanding or relief from a past trauma. Students with past trauma sometimes experience difficulties in meditation retreats because they have not worked the trauma through. They simply cannot undergo extensive periods of silence, and they have to leave the retreat.

Even among people with seemingly healthy egos there is a strong tendency to psychologically split into a person of insight who practices and another person who lives out daily life doing things the person of insight would never do. Alexis, a successful businesswoman, was quite dedicated to the dharma and had already attended a number of silent meditation retreats when we started working together. In her first interview with me, Alexis wanted to talk about how her meditation practice did not seem to enhance her daily life experience despite her many days of intense retreat practice. On retreat she was someone who just wanted to learn—she was patient, noncomplaining, and didn't think she knew much. So why with this good attitude was she not progressing—why did she not feel freer in daily life? It soon became apparent that Alexis had a "retreat personality" and a "worldly personality," and the two were hardly *integrated* at all.

Our discussions revealed that in her daily life, Alexis saw herself as a dynamo, someone who knew much more than everyone around her, and she had little patience with how "slow and dense" others were. She was so accustomed to having a compartmentalized life that it had not occurred to her that her worldly personality was resisting the realizations she had on retreat because they threatened her ego identity. Yet there was immense resistance, and it became clear to Alexis that she had to integrate these two aspects of herself. After a couple of years of struggling with feeling that she was not being tough enough or pushing enough, Alexis learned to allow her worldly ego to function without identifying with it. She now describes herself as being more relaxed in her daily life and far more able to enjoy her nonwork time. What most surprised Alexis was that bringing her practice into daily life did not diminish her effectiveness. "People like me so much more and seem to trust my good intention, so they cooperate without my constant pushing. That's amazing!" she recently told me.

Walking the Path Is What Your Life Is About

Committing to an integral practice also means that you view all your tasks in daily life as being more about practice than outcome. You integrate all aspects of the Eightfold Path into your daily activities such that they are reflected in how you respond internally and externally to various situations that arise in your life, from being cut off in traffic to being taken advantage of by someone you trust. This is a radical shift in orientation, and you may not yet be ready for this step even though you may have several years of meditation experience. *But if you continue to practice, the day will come when you realize that the only way life makes any sense with its endlessly changing cycle of gain and loss, pain and pleasure, is to view it as practice.*

Treating the Eightfold Path as integral practice transforms your everyday life into a type of monastic experience. Skillful living becomes your measurement for success, instead of how often you get what you want. This is a much better way to view your life! You are more relaxed, flexible, and you even experience more enjoyment. Some of your worldly goals will fall away or diminish in importance, but many will remain, although they are constantly changing. The radical difference is that your inner attitude shifts and how you manifest moment by moment as you go about attaining your worldly goals is dramatically different. Your experience of life itself is changed.

THE ELEVENTH INSIGHT:

This Noble Truth must be penetrated to by cultivating the Path.

CHAPTER 20

DEVELOPING INTENTION, YOUR ALLY ON THE PATH

DIRECTLY EXPERIENCING THE FOURTH NOBLE TRUTH

The Noble Eightfold Path is not a set of beliefs or laws but rather a practical, direct experience method for finding meaning and peace in your life. Think of it as an organic blueprint from which you organize and live your life. Each of the eight path factors defines one aspect of behavioral development needed for you to move from *suffering to joy*. Its eight factors function as an integrated system or *matrix* that supports and informs *all* parts of your life. By "cultivating" the Buddha means attending to, nourishing, and manifesting each of these factors of wisdom in your life.

RIGHT VIEW OR WISE UNDERSTANDING

It is taught that right view is understanding and framing your experience through the Four Noble Truths. Right view is also the understanding that your actions have consequences. Your first encounter with wise understanding may come from a personal experience of suffering so overwhelming that you realize there must be a better way to cope with life. Or it may arise out of an urgent need to find more meaning in your life that while not unhappy, seems superficial. Ajahn Sumedho says, "Right understanding is developed through reflection . . . with right understanding everything is Dharma." Through wise understanding you clarify what really matters to you and formulate a set of values by which to live.

Right view comes at the beginning of the Eightfold Path because without realizing that there is dukkha in your life and that you can do something about it, you would never be motivated to start. Wise understanding is also the continuous, cumulative result of practice. For this reason, it is useful to think of the Eightfold Path as both a sequence of eight steps that follow one after the other and as an interconnected set of eight energetic practices that relate *circularly* and *directly* to one another, such that wherever you start on the path is a *beginning*. Whichever aspect of the Eightfold Path you focus on, you engage all the parts directly or indirectly. And if you explore any one of the eight factors in sufficient depth, it will lead you naturally to another.

I sometimes use the phrase *deep understanding* instead of *wise understanding* to highlight the difference between "dharma understanding" and "regular knowledge." Regular knowledge is a *surface* understanding about events, which allows you to control conditions in order to fulfill your desires. In contrast, cultivating *deep understanding* enables you to find peace of mind in all circumstances, regardless of whether the surface conditions of your life are pleasant or unpleasant.

Right or Wise Intention

With wise understanding you gain increasing clarity about the nature of human existence and develop a deep aspiration to cease being a slave to your reactive mind. Based on your deep understanding of what constitutes the highest potential for a human, you develop *right intention*, which means that you live your life moment to moment based on values that reflect your knowing. In Buddhist terms practicing right or wise intention means making a commitment to not cause suffering for yourself or others, which requires renouncing those desires that would cause harm. You meet the world with compassion, loving-kindness, generosity, and integrity, and you strive diligently toward liberation. Your wise intention empowers you to align your thoughts, words, and actions with your deepest understanding.

Intention is the pivot point that allows you to dance with life. It is the bridge between understanding and action. Understanding without intention is conceptual and passive, no matter how profound it may be. *Wise intention, on the other hand, has an immediate, energetic, attentive quality.* Said another way, all your mental or physical acts involve *volition. Your intention is the ground from which all volition arises and is the primary determinant of whether your actions will plant beneficial or harmful seeds.* Intention quite literally affects all your mental formations—thoughts, associations, and emotions. Just as a shoemaker sees shoes, and an artist notices designs, you see what supports your wise intention and what does not, and you develop the strength to act accordingly.

Utilizing just this insight, one student completely altered his relationship with his wife. Doug, who had some meditation-retreat experience, started coming to my weekly meditation group because he felt desperately unhappy in his marriage and was looking for help. He and his wife had developed a habit of relating through blaming, competing to be right, and positioning themselves against each other. They have two young children and Doug wanted to stay married, but he was in despair over the unpleasantness of his relationship with his wife. He told me that being at home was more work than being at the office, so he was starting to avoid being at home. He and his wife were in marriage counseling, but with little to show for it. I talked to Doug about the Eightfold Path, in particular wise intention, and encouraged him to ask himself what his intention was before, during, and after each conversation with his wife. I advised him to not place such emphasis on his own goals when interacting with his wife.

It only took a few weeks of mindfulness of his intention for Doug to see his part in their problems. He was a superachiever type, and he discovered that he brought his goal-making power into the relationship such that he was always trying to get things to be just right, which often meant fixing his wife's actions and opinions. To him this had been an expression of love—he was making their life perfect. He started to see that he was not actually being with the real person in front of him, but with his projected ideal of what she should be—no wonder his wife was being difficult! This realization initiated a much longer exploration for Doug in which he found that he approached his spiritual practice in much the same way—every time he meditated, went on retreat, or even read a spiritual book, he set goals for himself.

As Doug discovered, there is a big difference between goals and right intention. Doug had wonderful goals for his family life, but he was so fixated on his future goal that he was not paying attention to the moment. He needed to learn to be mindful in the present and to be clear about his intention before speaking and acting.

The same is true for you as you learn to dance with life, particularly in your spiritual development. Your goals are your preferences for the future. Your goals provide inspiration and direction as well as determine how you allocate your time and resources. But your goals do not determine how you act right now. Instead, your intention determines how you actually think, act, and speak in any given moment. Just think of all the worthy goals you've had through the years and how often while pursuing those goals you've either spoken or acted in a way that was harmful to yourself or another.

The following analogy makes clear the distinction between goals and intention. Let's say you and a friend decide to hike up a mountain. You see the mountaintop and you know that reaching it is your *goal*—it provides direction and inspiration for the hike. It even informs your preparation and resource allocation—the time you need to set aside, how much water and food you will take along, how you will dress, etc. Therefore, committing to the goal is a vital part of the hike. But the actual experience of hiking is very different than reaching your goal, the mountaintop. Your journey up the mountain consists of a series of single steps, rest stops, moments of seeing nature, and sharing companionship. The hike happens in the present moment in each individual step, and each step is primarily defined by your intention. If all you focus on is the goal, you can easily miss being present for the hike.

The intention to stay with your goal in this very moment empowers you to keep taking steps toward the mountaintop. But it is crucial that you understand how you act *during* each step, which will determine whether or not you cause harm to yourself, another, or nature as you trek up the mountain. For example, if you injure yourself while hiking by not maintaining your intention to be mindful, it is less likely that you will make it to the mountaintop. As we saw with Doug, you can have quite lofty goals and still cause harm to yourself and others. It is also true that when you lose your wise intention and cause harm, you are much less likely to reach your spiritual goal.

I have witnessed students with admirable spiritual goals lose their way because they did not cultivate and maintain intention. When I encourage them to be more mindful of *just now*, they sometimes become frustrated with me because I'm not more excited about their ambition. Even though they are articulate and passionate about their goals, they refuse to cultivate the mindfulness, patience, and willingness to just start again that is required for practicing right intention. When you hear spiritual teachers say, "There is only the journey," they are not being glib; they are telling you to cultivate moment-to-moment awareness of your intention, which is the "ground" for your journey to the goal. *Each step on your journey is complete in itself.* Thus, finding fulfillment in living your intention is not dependent on you reaching your goal; rather, each moment you are awake and not clinging is liberation itself!

Another way to comprehend the *immediacy* and *attentive* aspects of intention is to realize that you are always *starting over in each moment*, even while you are continuing to walk toward your goal. Therefore, when you become lost, or lazy, or unskillful, it is not a sin or disaster; you have simply lost your intention. Now you remember it and just start over. Likewise, even in those moments when you are being mindful and present, and everything is going as you want it to go, you are still starting over in the very next moment. This understanding prevents complacency and boredom, as well as the creation of expectations, which can be obstacles to walking the path.

Wise intention with its immediacy of attention to the sacred now brings release from the pattern of wanting mind. T. S. Eliot described the transformative power of intention in these lines from *Four Quartets*, which he borrowed and adapted from the 13th-century Christian mystic Dame Julian of Norwich:

And all shall be well and
All manner of thing shall be well
By the purification of the motive
In the ground of our beseeching.

Eliot is telling us that we often think, speak, and act from motives that do not reflect our deepest intentions. But committing to purifying your motive—that is, learning to reconnect to your wise intention—brings a sense of well-being and ease into your life right now. The process of purification requires revisiting your intentions over and over again each day in the various situations of your life. Be curious and nonjudgmental, and align yourself as best you are able. In fact, the purification of motives is a lifetime activity—maybe many lifetimes.

Sometimes your worst failure of intention proves to be the most valuable in your purification process. For instance, you may do something that violates your own values, as happened with one yogi, Steve, who was horrified when he realized he had broken a confidentiality agreement in his workplace. Being trustworthy was one of his deepest intentions because he had witnessed so much suffering that was created by betrayal. Then he failed to honor his own intention! As Steve reflected on what happened, he saw that he had not been mindful of how hurt he had been by the circumstances that lead to his indiscretion. More important, he had failed to be with his hurt with compassion; instead he just dismissed it, telling himself that he was "moving on." But in truth, he had denied his feelings and they festered into bitterness, which lead him to abandon his intention. Rather than just feeling bad about his misstep, Steve saw the truth of his suffering in the situation. In the future he will recognize similar situations when they arise and not fall into reactive mind. Although his behavior was not to his standards, the situation did not actually cause any real harm, and by receiving it as a message, Steve deepened both his understanding and his practice. In the end, Steve was served by failing to live up to his intention.

RIGHT OR WISE SPEECH

The practice of right speech is built around meeting three conditions simultaneously: Say only what is *true* and *useful* and *timely*. If any one of these criteria isn't met, then *silence* is the wise form of speech. This is such a simple formula and easy to recall even in moments of strong emotion, but it is very hard to execute even under the best of conditions because the grasping mind corrupts speech faster than it does action.

You may not realize the aggressive nature of your speech until you try to make it a mindfulness practice. There are several factors that may interfere with your ability to know when you are being unskillful. For instance, you may feel that if you know something is true, then it is okay to speak it. But the Buddha was quite explicit in saying that when truth is spoken in an untimely manner it is not wise speech. Untimely speech is rampant between couples, in parenting, and in the workplace. For example, I know of a situation in which a man told his wife right before she was to give birth that he had doubts about their marriage. Although this was certainly the truth and something the wife would have wanted to know, his timing caused great suffering.

Applying the filter of saying only what is useful is even harder. We live in a culture where "speaking your truth" is promoted as a form of empowerment and good communication. Yet this is not the case if your words don't provide useful information or better understanding. In working with nonprofit organizations, I often encounter situations in which individuals vent their opinions and judgments about others in a manner that is quite harmful while rationalizing that they are speaking their truth.

There are endless opportunities for you to work with right speech in your daily life. For instance, you can vow for a week not to make a single comment regarding anyone who isn't present during any conversation. Or you can decide that you will not listen to gossip for a month. Or you can devote a period of time to saying only what is useful.

Practicing right speech includes actively refraining from giving unsolicited opinions or stating your view when it serves no purpose. It also means not positioning yourself by using faint or limiting praise or by stating the positive and then adding a qualifying limitation. Both of these forms of speech are passive aggressive in nature, and although what you say may be true, it is not useful. You also don't use the truth as a weapon for making yourself look better in comparison to another, or to put others in their place, or to be entertaining and clever at someone else's expense. Likewise, you don't use speech to satisfy your ego. Examples of this are "I told you so" talk, bragging or gloating, and positioning yourself while seeming to only be making an observation.

Right speech involves *listening from the heart*, that is, you give your full attention to the words of others and listen without judging, preparing a response, or comparing. Listening from the heart means that you listen with an attitude of compassion, kindness, and humility. This capacity is often best developed by practicing with a friend who is also doing the practice or in a contained situation with a few others, then gradually extending the practice to those with whom you have more complex, mutually dependent relationships.

At first practicing right speech can seem like expecting perfectionism, and it certainly is true that the harm resulting from unwise speech can seem slight at times. But as many students have discovered once they have truly engaged in this practice, the cumulative effect of unwise speech is quite dramatic, although mostly unseen. It drains your energy, and it encourages you to get caught in clinging to your views, to become lost in desire, and to become more aversive, vindictive, and defensive. And it causes others to pay less attention when you speak.

Many people believe they already use wise speech and are shocked to discover otherwise. It can be quite dismaying to find that you can't control your speech when you first try. I once suggested to a physician who came to my weekly meditation class that he practice right speech. First he told me with great indignation that he already practiced right speech as a caring physician. I replied that if that was so, it should be a really easy practice for him. He came back a week later and sheepishly admitted that he was needlessly critical of others, was often too impatient to listen from the heart, and worst of all, he was a gossiper! His newfound self-awareness gave him strong motivation to work at right speech. It would have been a disaster if he had announced he was doing this practice to his staff and colleagues, but by keeping it an "open secret," meaning visible but not named, he was able to quietly mature. His efforts were rewarded when one nurse observed that he must be a lot happier because he was acting so much nicer!

Right speech isn't only an external practice, but also an internal one. You may utilize right speech with others but have violent, unsettling, or crippling interior speech. If so, pay attention to what your mind's voices say and how they say it. Is this inner speech prone to judging and doubting you? Does it speak with fear of the future or of others? Does it assume you are in the wrong or that things will go badly? Is it explosive in its criticism of others, and does it defend itself by doubting others or by finding fault in their motives? Are there different voices in your head, some of which arise just to be negative? Is this unwise interior speech habitual? Wise interior speech would naturally include a healthy dose of compassion and loving-kindness as a result of seeing the truth of suffering.

RIGHT OR WISE ACTION

Through wise intention you are able to determine *wise action*. Wise action is any action that liberates the mind, moves you toward freedom from suffering, and supports a feeling of well-being that is independent of external conditions. It arises out of clear comprehension or sampajanna, meaning you are clear about what is needed, what is appropriate, and what is doable within your limitations. In order to take action with such clarity, you approach decisions with mindfulness and with awareness of the dharma.

Wise action doesn't just apply to big decisions, but applies to small ones as well. You see the truth of suffering and impermanence and that your immediate situation is caused by impersonal causes and conditions, and this larger dharma view allows right action to unfold. You cultivate being mindful of all your actions, even those that you don't ordinarily notice, such as how fast you walk, how you sit at your desk, how you decide what to eat, and how fast you eat it. Wise action is reflected in how you schedule and pace yourself, how you treat others, and how you nourish yourself.

Wise action is behavior that does not cause harm to yourself or others and includes all those activities intrinsic to your many roles as spouse, lover, parent, child, worker, friend, and so forth. The classical method for incorporating wise action into your life is to practice the Buddha's Five Precepts. The first of these training principles is to not cause harm through your actions.

The second is to take only what is freely given; in other words you don't steal, exploit others, or engage in deception. The third is to not cause harm or suffering by your sexual actions. The fourth is right speech, which I previously described in this chapter. And the fifth precept is to not intoxicate your mind with drugs, alcohol, or any other form of stimulation that would interfere with your ability to act wisely. By taking the Five Precepts you transform your daily life into a kind of spiritual retreat.

At times, students mistakenly view right action as a mere afterthought to cultivation of insight. They believe that if you are doing your practice correctly, right action happens automatically. But do not be lulled into such complacency; practicing right action often forces you to ask yourself, *"What is my intention?"*

Each time you practice right action you are manifesting right intention and temporarily fulfilling one of the goals of the path. Wise action acknowledges that you cannot control outcome and that you cannot know the ultimate outcome of any action. Your practice is to act with the wisdom you have available to you in this moment and according to your core intentions—that's all. Of course, you learn from the consequences of your action and gain more wisdom, which enables you to act more skillfully in the future.

RIGHT OR WISE LIVELIHOOD

Right livelihood specifically means not earning your living in a manner that brings harm to yourself or others, particularly if it involves killing. To me it also means not having a violent attitude in whatever you do for a living. For instance, if a man cuts someone open and the person dies, is this right livelihood? If it

was a thief who committed this act, then it is wrong livelihood. But if it was a surgeon trying to save a dying patient, it is
right livelihood. However, if that surgeon overbooked himself
and therefore made a mistake, or failed to wash his hands
between operations and infected the patient, then it is wrong
livelihood.

In our time, it is not usually the profession but rather the
manner in which the profession is practiced that creates wrong
livelihood. For example, if you recklessly drive your car while
commuting to work, or prey on the ignorance of others, or
mislead or trick others in order to earn a living, you are practicing wrong livelihood. In my view, any job that takes away
joy, either your own or others', also constitutes unwise livelihood, whereas any job that supports and nourishes well-being
and the sense of the possibility is wise livelihood. Wise livelihood matters as a practice because it brings freedom to the
mind now and in the future, while unwise livelihood thrusts
the mind into turmoil now and plants the seed for even greater
turmoil in the future.

As with wise action, right livelihood can be cultivated by
practicing the Buddha's Five Precepts. One student, Paul, who
is a salesman and is dedicated to living with integrity, adopted
the second precept to take only what is freely offered as his
practice. You can imagine the challenge that this presented him
at work. Paul's job is to convince customers to purchase his
products and to get signed orders. For the first two months
after taking the precept, nobody bought anything from him,
which confounded Paul. He realized then that he had to choose
his target list of clients more carefully, selecting only those people who he felt really should buy his product, then he was free
to vigorously work at educating them as to why this was so.
While he could push for their order, he had no right to manipulate them. At first Paul felt as though he was losing sales and

was quite nervous about what he was doing. He was careful not to tell his boss about his new ethical concern. Eventually, though, Paul felt a shift and noticed that he had gained a new "credibility vibe" with customers. He began to gain orders, but the big reward was that he liked himself so much more than before.

Paul reports that at least once a week there is a sales situation in which he sees the potential to manipulate a customer and that he has to restrain himself from doing so in the competitive heat of the selling atmosphere. "It thwarts my competitive juices to see the opportunity and not go for it, and I feel frustrated immediately afterwards," he once confided to me. "When will this tension around values stop?" I could only smile and tell him maybe next week, maybe never.

You, like Paul, may imagine that there will come a time when right speech, right action, and right livelihood will be so automatic that you no longer have to cope with your wanting mind. But it doesn't work that way. The tension you feel when following a precept is there as long as you have any clinging to outcome; however, working with the tension between what is right and what is expedient gradually becomes easier.

RIGHT OR WISE EFFORT

Right effort is directing your attention so that you are not helplessly caught in the various mind states that arise. The Buddha describes four kinds of wise effort: avoiding unhealthy mind states; abandoning unhealthy mind states once they have arisen; moving the mind to healthy mind states; and maintaining the mind on healthy mind states that have already risen. Attention is a function of the mind and is subject to training, although it often seems as if this is not so. However, *energy follows attention,* therefore whatever you place your attention on is what will receive energy in your life.

Right effort is classically associated with working with your mind in meditation, but it also applies to working with your mind states in daily life. If you have choice, you do not place your attention on thoughts that do not serve you, and you move away from thoughts that are obsessive, contracting, and limiting. Practicing these two forms of right effort doesn't mean that you should seek to never have difficult thoughts; it just means that you shouldn't stay stuck on them. You know how it is when you obsess about a future situation and keep planning it over and over or when you continuously replay a difficult experience of the past—these constitute unwise effort.

The other two types of right effort—moving your mind to a wholesome state and staying with wholesome states of mind—seem straightforward. But if you watch your mind, you may discover that you have mind habits that are quite different. When your mind is not occupied with wholesome thoughts, you may have a tendency to fall into worrying, or spacing out, or replaying the events of your day with harsh self-judgment. Wholesome mind states are a wise response to what is being called for in your life. They involve being flexible in how you respond to change, curious about your underlying mind states, and mindful of your deepest intentions toward yourself and others, combined with focus, concentration, gratitude, and humility.

Do not confuse right effort with a judging mind that rejects difficult mind states. In vipassana no mind state, emotion, or thought is unworthy of attention. Right effort has to do with how you are being with what has arisen. For instance, you may be really hurt by someone's actions and may be having terrible thoughts about him. The practice of right effort is not to reject those thoughts, for that would only push them underground and give them even more power, which will show up later as unwise words or actions when the conditions are right. Instead you would move your attention from identifying with the terrible thoughts to the suffering that is contained in the thoughts, which in turn will give rise to compassion and give you clarity to see how you are getting caught in whatever hurt you. Sometimes this chain of events will bring about psychological insights that free you from your emotional storm. Instead of being caught in reactive mind, you are able to accept that life includes such difficulty, i.e., "Betrayal feels like this." Do you see how this is right effort? Your external conditions and your emotional experience are no different, but you are no longer being defined by your emotional reaction. Amazingly, right effort really does work this way; it is not just some abstract idea.

One student in my Sunday meditation class, Janice, suffered from a steady barrage of negative thoughts about herself. If she was not focused on a task, her mind automatically began to review all of the ways in which she was inadequate. On meditation retreats this mental habit made her quite miserable because most of the time she had no task to occupy her mind, and in her daily life she was completely undermined by it. When Janice confided her difficulty to me, I suggested that during the upcoming week she spend a few minutes four or five times each day just listening to the negative thoughts when they first arose, feeling how they registered in her body, seeing what images accompanied them, and noticing whether it was her voice or someone else's that was uttering the critical comments. As it turned out, her inner voice was similar to her hypercritical mother's voice. Then for the next week I instructed Janice to notice the stress and discomfort she felt during a barrage of self-criticism and try to feel compassion for the part of her that had to suffer through this assault. Janice needed two weeks to even begin to find compassion for herself.

Next, I asked her to spend a week honestly examining whether the self-criticism served her. She reported that the criticism did not help her become more effective; all it did was reinforce that she could not ever afford to relax because of how incompetent the inner voice told her she was! Janice confessed that until this point she had always believed that the self-criticism kept her focused and alert to error; now she realized that this was a delusion.

Finally, we had reached the point where Janice could make an intention to stop harming herself with criticism. She had all the tools she needed for right effort. Her process was slow—many months went by before she sensed the first hint of a shift, and it was four years before she felt that she was free of her old mental habits. The process was not enjoyable, but, as I told Janice repeatedly, whenever she made the effort, even if she collapsed back into criticism, she at least for a moment stopped reinforcing the self-hatred. Janice may well have to work with this tendency toward negative mind states the rest of her life, but that is a very different reality than being defined and controlled by them. Just like Janice, you can apply right effort to those areas in your own life that cause harm through the use of mindfulness, investigation, and compassion.

RIGHT OR WISE MINDFULNESS

Right or wise mindfulness is much more than just paying attention. While wise mindfulness includes the *attention process,* which notices and stays with whatever is happening in the present moment, it also includes *investigation* of the experience, which allows you to see it clearly, and it includes the attitudes of *dispassion* and *compassion,* which give you the strength to fully receive the experience. It is through wise mindfulness that vipassana or insight arises and you see the characteristics of life that confuse the mind—constant change (anicca), the stress of clinging (dukkha), and the existential fact that the ego self is an illusion (anatta).

Wise mindfulness is present in every moment of wise living through wise intention. You are not always going to have mindfulness, but *it is your intention to be mindful that matters*. However life is manifesting, your mindfulness informed by your intention allows you to live wisely at every step. In any given moment you may be very misinformed or lost in emotion, and so you act quite unskillfully. But this action is just episodic; it is not what you are about. Once you discover through wise mindfulness that you have gotten off the path, you know how to get back on the path. Therefore, *even your unskillful moments become part of the path because you respond to them through wise mindfulness and wise intention.*

Martha, a student in my weekly meditation class, is a perfect example of the power of mindfulness to be transformational. Martha is a key executive in a large corporation, and she disagrees with some of its policies. Moreover, her boss, the chief operating officer of the company, is someone she doesn't respect because he frequently humiliates subordinates during management meetings. At the time Martha described her work conditions to me, she was painfully caught in her reactive mind much of the workday. She would become angry and depressed during meetings when she thought poor decisions were being made or when acts of inappropriate criticism occurred. Martha is a good dharma student and knew that her judging mind, aversion to her boss, and wanting things to be the way she desired were making a difficult situation more unbearable, but she didn't understand how to stop being reactive.

I worked with Martha to clarify how her values could manifest by being mindful of her intention while managing her own staff, in stating her opinion during controversial discussions with her peers, and in responding to her boss. Martha found a new orientation. She discovered that the more clearly she conveyed the values behind her views to her colleagues the less reactive she was, and the more likely her values were to prevail. There was a key moment in one management meeting in which she felt herself getting lost in her judgments, so she excused herself, pretending she needed a bathroom break. Stepping outside the meeting for just a few minutes gave her time to reconnect to her own intention. She recognized that the outcome of what was being debated was not in her control and that she had to let loose of clinging to it. Martha returned to the meeting, stayed mindful as she spoke about integrity, and was careful not to fall into reactivity when others took an opposing position. To Martha's surprise, they actually decided on the course she wanted! She realized that in the past her lack of mindfulness of her demeanor had often undermined the very values she was espousing. Things still often do not go her way, but she has found a new ease at work and feels that she is having a humanizing effect on the company.

RIGHT OR WISE CONCENTRATION

Right concentration is the last of the eight factors and empowers your sense of presence in every other aspect of the path. Right concentration is the ability to *collect and unify the mind*. It enables you to direct your attention to an object of your experience and stay focused on it. In daily life wise concentration supports right intention in thought, speech, and action with a feeling of *collected purpose*; without it your mind would not be able to stay connected to your intention. However, it's not so easy to develop steady concentration; therefore, you cultivate it in meditation.

There are two general types of meditation for establishing the steadiness of concentration that allows you to practice mindfulness: open field attention and deep absorption. The first of these, open field, is what the great Burmese meditation teacher Mahasi Sayadaw referred to as "momentary concentration," in which your mind is briefly concentrated on a single object. He taught that such short-term concentration is sufficient for gaining insight from mindfulness practice. Momentary concentration means that your mind is collected and unified such that you can know what it is experiencing. For the mind to be responsive rather than reactive to what it perceives, it is important that you develop what I call "relaxed attention," which is the quality of concentration that allows the mind to "soften into the experience" rather than contract around it or disassociate from it.

For many people it is skillful to begin meditating by focusing on a single object such as the breath and repeatedly returning to it when the mind wanders. (For instructions on how to practice this technique, refer to Chapter 2.) With practice, your ability to establish and maintain attention on an object that arises in the mind becomes sufficiently stable so that you are able to fully receive and investigate your experience of it. For instance, suppose an upsetting thought about a situation at work arises in your mind during meditation. Ordinarily, you become so anxious that your mind starts jumping from one worrisome thought to another, and you miss the opportunity to notice the nature of the original experience. But if you have cultivated stability of attention, you can concentrate on the experience of the upsetting thought and know it more fully. Maybe you will recognize it as just a recurring thought that may or may not come true in the future, and that there is nothing you can do about it anyway. You realize that your mind is contracting and suffering around something that doesn't exist and therefore serves no purpose. With this realization or insight, you let go of the upsetting thought of the future and experience clarity and ease of mind instead.

Such an investigation can't happen if your mind isn't collected and unified at a certain minimal level. Over time your mind has this kind of stability more and more often even during daily living and you do not get caught so often or so deeply in wanting or rejecting what is happening to you.

The second approach to practicing formal mindfulness meditation is to start by attaining *absorption* concentration, which in the Theravada tradition is called "jhana." In jhana practice your mind becomes fully concentrated on a meditation object for an indefinite period of time, then moves to ever more subtle levels of awareness. After achieving an intense state of stillness and one-pointedness, you then begin to practice mindfulness.

In my experience a certain amount of deep absorption can arise spontaneously even while practicing momentary concentration. For instance, your mind might stay with the breath for many minutes, during which time thoughts only occasionally arise. Or you may discover that your attention is resting in body sensations and is totally calm and peaceful, despite some of the body sensations being unpleasant. Or your mind can become stabilized with a quiet sense of well-being that lasts long after you stop meditating. Some teachers call this noninduced stability of the mind a form of jhana; but regardless of how it is labeled, it is often present when insight starts to progress toward the realization of the arising and passing of phenomenon, and other realizations that lead to cessation.

The importance of being able to achieve fully absorbed meditation states to attain deepening insight is debated among meditation teachers. There are also differing views as to what level of one-pointedness characterizes such states. But there is no debate about the importance of being able to collect and unify your mind in meditation in order to practice mindfulness. Unfortunately, in my years of experience conducting interviews, I've seen that only a modest percentage of students ever develop the concentration potential they naturally have. If you want to develop more concentration capacity, I recommend attending a concentration-oriented meditation retreat, and leave all your ideas about why you can't concentrate at home.

You can be *unwise* about concentration. Sometimes students become "hungry ghosts" looking for certain altered states of mind that come during absorption meditation. Some students fall into delusion about their attainments simply because they have had a few ecstatic states during meditation. Still others abandon their practice because they have a mistaken notion that they lack the concentration required for progress.

Robert's experience illustrates the importance of taking a nongrasping approach to concentration practice. In his own view, Robert had never been good at getting concentrated. To his disappointment he had never once experienced any altered states, despite attending a number of retreats. However, his clarity of mind had grown by practicing mindfulness, and he knew it was making a difference in his life, so he kept coming to retreats. One afternoon while meditating after lunch, Robert felt his usual sleepiness coming on. At first, he had a couple of self-critical thoughts and felt disappointment, but then he realized that it didn't matter if he dozed, he was practicing as best he could, so he just *relaxed*. Robert's mind then shifted into a state of *surrender to the moment* and became totally still, in a manner he did not know was even possible. By keeping his attention gentle, combined with all his previous experiences of "not getting any concentration momentum," he was able to yield to an incredible experience. For the next hour he went through one deep level of altered reality after another. Then it happened again that evening during a meditation, and this pattern continued for several days. Robert was so amazed and so happy, but to his credit he never grasped to keep his concentration going. He has not yet had another moment of such strong concentration on subsequent retreats, but it has not mattered to him. He reports that the insight and confidence he gained during those days continues to serve him in daily life and on meditation retreats.

Eight Factors in a Single Path

The Noble Eightfold Path is truly a lotus blooming among the confusing muck of life in this ever-changing world. You can't grasp after achieving the Eightfold Path; you can only approach it slowly and with humility, doing a little practice at a time. Eventually a little insight will arise, and you will really know something about life. From this initial taste of insight, you may naturally wish to go deeper, so you explore some more. At first your practice is somewhere "over there" while your ego experiences life as being "over here." But gradually you realize that it is wise living to treat more aspects of your life as an opportunity to practice. Finally, your view evolves and you realize that life is simply practice. Now you can be a true beginner. Your mind is sufficiently empty of concepts and opinions and fully open to insight. You are simply dancing with life!

THE TWELFTH INSIGHT:

This Noble Truth has been penetrated to by cultivating the Path.

CHAPTER 21

NOW THAT YOU KNOW, WHAT IS IT THAT YOU KNOW?

KNOWING THAT YOU KNOW THE FOURTH NOBLE TRUTH

As you begin working with the twelfth and final of the Buddha's insights, you are nearing the end of your search to know how to live wisely. In your journey you have utilized mindfulness to explore the experiences of your mind and body, which has allowed you to directly know the emotional, psychological, existential, and spiritual dilemmas of daily life. You are no longer deluded—you no longer have the mistaken belief that your mind has to be trapped in stress and reactivity for the rest of your life. You now know that freedom is truly possible, and you "know that you know" effective ways to respond to desire and difficulty when they arise in your life. You know that a *path* to cessation with its eight factors exists; you know its parts; you know you are capable of practicing it; and you know that it works for you!

You now also know that practicing the Noble Eightfold Path and developing direct knowledge of cessation are inextricably entwined: The cultivation of one supports the cultivation of the other. As you practice the Eightfold Path, you will have moments of temporary cessation, which will allow you to overcome desire, withstand fear, and stop your mind from falling into turmoil. For instance, one student who struggled with right speech and right action due to being "compulsively competitive," as he described it, finally freed himself from his compulsion by learning to focus on the arising and passing of each of his impulses instead of speaking and acting. He spent a very frustrating two years practicing this way. But the day finally came when a situation arose that in the past he would have reacted to unskillfully. Instead, he reports that he watched his desire to dominate and to be "the smart one" arise, but he did not get caught for a single moment and stayed in touch with his deeper intention. "It was so liberating," he told me. "Once the impulse was gone, there was no frustration, no sense of losing—there really is cessation!" Ultimately, practicing the Eightfold Path leads to the full realization of cessation and its fruit. At that point, you have completed the Eightfold Path.

The Goal of No-Goal

My preconceived idea of the Eightfold Path before I gave myself over to it was that it was simply a means to a *goal*—to achieve liberation in the future. Such a view can be inspiring and highly motivating, and I thought I would just naturally respond and embrace this view. But I quickly discovered that it is also possible to walk the Eightfold Path as a moment-by-moment goal that is not *future* oriented, but is *now* oriented. This "just now" perspective will serve you well if, like me, you have a tendency to get fixated on the future at the expense of the present.

For this reason, I took the goal of having *no goals* (even spiritual ones) as my primary practice in the years immediately following my departure from *Esquire*. All my adult life I had been organized around making goals for the future, and I had the ability to realize many of them. But the trouble with goals, at least for me, is that they tend to elicit a sense of identity bound up in time. The ego will usurp even your loftiest goals and use them to further entrench itself at the center of your being when it really belongs in a supporting role.

My practice during this period, which I call my time of wandering in the desert, was to focus my *attention* on the *intention* of just being fully present for *this* moment, *this* step, on the path, as best I was able. It was a difficult practice, and it was impossible to explain to others how "nondoing" represented a profound practice. I had spent 20 years in the larger-than-life roles of editor and entrepreneur. What I accomplished was "heroic" in the eyes of the media world and those around me. I naively thought that once I surrendered my worldly position, I would have a new ego identity, that of someone who was a seeker of answers to life's big questions. Instead, for the first five years after I entered my new life, it was my "hero" identity that would wake up most mornings ready to slay dragons. This well-established ego identity wanted and needed a sense of purpose that involved action, challenge, and ego satisfaction. But there was nothing for him to do! It made my mind restless and unsure. My ego would constantly criticize what I was doing. I never regretted leaving publishing to pursue the inner life, but during those early years I constantly questioned the manner in which I was practicing. Was the goal of *no goal* wise, or should I use my hero energy to create a spiritual identity?

But I couldn't do it; it seemed artificial. As I have pointed out numerous times in this book, *you have to start where you are, not where you would like to be.* So given my desire to accomplish and become, my only genuine course seemed to be the path of nondoing. Acting solely on intuition, I would urge myself, "Just now. Just be present in this moment." I repeated this many times each day, week after week.

Periodically I "fell off the wagon" and got involved in various projects that gave me ego satisfaction, but I always came to my senses, dropped the projects, and resumed my moment-to-moment practice of living without goals. After several years, a shift in my ego identity occurred that felt as though part of me had died. Initially it felt like a great loss. But eventually a new internal organizational structure emerged that felt spacious and freeing. For the first time I felt capable of meeting life just in the moment, rather than compulsively seeing and interpreting every experience in the context of future goals. This inner change was the genuine beginning of the path I had long sought.

Ironically, once I ceased to identify with goals, I had much more capacity to pursue goals without clinging to them and without getting caught in concerns about the future. Had this freedom of mind been present at the time I left *Esquire*, I would have been more involved in social activism and those years would have been less tumultuous. But as I've said, you start where you are. Although I intellectually had a larger view of what was possible, my identity was not engaged in that larger view, so I had to take a more difficult and frustrating path.

It may well be the same for you. *You have to let go of those places in which you cling to an identity.* It doesn't matter if you already have a great understanding in the theoretical sense. It is the actual "felt experience" that determines how you walk the path. I cannot stress this enough: *You begin with yourself, just as you are, acting compassionately toward yourself, but willingly submitting your ego's identity to its defeat.*

Once you've found resolve with one type of clinging, your reward is that you get to work with another aspect of your suffering! Then another and another as you walk the Eightfold Path. At least, this has been my experience. Like peeling the layers of an onion, your heart becomes progressively lighter as you move towards your core. You will have no trouble knowing that your heart is becoming less burdened—there is such a feeling of relief!

The Call to Surrender Your Ego

In *Four Quartets*, T. S. Eliot points to the necessity of letting go of your *ego's attachment to its own importance*. Initially, it can be humiliating for your ego to discover that there is a greater purpose to your life than attending to its own sense of well-being. Eliot states it this way:

Old men ought to be explorers
Here and there does not matter
We must be still and still moving
Into another intensity
For a further union, a deeper communion . . .

Eliot is calling for the inner stillness of meditation and inner inquiry at the cost of the ego's self-aggrandizement. By "old men" he means those who are ready for their second half of life's great task—to resolve the inner disquietude that comes from the mind's reaction to the stress and dissatisfaction of ordinary life with its endlessly changing opposites of happiness and sadness, gain and loss, pain and pleasure. Only you can know when you are ready to begin this task—it may be when you are 20, 30, 40, 50, 60, or even just before you die.

It was laying down the hero's sword that gave me the humility necessary to become an *explorer*. This *voluntary submission to the defeat of the ego* allowed me to be *initiated* into another *intensity*, and my life slowly transformed into path. I had not understood at the outset of my journey that the manner and timing of that initiation and transformation would in no way be of my choosing or under my control. Only after this involuntary defeat of the ego (which felt awful) did I really surrender the idea of there being a "me" who is in charge.

You don't necessarily need to practice the goal of having *no goals* as I did. This was my first step because of the causes and conditions of my childhood and how I had responded to them. It was my karma. Your path will be determined in part by your unique karma. Based on my years of experience of working with students, you most likely have some psychological/ emotional issues that create an inner sense of scarcity or need in your ego identity and that must be worked with before you can finish walking the Eightfold Path.

I can say with confidence that *if you look honestly and with patience, you will discover that there is something that makes it challenging for you to embrace wise intention as the axis of your life.* Maybe it is that you are fear based or self-righteous, therefore the call to surrender means to give up defending yourself. Or you may be emotionally needy or insistent on having things your way, and this self-centeredness needs to come out of the shadow. Or you may keep losing yourself in others or be driven to accomplish, therefore clinging to your hero-martyr or hero-mother-father complex must be surrendered. *What matters is that you allow yourself to know what must be surrendered and voluntarily surrender it.*

Working with your core attachment is your equivalent of my practice of no goals. It is what must be released so that something new beyond your ego's imagination and capacity can enter and flourish. You do not necessarily have to act in a dramatic fashion. Most likely, walking the path will consist of small steps for you—practicing right speech, changing how you allocate your time, increasing your mindfulness of body and mental activity—until a sense of being at the threshold of change arises.

It is difficult and confusing to work with your ego's limitation, no matter what it is. This is because you need the ego's cooperation in order to act in a manner that at times seems contradictory to its own interest. As T. S. Eliot says in *Four Quartets*:

> In order to arrive at what you are not
>> You must go through the way in which you are not.

The journey feels as strange as Eliot's words because by definition you are "not being yourself," yet you are being very genuine in not being yourself! This is the paradox of the inner journey. It requires stopping the ordinary mind while maintaining conscious mindfulness, and you have to do it for an extended period of time.

Ajahn Sumedho says, "Your personality never gets enlightened." When you are characterized by personality, but not defined by it, there is freedom in your response to life that comes from wisdom and compassion. You aren't supposed to build your practice around "destroying your ego limitation," rather you consciously go through your ego limitation in order to be freed from it. Knowing that you know the twelve insights in the Four Noble Truths are intellectually, emotionally, psychologically, and spiritually true empowers you to make the ego sacrifices necessary to walk the path. You have taken refuge in the dharma and in your own Buddha nature. You are on the path to freeing your mind and heart.

CHAPTER 22

THE COURAGE
TO BE HAPPY

The Wisdom of the Fourth Noble Truth

A few years ago I was teaching a silent meditation retreat attended by a student named Thomas. I had been Thomas's teacher at his first retreat the prior year. That retreat had been difficult for him, but he showed willingness to hang in there with body pain and some difficult memories from his childhood that kept coming up. Since then Thomas had attended one other retreat, and now here he was sitting with me again. During our one-on-one interviews, Thomas spoke about his practice in the same way he had on his first retreat. All he mentioned was what was wrong with his practice—how he lost his mindfulness time and again, how he started judging others, and how he could not stay with his breath. Yet, when I questioned him it was clear that Thomas had actually progressed in his meditation practice—his mind was a lot less restless, he did not complain about his body hurting, and he was beginning to have insights. He was actually having a fine retreat, but you would never know it by what he said. Finally, I asked Thomas why he never reported any mindfulness of his good moments on the cushion. I pointed out that if I did not question him, I would never know that he ever had pleasant moments in his practice! Moreover, I observed, he seemed to be benefiting from his hard work, but why did he not appreciate his progress?

After much inquiry, Thomas came to the conclusion that he almost never stayed mindful during his good moments, partly because he had an unconscious belief that good moments are the way life is supposed to be, so when they occurred it simply indicated that he was finally functioning at his minimal level of capacity. I was amazed by this response and asked Thomas what was beyond the minimal level. He explained that it was great clarity of mind, total calmness, and feelings of ecstasy! We laughed together as he uttered these words, and I told Thomas he had just had an insight about clinging to views and expectations. Further exploration revealed that Thomas was also afraid that if he focused on the good moments in meditation or in his daily life he would become lazy and lose his motivation to both succeed in the world and to practice.

Working with Thomas led me to start noticing how many people in my weekly sitting group skip over their good moments of meditation. Then I began being mindful of how many people in casual daily conversation seldom mention enjoying something, being in a good mood, or feeling gratitude or appreciation for their many blessings. What it revealed to me is that people are afraid or at least ambivalent about being present for their own happiness!

Throughout this book I have focused primarily on mindfully working with dukkha—the stress, disappointment, and dissatisfaction in your life—as a gateway to finding freedom. But it is also true that you can find liberation in being mindful of *sukha*, the pleasant and happy times in your life. You may not realize that joyful, meaningful moments can provide the same liberating insights as those that are filled with angst and anxiety, but they unquestionably can. You may also have a slight and unnoticed aversion to staying aware when you are feeling happy because you unconsciously mistrust your periods of well-being, believing that feeling good is innately delusional or inherently clinging. But this isn't so. Your moments of satisfaction, enthusiasm, and fun are to be enjoyed, appreciated, and even celebrated, when they are arising from wholesome actions. Your challenge is to fully receive such temporary moments of well-being without devolving into clinging to them and to maintain sampajanna (clear seeing).

The Buddha mostly focused on the temporary nature of material happiness, how "pleasant" elicits clinging and how ideas about being happy can lead to delusions of being an unchanging self. However, at various points in the *Anguttara Nikaya*, the book of lists, he talks about happiness in the *here and now*, and enumerates the various kinds of happiness that are possible in the mundane world. For instance, he says there are four kinds of happiness: that of possession, enjoyment, debtlessness (yes, even in the Buddha's time), and blamelessness. At another point he classifies two types of happiness—that of home life and that of monkhood. In the *Majjhima Nikaya* he names five desirable things: long life, beauty, happiness, fame, and rebirth in heaven. He also names the joys that arise from each sense door.

I suspect that in the Buddha's time there was not the ambivalence about happiness that exists today. It would not have occurred to his students to feel uneasy when they felt good; today, however, uneasiness with well-being is quite common. For the Buddha your highest happiness comes from *virtue* because it leads to *nonremorse*, which leads to *gladness and joy*, which in turn brings *serenity and happiness*, which allows for the kind of *dispassion* and *concentration* that bring knowledge, vision, and liberation.

You may already be telling yourself that you certainly are not afraid of your happiness. You might be right, but I suggest that you pay more attention to how you handle your moments of happiness before reaching such a conclusion. In my observation ambivalence, defensiveness, and even aversion toward happiness is quite pervasive. Even among people who talk about wanting to be happy, there is a tendency to distance themselves and take their actual felt experience of happiness for granted.

There are many reasons for this unease. First of all, you might feel guilty that your life is going well when there is so much disease, poverty, inequality, and oppression in the world. You might also be superstitious, fearing that if you open to happiness you will jinx it, or that it will attract envy, or that someone will try to take it from you. In order to avoid giving the impression that you are flaunting your happiness, you may distance yourself from it. Likewise, you may be afraid to open to joy and well-being because receiving joy requires being vulnerable and fully present; therefore, losing the happiness or even the thought of losing it can seem devastating to you. You might also be afraid of falling into craving if you fully receive joy and want more of it, becoming a hungry ghost who can never be satisfied. This represents a misunderstanding of the Buddha's teaching and reflects a nihilistic view of the world.

Your times of happiness and joy are just as valuable, just as authentic, and possess just as much potential for insight as your difficult moments. As with dukkha, you are called upon to have courage in order to be fully present in those moments of well-being. You are to feel them fully in your body, to know the quality of the mind when well-being manifests, and to learn the nature of this worldly existence as revealed by your sukha. Ask yourself, are you genuinely staying mindful during your times of sukha in this manner? Do most of your moments of sukha even register in your awareness, or are you taking them as a given and looking ahead for the next fulfillment? Do you have a habit of acknowledging sukha, appreciating the feeling of well-being, and cultivating gratitude for it?

Sometimes students resist my instructions to be mindful of their sukha moments because they mistakenly believe that if they bring mindfulness to their joy it will disappear! When I first encountered this belief it took me by surprise. *Your happiness will not be diminished by becoming fully present with it; it will be enhanced.* It is true, however, that your mindfulness of the pleasant will reveal whether you are *clinging* during times of happiness, or if your *euphoria is false,* or if your pleasure is coming from *unskillful acts* that will bring harm.

THREE KINDS OF HAPPINESS

To practice being mindful of happiness and courageously work with it, you need to develop clarity about the various kinds of happiness that you feel. In my experience, there are three kinds of happiness: the happiness that arises when conditions in your life are what you desire them to be; the well-being that comes when your mind is joyful and at ease, regardless of the conditions of your life in that moment; and the unbounded joy you feel when your mind has reached final liberation or cessation of all clinging.

It is easy to recognize the first kind of happiness; you know full well how much you like it when conditions in your life are just as you wish them to be. What you may not do so well, however, is know how to use your happiness based on conditions to find genuine freedom. The second kind of happiness is experienced on those occasions when you are *temporarily* in such a good mood, or so centered, or so quiet, or so appreciative that when you encounter an unpleasant person at work or a frustrating situation at home, you aren't overwhelmed. Life isn't the way you would prefer it to be, but you feel just fine right now and you are not being *defined* by unpleasant conditions. You have had many such moments in your life, although you may not have noticed them and therefore never had the chance to cultivate them. I characterize this second kind of happiness as *being centered in a state of mind that is happy* in order to distinguish it from happiness that is *dependent on conditions being just as you want them to be.* It is obvious that your mind is clearer, your heart is more open, and you have more freedom in the second kind of happiness than in the first kind, which is condition based. Yet, even the second kind is nowhere near the level of attainment of the third kind of sukha, the well-being of full realization.

Notice that when you are happy because the conditions of your life are pleasant (the first kind of happiness), your well-being is *dependent* on conditions, and therefore ultimately is not reliable or lasting. As the Buddha taught, you cannot control conditions or prevent sukha from being replaced by dukkha. Still, who isn't happy to be healthy, or safe, or loved, and so forth? By contrast, when you are temporarily centered in well-being that is not dependent on conditions being right (the second kind of happiness), your happiness is dependent on your *state of mind.* But this second kind of happiness is also unreliable, just as the Buddha said. Yet it too can be received and enjoyed and teach you the dharma. The well-being that arises when you begin going through the various stages of nibbana (the third kind of happiness) is not subject to conditions or to the state of your mind. You can be having a lousy time and your mind not be in an exalted state, yet the mind is unruffled. This is a mind that is liberated. There is nothing temporary about it. *This third kind of well-being is independent of any external or internal factors.*

Do you see the difference between the first two kinds of

happiness, which are temporary and dependent, and the third kind, which is lasting and nondependent? Traditionally, it is taught that there are two types of sukha—relative and absolute—but if you can also make the distinction between *condition-dependent* and *mind-state-dependent happiness,* you give yourself the opportunity to grow and be transformed long before you reach a transcendent stage of awareness. By cultivating awareness of the limitations of condition-dependent happiness, you can break your attachment to getting conditions just right, and mind-state-dependent happiness will start to arise spontaneously.

I have seen many students make a significant shift in their sense of well-being in just a year or two of practicing awareness of sukha; you can too. You may have heard of behavioral studies that show people are born with a certain predisposition to happiness and that they tend to consistently report experiencing their innate level of happiness regardless of their circumstances. Mindfulness and compassion practice allow you to affect this kind of core programming and, in my experience, this is particularly true in working with sukha.

Allow Happiness to Be Your Teacher

There are many reasons to practice being mindful of happiness. First of all, *if you fail to be fully present when your mind is feeling sukha, you are not being mindful* much of the time because there are many moments in your life that are pleasant, although most of them are quite short. Secondly, by not working with them mindfully you are *missing to a significant degree the fullness of the best moments* of your life. *Only by being fully present for your moments of well-being can they be received as a blessing and thus empower you.* A sense of well-being or sukha is also the *proximate cause* (a term meaning what conditions or leads to something) of concentration; therefore, when you feel good, you are more able to gain concentration both in formal meditation and in daily life. Another reason to be mindful of happiness is that moments of *wholesome happiness create the karmic seeds that will affect future moments* and bring even more happiness into your life. By awakening to happiness you also awaken to the truth of suffering. *Happiness also brings the motivation to be kind and compassionate.* The Buddha said that someone who is happy would never hurt another. And finally, the insights you gain from seeing dependent happiness *lead you to the nondependent happiness* of cessation.

You can realize insight in your moments of well-being by making the feeling of them your object of mindfulness meditation, then investigating the qualities of the particular kind of sukha you are experiencing. In addition, through mindfulness and investigation, you develop inspiration and gratitude and allow these feelings to condition the moment and the future.

Sometimes you will discover that you are getting in the way of your own happiness. Other times you may find that the price you are paying for happiness is too high. Or you will realize that what you thought was happiness is actually suffering or *sukha-sanna*. To initiate the process of investigation, ask yourself if your sukha feels heavy or manic. Is it being diluted by thoughts about the past or future? Is anxiety present, and if it is, what happens to that anxiety when you accept that it is just fine for it to be there? Is this sukha causing suffering now or later to others or to you? What else might be diluting your full acceptance of this moment of well-being? If appropriate, remember how you wish to manifest moment by moment in your life. What might you gain from asking these kinds of questions? You might see that you are spending money you can't afford, or that you are guilty of false modesty, which is preventing you from fully letting in the appreciation you are receiving from a friend. You may discover that what you are doing in the name of feeling good is a way to distract yourself from a strong emotion that you are reluctant to be with.

MOMENTS OF SUKHA BASED ON CONDITIONS

The happiness you are probably most familiar with is the kind that arises when conditions in your life are just as you want them to be. It may be a good dinner, a hike, an intimate conversation, a delightful moment with your child, getting a difficult job done right at work, receiving praise or a good bonus, or feeling the serotonin high of a vigorous physical workout. Each of these moments of fun, closeness, accomplishment, or recognition can be received with mindfulness. Specifically, bring awareness to your moments of conditional happiness without judging them as inferior or dismissing them as mere clinging. Accept your feeling of sukha, but do so with recognition of the truth that all conditions change and that *the good feeling you are having will be replaced with one less pleasant.* Second, be mindful of *clinging to the conditions underlying your happiness.* For instance, let's say you are with a good friend and having a wonderful conversation. Do you keep prolonging its ending? Are you making yourself tense by trying to soak up more of it than is possible? Are you expending part of your attention trying to figure out how to have more of such conversations or judging yourself for not doing this more often? You can repeat this same process of inquiry while enjoying a good dinner, a sweet moment with your family, or a satisfying interaction at work. You are not trying to cease having pleasant feelings or trying to be indifferent to them. All you need to do is be mindful when these moments are occurring, and *be particularly aware of how the sukha registers in your body.*

Next turn your attention to awareness of the *qualities* of the sukha itself. How does it feel to you? By investigating the qualities of the happiness, you learn to differentiate between wholesome happiness (even though it is based on conditions) and unwholesome happiness, which is arising because you are acting unskillfully or are clinging in a manner that is going to cause much suffering later on. You will discover that *qualities of lightness, sweetness, and freshness tend to arise during condition-dependent happiness when there is no clinging or unwholesome behavior.* Then examine how your thoughts about the past or future are diluting or polluting this moment of sukha. For instance, are you starting to want more of this good feeling in the future, and is the wanting lessening your opportunity to fully enjoy what is true at this moment? Then see what happens to the quality feeling of the sukha when you acknowledge that it is temporary and not to be clung to. Does this exercise in contemplation disturb your sense of well-being or make it more available? In time, you will discover that just being with your moments of conditional happiness without thought of duplicating them in the future or prolonging their duration makes them even more satisfying and poignant.

Now, *acknowledge your gratitude* that in this moment you have a sense of well-being—really appreciate it for a brief moment, even if it is only enjoying a cup of coffee or finding a parking space. Notice the effect of this acknowledgment. Does it make you uncomfortable? If so, why? If you do this exercise for a few months, you will start to feel less and less discomfort, and begin to notice what is left—often it is a feeling of relief, of having received a bounty from life. Does this gratitude lead you anywhere? Many people report that after doing this gratitude practice for a while, they start feeling a desire to share their good fortune, even if it is only small things. One person found that it was much easier to be kind to the difficult people in her office. Another person who had just gotten a great job took an interest in helping his juniors work through their limitations. From a Buddhist point of view, these are acts of compassion coming from gratitude for well-being. These individuals are responding to their good fortune by *passing it forward* to others. The inclination toward generosity arose in them in no small part because they are practicing mindfully staying with moments of sukha.

There is one final way to work with moments of well-being based on conditions and that is: *Remember that your deepest intention is your movement toward liberation of your mind.* Even in those times when conditions are what you want them to be, you stay focused on *moving up the ladder of types of happiness.* You can relax and enjoy the pleasant feelings but know absolutely that what you are really about is moving toward an ever more independent sense of well-being. It is crucial that you come to have faith that this coexistence of sukha and spiritual aspiration is truly possible. I cannot convince you that this is so, but your own mindfulness and investigation will prove it to you. Can you see that if you do not have this faith, you are thrown into ambivalence about moments of well-being, which does not serve you; it wastes the joy, and it makes you resentful of your inner aspiration.

Of course there is always the danger of falling into shadow around sukha that's based on conditions. For instance, you can rationalize living for the moment where happiness based on conditions is all you focus on. You can also harbor a secret cynical view that nothing really matters, so why not get what sukha you can out of this hopeless and pointless life. I have encountered both views in students who were shocked to discover they held them. Both views are nihilistic and are not the dharma. Likewise you can discount any temporary feelings of well-being you have, believing they have no value—all that matters is your reward after death, either in heaven or in a great rebirth, depending on your belief. Such a view is eternalism, and this also is not what the Buddha taught.

The other mind-set that can ensnare you is succumbing to past trauma or present fear and becoming numb to feeling the sukha in your body and therefore not being able to fully explore it, nor let it inspire you into a state of appreciation and compassion. I've known students with this mind state who claim that they have conquered the arising of pleasant and therefore never cling! This numbness represents denial of life and can be a result of past trauma or present fear. It is not a healthy state of mind and needs your attention. The alternating cycle of sukha and dukkha moments is the tide in your life—to not be fully present for both is missing life. *Indifference in the form of numbness or lack of affect is not liberation.*

STATE-OF-MIND-DEPENDENT HAPPINESS

Experiencing states of well-being in which you are not thrown off by conditions being unpleasant is certainly a step forward in your journey toward freedom. These states, even though temporary, are exalted states that are to be understood, cultivated, and appreciated. You have many such moments in your life, although you may not be aware of them. For instance, you receive a piece of bad news, but rather than get anxious or sad, you remain feeling good about yourself and life. *The bad news conditions the moment, but it does not define you, therefore your sense of well-being stays intact.* Or let's say a project goes badly at the office, and you are going to have to work over the weekend although it was not your fault. Rather than getting resentful or falling into self-pity, your mind stays calm and the sense of well-being in your life stays strong. You would rather not have this unpleasant situation, but it does not control your mood. It is bad enough that you have to do the extra work, but your inner wisdom tells you that there is no reason to let it ruin your weekend.

You work with sukha moments that are independent of conditions but still based on your state of mind using the same three tools of mindfulness, investigation, and appreciation that lead to compassion. To begin with, you bring mindfulness to the feeling of well-being and note its nature. Then you contrast the unpleasant condition with that of your pleasant mind state, noting the differences. You are not trying to hold onto your equanimity. Rather, you are making it more conscious such that you see that your well-being is not dependent on conditions and that even in your current stage of development you can make this separation between mind and condition, which is a very encouraging awareness once you truly experience it. You acknowledge the temporary nature of your well-being and notice whether you are clinging or identifying with this feeling of centeredness, thereby creating a sense of "this is who I am." Again, the practice is in the mindfulness itself and noting how this type of sukha feels in the body.

Now, begin to investigate how well-being that's not dependent on conditions arises in the first place. Note the qualities of your unperturbed mind. Is there an underlying vitality, a feeling of acceptance of how things are, a feeling of trust that no matter what you will be okay? Name the unpleasant feelings that register in your body when the underlying mind state remains basically sukha.

Next, become mindful of how fortunate you are to have such independence from conditions. Reflect on the ease that is present in your mind and that *you know you know* such ease exists and therefore can be cultivated in your practice. Take time to fully appreciate the blessing that such temporary freedom genuinely represents. Then see what impulses arise from your state of well-being. Deliberately expand whatever warm feelings you have toward others by reflecting on their positive traits, on the challenges they too face in attaining well-being that isn't dependent on conditions, and act in the moment or later in ways that might help others find this state of happiness. By helping others you are acknowledging and showing gratitude for your own blessings. It is not something you owe, but rather a spontaneous creative expression of your own sukha.

Finally, even if you have reached a point in your development in which you have prolonged periods of centeredness and are seldom affected by even the most difficult conditions, remember your intention to keep opening to freedom. This intention would be to cultivate more periods of being temporarily in a state of well-being regardless of conditions, and it means that you do not identify with these exalted states. Instead, you stay focused on your ultimate goal—not being defined and imprisoned by ever-changing conditions and mind states.

NONDEPENDENT HAPPINESS

You may have already had a taste or a brief moment of sukha that was completely independent of either conditions or your state of mind. If not, this type of sukha may arise as you continue with your practice. This is the sukha that comes from the deathless, from residing in your true Buddha nature. I sometimes call it *sukha sukha* or the *happiness of realization*. The esteemed Thai Buddhist teacher Ajahn Jumnian refers to this state as "happy happy." Such a moment of well-being gives you the sense of what is possible and provides faith and inspiration for your practice. Sometimes it can happen to you on a long meditation retreat, or it can follow a life-threatening illness, accident, or a near-death experience in your life, or it can arise out of a spontaneous full relaxation into the *sacred now*, without your having a clue as to why it occurred.

The common factor in moments of realized well-being is a *surrender of the ego into being present with what is without resistance*, followed by a shift in perception that is too mysterious to describe. The result is a sense of well-being that is incomparable, unsurpassable, and far beyond anything else you have known. If you are fortunate enough to have such a moment, you will not have any trouble distinguishing it from the far more common happiness of a temporary mind state that is free from conditions.

If and when you have a moment or a series of moments of nondependent sukha, there is not much of anything for you to do. Only afterward do your mindfulness, investigation, and reflection on gratitude and compassion come into practice. Your first reflection is to just *appreciate* it, remembering as best you can what it felt like and noticing how this sukha is different from the other two. Next, you check to see if you are clinging to the memory of it or falling into the trap of wanting to know it again. You look carefully at whether your ego is starting to hijack your moment of grace and redefine it as an achievement of the ego. (Sometimes the ego can take months to start claiming such a victory, so you must stay diligent in this regard.) The signs that your ego is making a false claim can be very subtle. They take the form of a sense of superiority without actual thoughts, finding ways to mention it to others, and listening to others while secretly comparing your mind and experience to theirs.

You utilize your knowing of sukha that is dependent on neither mind states nor conditions to reflect on the Twelve Insights, allowing your new knowledge from direct experience of sukha sukha to deepen your understanding of what you have learned. For instance, there may be a specific practice that you now feel called to do. One student was drawn to deepen body awareness, another to meditate on death, another to immerse herself in knowing arising and passing.

One point for you to reflect upon is that this type of absolute sukha is also temporary; after all it is no longer present, so why is it not the same as noncondition-dependent happiness? What you will discover is that the qualities of cognition and awareness are quite different. In sukha sukha there is not a sense of an "I" or of objects that are separate, nor does the well-being feel localized in you as a particular person; *it just is*, impersonal and without boundaries. You can only experience sukha sukha temporarily at this point, but you know from direct experience that it is the underlying condition of your mind.

Of course you take the gift of this sukha as inspiration to practice all three types of happiness. Now, you really have some perspective on condition-based happiness, and you have more of a foundation for reaching temporary states of noncondition-based happiness. It is important that you immediately start living from your new level of experience; otherwise the stimulation of daily life combined with your old habits will wipe out much of what you've been given.

Following the acknowledgment and mindful examination of your sukha sukha moment, you cultivate your gratitude, which is usually quite strong unless your ego has taken control of the experience. Your gratitude is without bounds, and by reflecting on it your compassion for others can reach a whole new level. For the first time *you may truly know that your own practice is of benefit to others*. This realization is a key part of your bodhicitta, that is, your heart's intention to practice. You may realize that helping others and being of service in some way is all that is really worth doing in life. (You can be of service in many ways in life, including creating beauty and harmony, safety and security, and opportunities for others to develop.) You may be drawn to the Bodhisattva vow that you will not take full enlightenment until all beings are liberated. You may now be able to see that helping others find moments of condition-based happiness also inspires them to develop the capacity for nondependent happiness and ultimately to seek liberation (although all that may be on their minds is the need to feel seen, or to be fed, or safe, or listened to).

Do you recognize how patiently working with dukkha has prepared you to fully embrace sukha? Now that you understand the depth and subtlety of sukha practice, I hope you can see how challenging it is to your mind to embrace it and that you can also see how it will benefit your life. You will start to feel the effects within just a few months. *It can be your quiet practice, your open secret, visible in your feeling tone, words, and actions, but never directly stated to others.* One student recently told me that she felt a responsibility to pursue happiness, having been given the gift of conscious life and the circumstances in which well-being could arise. Please do not deny yourself this gift of wonderment and joy; being fully present with your sukha is a vital part of dancing with life.

EPILOGUE

THE CALL TO SURRENDER
YOUR INNOCENCE

Our time together has come to an end. What you do with these teachings on finding freedom through mindfulness and compassion is your decision. The one thing you must acknowledge, however, is that you *are making a choice*, whether consciously or unconsciously, as to how you are going to *reconcile* the truth of the arising and passing of dukkha and sukha. Your *choice* will then define how you live and what will give meaning and relatedness to your life. The making of this *choice* and its unfolding has been the inspiration for great literature, music, and art throughout human history. Be assured that from the perspective of the interconnected nature of reality your life and your choices are just as worthy as any other person who has ever lived.

You do not have to choose the path of mindfulness. You can decide to distract yourself with pleasure or ego fulfillment, or to fixate your attention on a problem, or a worthy goal, or an enemy. I used to disdain such choices because I thought they were forms of denial and avoidance, but I no longer feel that way. I was being judgmental, thinking I knew what was best for other people and wanting them to be something other than they were. Such an attitude on my part was neither productive nor kind, and lacked humility, which is the most appropriate attitude toward the mysteries of this life. How can I know how you should choose to live your life at this time? But I do know that in order for you to have a *genuine choice*, you need to discover in your own unique words and images that *freedom is truly a possibility* and that *you can dance with life*. If this book has in some small way helped you realize this possibility, then it has served its purpose.

In the course of writing this book, my younger sister died unexpectedly, another family member suffered a major health challenge, and my significant other discovered that she has breast cancer. She and I are still fully consumed by this challenge and all the uncertainty that it entails. Of course I did not want these heartbreaking events to happen to those I care for. But they did, and they changed the *surface appearance* of my life. I had planned to devote my time one way, but it is being lived out in another. It has been a hard, often sad and exhausting three years, yet I have felt no less insight, no less compassion, and no less loving-kindness than if all had gone well. Why? Because I stayed mindful of the truth that this life with its fortune and misfortune is the only life I have. Therefore, if I did not have *enthusiasm* (passion) for it, if I did not bother to be *fully present* for its sadness and loss, *then there is no life to be lived*, and I would fail to bring meaning to the dukkha of those I care for.

It is the same for you; if you do not choose to be fully present for your life, then what are you about? Are you willing to embrace your happiness and your sorrow with equal measure, mindfully living through both in order to discover meaning and joy that are beyond conditions? Making this mindful choice will lead you to wholeness, transformation, transcendence, and far, far beyond.

As the Buddha lay on his deathbed, his students questioned him about how they should continue without him. In his final discourse he gave them the following advice: "Be a lamp unto yourselves, be a refuge to yourselves, do not turn to external refuge, hold fast to the Truth as a lamp, hold fast to the Truth as a refuge. . . . It is those [who do so] that will reach the very topmost height. But they must be anxious to learn." (*Digha Nikaya*, XVI, 2.26) There have been many translations and interpretations of these words, but for me they are a call to examine, to reflect, to discover, and to consciously know the mystery of this human life in this very moment. These words reflect the heart of the Buddha's teaching—that you have the power and the responsibility to resolve the many contradictions and paradoxes of life through insight and direct knowing.

To be "anxious to learn" means that you have the passion, the enthusiasm, to gain freedom. It means that you are willing to surrender even your innocence to conscious suffering. By innocence I mean that part of you that has done nothing wrong, has not been caught in clinging, and has stayed connected to your ideals. Your innocence has the capacity to truly be present in the moment, no matter how difficult conditions are. Guilt, self-pity, and blame are, as Helen Luke says, *false suffering*. Each of these reactions removes you from being fully present with *what is happening right now* by inserting a story or concept between your heart and your direct experience of *now*. The part of you that is innocent rests in emptiness, meaning it is *empty* of any story or concept that limits you to a personal identity. Therefore, that which is innocent in you can have the passion and enthusiasm to realize the Twelve Insights of the Four Noble Truths.

Meditation, mindfulness, and compassion bring you into the *stillness in which your innocence is most unguarded and available*. It is here that you can most deeply experience insight as to what genuinely matters, or as C. G. Jung stated, "It is the individual in stillness who constitutes the meaning of the world."

To make a journey of exploring your own inner stillness is the most refined and subtle form of dancing with life. Within this stillness lies your reconciliation with all of life's movement. Although you will travel far in your journey, you will not really go anywhere, for as T. S. Eliot says in *Four Quartets*:

> We shall not cease from exploration
> And the end of all our exploring
> Will be to arrive where we started
> And know the place for the first time.

The words in this book exist to help you conduct your personal exploration of transforming suffering into joy. If you choose this path, you will find many well-trained teachers and students along the way who stand ready to help you and to be your companions on the journey. Maybe at some point even our paths will cross. I wish you well on your journey.

—Phillip Moffitt
Northern California
March 2007

APPENDIX 1

THE TWELVE INSIGHTS
OF THE FOUR NOBLE TRUTHS

You may find it helpful to refer to all Twelve Insights of the Four Noble Truths as you practice. Reading them as a whole reveals how each one supports, enables, and naturally leads to the next. Seeing each in context also reminds you that you are engaged in an actual practice, not just thinking about it. This kind of contemplative reading is akin to reading poetry or listening to music by allowing it to settle into you rather than you trying to comprehend it. May these Twelve Insights serve you as they have served me.

FIRST NOBLE TRUTH

What is the Noble Truth of Suffering? Birth is suffering, aging is suffering, and death is suffering. Disassociation from the loved is suffering, not to get what one wants is suffering . . .

First Insight
There is this Noble Truth of Suffering: Such was the vision, insight, wisdom, knowing, and light that arose in me about things not heard before.

Second Insight
This Noble Truth must be penetrated to by fully understanding suffering . . .

Third Insight
This Noble Truth has been penetrated to by fully understanding suffering . . .

Second Noble Truth

What is the Noble Truth of the Origin of Suffering?

Fourth Insight
It is craving . . . accompanied by relish and lust, relishing this and that . . .

craving for sensual desires, craving for being, craving for non-being. . . .

Fifth Insight
This Noble Truth must be penetrated to by abandoning the origin of suffering. . . .

Sixth Insight
This Noble Truth has been penetrated to by abandoning the origin of suffering.

Third Noble Truth

What is the Noble Truth of the Cessation of Suffering?

Seventh Insight
It is the remainderless fading and cessation of that same craving; the rejecting, relinquishing, leaving, and renouncing of it. . . .

Eighth Insight
This Noble Truth must be penetrated to by realizing the Cessation of Suffering. . . .

Ninth Insight
This Noble Truth has been penetrated to by realizing the Cessation of Suffering.

FOURTH NOBLE TRUTH

What is the Noble Truth of the Way Leading to the Cessation of Suffering?

Tenth Insight
It is the Noble Eightfold Path . . . Right View, Right Intention, Right Speech, Right Action, Right Livelihood, Right Effort, Right Mindfulness, and Right Concentration.

Eleventh Insight
This Noble Truth must be penetrated to by cultivating the Path . . .

Twelfth Insight
This Noble Truth has been penetrated to by cultivating the Path . . .

—*Samyutta Nikaya* LVI, 11[23]

---

[23] Ajahn Sumedho, *The Four Noble Truths.* Amaravati Publications, 1992, pp.14, 29, 38, 50.

APPENDIX 2

GLOSSARY

This glossary is not intended to be a definitive source of Buddhist terms, but rather to be a quick reference only. For more complete information, I recommend that you obtain a copy of Nayantiloka's *Buddhist Dictionary* (Buddhist Publication Society, 1997).

Ajahn: honorific title meaning "teacher" or "mentor."

anatta: not-self; the realization that much of what you previously identified as "you" is actually "neither me nor mine."

Anguttara Nikaya: the book of "lists" in which the Buddha describes the qualities of luminous mind and enumerates the various kinds of happiness, among many other things.

anicca: the rapid and endlessly changing nature of all things in life.

arahant: someone who has realized nibbana; one who is completely free of the darkness of ignorance that leads to clinging and suffering.

avijja: ignorance; the misperceptions and delusions that your mind has about its own nature and the world.

beginner's mind: when your mind is free of preconceived notions about what it is supposed to be and expectations as to what it can achieve.

bhavana: mental cultivation through meditation.

bhava tanha: the desire for existence and for becoming what you are not.

bodhichitta: pure love that is not corrupted by desire.

brahma-viharas: the four "divine" abodes the Buddha taught for overcoming feelings of separation from others; they are loving-kindness, compassion, sympathetic joy, and equanimity.

Buddha nature: the transcendent state of pure awareness that lies beyond your ego personality.

chanda: desire

clear comprehension: see *sampajanna*.

clear seeing: see *satipatthana*.

compassion: see *karuna*.

concentration: the ability to direct your attention and to sustain it.

damma (Pali) or **dharma** (Sanskrit): truth; the universal insights that constitute the Buddha's teachings.

deathless: the state of being in which you are no longer defined by, living from, or identified with that which is arising and passing; the mind is unperturbed by the perturbations of life.

dependent origination: the chain of events that is created by the mind's reaction to stimuli and which leads to clinging.

dukkha: your mental experiences of discomfort, suffering, pain, stress, anxiety, frustration, hardship, disappointment, and sorrow. The Buddha identified three kinds of dukkha: the dukkha of physical and mental pain (dukkha-dukkha); the dukkha of constant change (viparinama-dukkha); and the dukkha of life's compositional nature (sankhara-dukkha)

emptiness: see *sunnata*.

ego: the complex within the mind that serves the management function in daily life.

equanimity: when the mind is unperturbed by whatever experience is arising.

hindrances: see *nivarana*.

ignorance: see *avijja*.

impermanence: see *anicca*.

insight: a profound level of understanding that transcends mere intellectual cognition and can only be known by experiencing it.

jhanas: deep mental absorption states.

kalapas: in deep meditation experience, an altered state can arise in which the mind completely breaks through the illusion of ordinary seeing and is able to see what are called *kalapas*, or what seems like a stream of atom-like elements that make up all experience.

kama tanha: desire for the six kinds of sense pleasures.

karma: the seeds of consequence that will bloom in the future when conditions are suitable.

karuna: compassion, or the heart's response to suffering; one of four brahma-viharas or "divine" abodes the Buddha taught for overcoming feelings of separation from others; both a form of meditation and the emotional quality that is cultivated by practicing this form of meditation.

loving-kindness: see *metta*.

luminous mind: the change in consciousness that manifests when the mind has realized full cessation and has become transparent to the delusion of ordinary reality.

metta: loving-kindness, or the intention of goodwill toward yourself and others; one of four brahma-viharas or "divine" abodes the Buddha taught for overcoming feelings of separation from others; both a form of meditation and the emotional quality that is cultivated by practicing this form of meditation.

mindfulness: the ability to be fully aware in the present moment. Mindfulness enables you to go beneath the surface level of your moment-to-moment life experience, which is clouded with emotions, to clearly see the truth of what is happening.

nibbana: literally means "cooled"; the state of being when the mind is free of wanting, ill will, and delusion and is no longer consumed by suffering.

nirodha: the state of fully-realized cessation.

nivarana: the five hindrances that cloud the mind and prevent you from knowing the cause of your suffering: sensual desire (kamacchanda), aversion or ill-will (vyapada), sloth and torpor (thina-middha), restlessness and worry (uddhacca-kukkucca), and doubt (vickiccha).

non-attachment: the state in which you have momentarily let go of clinging.

not-self: see *anatta*.

panna: wisdom.

parami: ten qualities that one cultivates to "perfect" one's character, such as diligence, patience, and equanimity.

sacred now: the state of being fully present such that you are both "in time" and "not in time."

samadhi: the practice of concentrating the mind to achieve deep mental absorption states, or jhanas.

sankharas: the collections or composites that make up all conditional existence.

sampajanna: clear comprehension; the ability to see clearly what needs to be done, what you are capable of doing, and how it relates to the larger truth of life.

samsara: the cycle of clinging and taking birth in one desire after another.

Samyutta Nikaya: book of the Buddha's teachings that contains his discourse on the Four Noble Truths.

sangha: a community of Buddhist meditation practitioners.

satipatthana: mindfulness.

Satipatthana Sutta: Buddha's discourse on the Four Foundations of Mindfulness.

sila: non-harming, ethical behavior.

stream enterer: someone who has reached the first stage of enlightenment.

sukha: the pleasant, happy moments of your life.

sukha-sanna: the perception of happiness in what is actually suffering.

sunnata: emptiness; the realization of total cessation.

sutta: a discourse or sermon by the Buddha or one of his contemporary disciples.

tanha: craving

tathata: the "suchness" of the moment or "the way things are."

Theravada: one of the earliest schools of Buddhism to have survived till the present; it is the predominant form of Buddhism practiced in Thailand, Burma, and Sri Lanka. Also known as the "forest tradition" and the "tradition of the Elders."

unity: the state of being unified with your Buddha nature in which you directly experience your oneness with everything in this realm of existence.

vibhava tanha: the desire for non-existence.

vicara: the ability to sustain your attention; one of the Factors of Enlightenment.

vijja: knowledge.

vipassana: the primary meditation technique used in the Theravada Buddhist tradition; also known as "insight practice."

vitakka: the ability to direct your attention; one of the Factors of Absorption.

wholeness: the state of having integrated your psychological and spiritual insights into your being.

APPENDIX 3

RESOURCES AND MEDITATION RETREATS

BOOKS

Ajahn Chah. *Everything Arises, Everything Falls Away: Teachings on Impermanence and the End of Suffering.* Shambhala, 2005.

Ajahn Sumedho. *The Four Noble Truths.* Amaravati Publications, 1992.

Ajahn Sumedho. *The Mind and the Way: Buddhist Reflections on Life.* Wisdom Publications, 1995.

Amaro Bhikkhu. *Small Boat, Great Mountain: Theravadan Reflections on the Natural Great Perfection.* Abhayagiri Monastic Foundation, 2003.

Analayo. *Satipatthana: The Direct Path to Realization.* Windhorse Publications, 2003.

Bhikkhu Nanamoli and Bhikkhu Bodhi. *The Middle Length Discourses of the Buddha: A New Translation of the Majjhima Nikaya.* Wisdom Publications, 1995.

Fronsdal, Gil. *The Dhammapada: A New Translation of the Buddhist Classic with Annotations.* Shambhala, 2005.

Geshe Tashi Tsering. *The Four Noble Truths: The Foundation of Buddhist Thought,* vol. 1. Wisdom Publications, 2005.

Goldstein, Joseph. *One Dharma: The Emerging Western Buddhism.* HarperSanFrancisco, 2002.

Kornfield, Jack. *A Path with Heart: A Guide through the Perils and Promises of Spiritual Life.* Bantam Books, 1993.

Kornfield, Jack and Paul Breiter. *A Still Forest Pool: The Insight Meditation of Achaan Chah.* Quest Books, 1997.

Kornfield, Jack, ed., with Gil Fronsdal. *Teachings of the Buddha.* Shambhala, 1996.

Luke, Helen M. *Old Age*. Parabola Books, 1987.

Luke, Helen M. *The Voice Within: Love and Virtue in the Age of Spirit*. The Crossroad Publishing Company, 1987.

Mitchell, Stephen. *Tao Te Ching*. HarperPerennial, 1991.

Salzberg, Sharon. *Loving-Kindness: The Revolutionary Art of Happiness*. Shambhala, 1997.

Suzuki Shunryu. *Zen Mind, Beginner's Mind*. Shambhala, 2006.

Thanissaro Bhikkhu, trans. *Handful of Leaves: An Anthology for the Digha and Majjhima Nikayas*. The Sati Center for Buddhist Studies and Metta Forest Monastery, 2002.

Thanissaro Bhikkhu, trans. *The Wings to Awakening: An Anthology from the Pali Canon*. Dhamma Dana Publications, 1998.

Thera, Nyanaponika. *The Heart of Buddhist Meditation: A Handbook of Mental Training Based on the Buddha's Way of Mindfulness*. Samuel Weiser, Inc., 1996.

WEB SITES

www.accesstoinsight.org
Contains an extensive collection of books, essays, and sutta commentaries by well-known Theravada Buddhism teachers, including Ajahn Chah and Thanissaro Bhikkhu, as well as a Pali-English glossary.

www.bps.lk
This Web site of the Buddhist Publication Society has an extensive library of works by such notable Buddhist teachers as Nyanaponika Thera and Bhikkhu Bodhi, as well as an English-Pali dictionary.

www.buddhanet.net
This Web site by the Buddha Dharma Education Association contains the World Buddhist Directory, a comprehensive listing of Buddhist centers and communities around the world; an extensive

library of e-books, including *The Four Noble Truths* by Venerable Ajahn Sumedho; and audio recordings.

www.dancingwithlife.org
Submit any questions you may have about *Dancing with Life* or your practice to the newly created Web site and Phillip will post answers to questions once a week. Here you'll also find a schedule of Phillip's book tour.

www.dharmaseed.org
Offers nearly 500 audio recordings of dharma talks by vipassana meditation teachers.

www.lifebalance.org
This is the Web site for Life Balance Institute, where you can find articles by Phillip, audio files of some of his dharma talks, and a schedule of retreats and workshops he is teaching around the U.S.

www.sacred-texts.com
Includes online electronic versions of *The Sacred Books of the East*, a 50-volume series published by Oxford University Press between 1879 and 1910 containing translations of key sacred texts of Buddhism, Hinduism, Taoism, Confucianism, Zoroastrianism, Jainism, and Islam.

Vipassana Meditation Retreat Centers

Abhayagiri Buddhist Monastery
1620 Tomki Road
Redwood Valley, CA 95470
707-485-1630
www.abhayagiri.org

Amaravati Buddhist Monastery
St. Margarets Lane
Great Gaddesden, Hemel
Hempstead
Hertfordshire HP1 3BZ
England
www.amaravati.org

Barre Center for Buddhist
Studies
149 Lockwood Road
Barre, MA 01005
978-355-2347
www.dharma.org/bcbs

Cloud Mountain Retreat
Center
373 Agren Road
Castle Rock, WA 98611
888-465-9118
www.cloudmountain.org

Gaia House
West Ogwell, Newton Abbot
Devon TQ12 6EN
England
+44 (0) 1626-333613
www.gaiahouse.co.uk

Insight Meditation Society
1230 Pleasant Street
Barre, MA 01005
978-355-4378
www.dharma.org/ims

Southern Dharma Retreat
Center
1661 West Road
Hot Springs, NC 28743
828-622-7112
www.southerndharma.org

Spirit Rock Meditation Center
P.O. Box 169
5000 Sir Francis Drake Blvd.
Woodacre, CA 94973
415-488-0164
www.spiritrock.org

FURTHER RESOURCES

Visit dancingwithlife.org and dharmawisdom.org
As I stated many times throughout *Dancing with Life*, the 12 Insights of the Four Noble Truths are a practice. Therefore, I've developed the following tools to help you sustain your mindfulness practice in daily life.

"A Year of *Dancing with Life*" e-Teachings
Receive a visually inspiring teaching based on *Dancing with Life* in your e-mail inbox each week for a year. Each teaching contains a key passage from the book with questions for further reflection and self-study.

Teacher's Guide to *Dancing with Life*
If you're a meditation teacher and would like to use *Dancing with Life* as a teaching text, you can access a teaching guide on the Web site www.dancingwithlife.org. The guide includes recommendations for how to teach the material in the book, advice for addressing challenges your students may encounter, and sample curricula. You can also purchase books at a discount from the publisher.

Dancing with Life Study Guide for Book Groups
If you're interested in reading *Dancing with Life* in a book group, want to start a book study group, or simply want to study the book in more depth on your own, sign up to receive free access to this online study guide, which offers suggestions for structuring your approach to reading the book and includes an audio recording of a dharma talk by Phillip Moffitt.

Other Resources Available on dharmawisdom.org

- Listen to talks and read articles about mindfulness and living the dharma in daily life.
- Find information about Phillip Moffitt's teaching engagements.
- Learn where to go on a meditation retreat.
- Find other books that can help you in your spiritual journey.

APPENDIX 4

THE SUFFERING OF
AMBIVALENCE AND AMBIGUITY

Since the initial publication of *Dancing with Life* in 2008, a large number of meditation students who are psychotherapists and many meditation students who are utilizing psychotherapy have asked me how Buddhist psychology can augment Western psychotherapy. In response to these inquires, I have written this appendix to the paperback edition. Its purpose is to illustrate how mindfulness and insight practice can help provide clarity and direction to anyone dealing with difficult emotions and to offer examples of how psychotherapists can utilize the Buddha's wisdom in working with clients.

Please bear in mind that I am writing this as a dharma teacher and not as a psychotherapist. I don't speak the language of psychotherapy, but rather I speak the language of vipassana insight practice. For example when I use the word *ego*, I am referring to the definition I presented in Chapter 6: "[The ego is the] complex within the mind that serves the management function in daily life. It uses the language of 'me' and 'mine' in order to operate in the relative world. In an un-liberated mind, the ego suffers from the delusion that its existence has permanence."

The aim of Buddhist insight practices is to liberate the mind from the ego's constant clinging to what it desires. My teacher, the venerable Ajahn Sumedho, calls this state of freedom "Buddha knowing the dharma" and describes it as having a relationship to the mind that transcends merely satisfying the ego's goals of maximizing gains and minimizing losses. When the mind is liberated, your sense of well-being isn't dependent on the conditions of your life being favorable or on your ego's desires, even its healthy ones, being met.

These same Buddhist insight practices that lead to a liberated mind also foster psychological development, therefore Buddhist psychology can complement and enhance Western psychological techniques. In fact mindfulness practice is now widely utilized in psychotherapy to help individuals learn to observe their emotions and behaviors in order to break destructive patterns of thoughts and actions. And mindfulness practice in combination with Western psychological treatment has been shown to be a much-needed and effective tool in certain psychological conditions such as borderline personality disorders.[1]

The excellent book *Mindfulness and Psychotherapy*, edited by Christopher K. Germer, et. al.,[2] traces the integration of mindfulness into modern psychotherapy practices, including cognitive-behavioral psychotherapy, psychodynamic psychotherapy, humanistic psychology, and others. Christopher Germer writing in the book defines mindfulness as "(1) awareness of (2) present experience with (3) acceptance" and states that all three of these conditions must be present together. The book also makes the important point that many psychotherapists now study and practice mindfulness and Buddhist psychology and consider the Buddha to have been a brilliant psychologist. It also repeats the story of America's most famous psychologist William James who upon seeing a Buddhist monk from Sri Lanka in his audience said to him, "Take my chair. You are better equipped to lecture on

---

[1]   Linehan, Marsha. *Skills Training Manual for Treating Borderline Personality Disorder.* New York: Guilford Press, 1993.

[2]   Germer, Christopher K., PhD; Ronald D. Siegel, PsyD; and Paul R. Fulton, EdD., editors. *Mindfulness and Psychotherapy.* New York: Guilford Press, 2005.

psychology than I. This is the psychology everybody will be studying . . . " Indeed, James was prescient in this regard.

In general, mindfulness practice combined with loving-kindness practices produce clarity and resilience in the mind, which are of immeasurable benefit to psychological health and maturity. These practices train you to:

1. Stay present in times of difficulty as well as in joyful times.
2. Cease interpreting defeat and ego setbacks as personal failures.
3. Direct and sustain your attention on any experience.
4. Recognize, name, and investigate any experience of the mind or body.
5. Be patient and tolerant toward people and situations that are unpleasant.
6. Shift your attention toward what is most skillful in any situation.
7. Set intentions in your life and live them out.
8. Attenuate envy with sympathetic joy.
9. Relieve aversion with compassion and equanimity.
10. And most important, you recognize how you create your own suffering and learn how to stop doing it (this is the psychological application of the Twelve Insights of the Four Noble Truths).

THE DIFFICULT MIND STATES OF AMBIVALENCE AND AMBIGUITY

In order to illustrate the effects insight practice can have in psychotherapy, the rest of this appendix will focus on two difficult mind states, *ambivalence* and *ambiguity*, that are not often worked with directly as mind states themselves in psychotherapy. These two unsettling mind states can severely limit a person's resilience and render them unable to respond freely to life's joys and challenges.

I became cognizant of the pervasiveness of these two mind states in the course of conducting thousands of meditation interviews over a fifteen-year period and in hearing stories from psychotherapists about clients who struggle with ambivalence and ambiguity. Motivated by their comments, I began an in-depth study of ambivalence and ambiguity. What I discovered is that both of these mind states can be attended to with various mindfulness practices. Moreover, I found that the combination of mindfulness practice and psychotherapy can enhance the ego's ability to function effectively.

The Differences between Ordinary and Debilitating Ambivalence and Ambiguity

Everyone experiences what I call *ordinary* ambivalence and *ordinary* ambiguity at various times in their life, but when these mind states occur frequently with great intensity and last a long time to such an extent that they dominate the mind, they can inhibit or even prevent psychological growth. If they persist and are left unattended, they can deteriorate into devastating limitations that interfere with key perceptual and interpretative functions of the mind. When this happens, ordinary ambivalence and ambiguity become what I call *debilitating* mind states.

From a Buddhist psychological perspective, when you are caught in debilitating ambivalence or ambiguity, your mind is either deluded and clinging to a desire for your life to be perfect; or it is afraid and wanting a guarantee that what you are doing is the right thing to do; or it is refusing to participate in the dance of life due to some conscious or unconscious aversion to uncertainty and potential loss. (These insights are contained in the first two Noble Truths.) Thus, if your mind is frequently dominated by ambivalence or ambiguity about a particular area of your life, then these mind states begin to limit your capacity to live fully and you are less effective in meeting your goals in the areas where they manifest. You may develop a general feeling of unease, vagueness, or uncertainty about your life. You may become depressed or feel disassociated, aimless, or powerless. Additionally, your ambivalence and ambiguity may start to inhibit severely your development of an inner life, which seems to be quite common.

You can have an episode of debilitating ambivalence or ambiguity about a past or present situation or about the future. Almost everyone has struggled with the pain and confusion caused by debilitating ambivalence and ambiguity at some point in their life. Sometimes both can be present in your mind and so entwined that they can seem to be one. However, they are actually distinct mind states and each can be treated using the mindfulness tools of recognition, directed attention, and intention.

The destructive effects of ambivalence and ambiguity are usually identified as *symptoms* in psychotherapy and are not defined as illnesses in the Diagnostic and Statistical Manual of Mental Disorders (DSM-IV). Therefore ambivalence and ambiguity often go unrecognized as psychologically difficult mind states in and of themselves. Yet they may have formed first and been the source of what later developed into a larger psychological problem. Ambivalence and ambiguity can become so embedded in someone's life that they can continue to exist independently even when the conditions that first created them are no longer present.

Psychotherapists have told me that clients who complain of

anxiety and depression are oftentimes fuzzyheaded when asked to characterize their situation. They describe feeling as though they are immersed in a soup of emotions and thoughts that they cannot sort out. The psychotherapists also report that these clients are frequently ambiguous about their goals for psychotherapy and are often seeking help in resolving their ambivalence regarding a spouse, a parent, or their career.

Psychotherapists also report that clients are often ambiguous about what they wish to achieve emotionally and the qualities they are looking for in a friend or a romantic partner and may even be ambivalent about whether they want certain types of relationships. For instance, one psychotherapist described a woman who was desperate for a relationship with a man but had such ambivalence that she wouldn't put herself in any situation where she might meet a man. She suffered in the same way around having excitement in her life; she claimed to want it but consistently avoided any possibility of it occurring. When she entered psychotherapy, she had no awareness of her ambivalence—she simply wanted to be happier. Moreover, when confronted with her ambivalence, she would retreat into ambiguity, saying that she was okay with her life as it was and that it wasn't clear what would make her happier.

The psychotherapist, who had been practicing insight meditation for more than ten years, started teaching the patient to be mindful of her ambivalence, not in order to immediately relieve her symptoms of ambivalence, but as a worthwhile goal itself. As the client became clearer about her ambivalence, the psychotherapist then had her begin to notice and explore her ambiguity. Simultaneously, she had the client work with her negative self-image by becoming mindful of when she was caught in it, recognizing that her negativity was only a deluded thought, and using right effort to move beyond the social inhibitions that had limited her for years. Over time, the client developed clarity about what she desired and showed dramatic improvement in her ability to move toward what she desired.

Such changes are not unusual. When ambivalence and ambiguity are addressed directly and the clinging in the mind that is associated with them is released, major positive changes can occur in the psyche. Improvement can happen independently without the client necessarily understanding how the ambivalence or ambiguity originally developed. It's as though resolving ambivalence and ambiguity empowers the psyche to heal itself or bring itself back into balance. Additionally, the client will often spontaneously realize the sources of ambivalence and ambiguity in their emotional history.

The Dukkha of Ordinary Ambivalence

Different schools of psychotherapy define ambivalence in varying ways. What I'm talking about is ordinary ambivalence, which is characterized by fluctuating feelings, indecisiveness, and second-guessing and shows up in your speech and thoughts in a variety of ways: "I am of two minds," "I run hot and cold," or "I have a love-hate relationship with so-and-so." You may feel as though you are being "torn apart" or "pulled in two directions." You are alternately "attracted to and repelled by" someone, or "go back and forth," because you're afraid to say yes and unable to say no. You can't make a decision, take a stand, or even be comfortable with a decision once you've made it. You are reduced to being passive, which can either be a temporary state or become an ingrained pattern of behavior. Your passivity conceals the hard truth that even when you can't make a decision you are still deciding by default, which means that if things turn out poorly you don't even have the comfort of having acted to the best of your ability. Moreover, by dithering and being passive, you limit how much you can learn and develop, since good judgment comes from first making bad judgments.

There are many circumstances where ambivalence is an appropriate response for a period of time or to a limited degree. At various points throughout our lives, we experience ambivalence about certain people, situations, and our goals for valid reasons. For instance, you may not have enough information or experience to clarify your opinion about a difficult person in your life or to evaluate a sticky situation. Sometimes situations will arise where having mixed feelings is an appropriate response. You can have conflicting desires and not be able to let loose of either possibility. You can also have contradictory priorities, and when faced with a decision, you may struggle to choose one priority over the other. Similarly, you may have mixed feelings about parts of your personality; sometimes you can accept your limitations, but other times you experience strong feelings of rejection of those same characteristics.

THE DUKKHA OF DEBILITATING AMBIVALENCE

Even in situations where a certain amount of ambivalence is appropriate, if it becomes your predominant experience, it can become debilitating. You can't proceed with making a decision, even if there is an immediate need to. Such conditions often arise at work or in your home life. You become frozen in indecision, and then others end up making your decisions for you, often to your disadvantage. In such circumstances you have, according to Buddhist psychology, become identified with your ambivalence. It's a terrible feeling that can feed upon itself. Even when you are able to decide finally, you still harbor the ambivalence, which drains your energy and enthusiasm. This means that you will not be effective in living out your decision.

Debilitating ambivalence is a combination of your mind's reactivity and a weakened capacity to respond to the *emotional charge* associated with the subject of your ambivalence. Energetically, it can manifest as anxiety, restlessness, racing thoughts, rapid speech, or sudden emotional changes. Or you may feel it as dullness, apathy, mental blankness, spacey vagueness, or disassociation.

Debilitating ambivalence robs you of your agency, your ability to effect your own life and to participate effectively in its unfolding. The loss of agency, which so many people have to endure, is one of the reasons I call it debilitating ambivalence. In Western literature, the most famous character to suffer debilitating ambivalence is Shakespeare's Hamlet who in his frozen mind state couldn't decide whether to act or not. His lack of agency ultimately led to tragedy for himself and many others.

When you are in the throes of debilitating ambivalence, you may become frequently frustrated, angry, resentful of others, or self-doubting. You may develop learned helplessness and abandon your goals, act against your self-interest, alienate others, or repeatedly behave unskillfully. You may lose touch with your intuition or cease to connect to your deepest values.

If your ambivalence is about another person, you may alternately push them away and then pull them toward you, or participate in and then abandon the relationship. You may feel close one moment, then claustrophobic the next. Left unattended, the ambivalence grows more intense and your reactive mind states become more difficult to contend with.

If you reject the life you currently have as unacceptable, you may experience debilitating ambivalence. You may refuse to try to find satisfaction and happiness in your current circumstances and insist on having a life that only exists in your imagination. As a result it may be a struggle for you to commit to and live out your goals, or you may be negative or disinterested in your work and removed or denigrating in your relationships with others.

Even people who appear to be successful and decisive will often complain of feeling disappointed or disinterested in life. They report being anxious that their good fortune will come to a sudden end. As a result they're ambivalent about their success. Or else they report that despite their success, their lives don't offer much meaning. They're ambivalent because they have yet to discover what genuinely gives meaning to their lives. In each instance, their ambivalence can become so overwhelming that it is debilitating.

Debilitating Ambivalence Obscures Reality

If you suffer from debilitating ambivalence, it means your mind is assaulted by conflicting feelings or attitudes about a person, group, institution, place, object, or situation. Your mind is clouded, and your judgment is distorted. For example, you may be ambivalent about a close friend because you envy their success and can't face the fact that you're envious, but you have no idea why you have such mixed feelings toward your friend. Or maybe you want to own your own business, but you don't want to take the risk or make the sacrifice that's required to start up a business. You become paralyzed by your ambivalence about going out on your own. You can't let loose of the desire, nor can you take action. Over time you may lose any sense of the underlying fear that gave rise to the ambivalence. Or maybe your marriage doesn't meet your expectations, and you don't address it; your disappointment can turn into ambivalence toward your spouse that is deadening to both of you. You may desire achievement and recognition, but because you're ashamed of your ambition or are afraid of failing publicly, you won't commit fully to making the effort to succeed and you become marked by your ambivalence toward success. You may remain stuck with these ambivalent feelings for years without understanding why they exist.

When ambivalence is debilitating, your mind is in a flu-like state and reality is obscured. You feel stuck, dissatisfied, restless, or uncertain. In the language of Buddhist psychology, you lack clear comprehension (*sampajanna*) of what is being called for and how you might respond to that call. You are caught in the hindrances to such a degree that your mind isn't unified and you've taken birth in your ambivalence, meaning you've become so identified with your ambivalence that it is defining your life. As a result you may be rendered ineffective, unable to be fully present for your relationships, your work, or even yourself; or you may be frozen in place and unable to move toward or away from the object of your ambivalence.

Ambivalence in one part of your life can inhibit your experience in other parts; for instance, you may be unable to decide about committing to a relationship and be so distracted that you do not do your job well or cannot make career decisions until your question is resolved.

Sometimes you recognize your ambivalence; other times you are unconscious of it, and it becomes expressed indirectly through strong emotions or behaviors that you cannot explain. Ambivalence and the feelings it stirs up create suffering for others, as well as for you. Although you may be able to override your ambivalence in the short term, over time it disturbs your focus and renders you less effective and less available to learn, to have insight, and to relate to others. It also causes others to doubt you. For all these reasons, it is truly debilitating.

THE CAUSES AND EFFECTS OF DEBILITATING AMBIVALENCE

When you apply the Second Noble Truth to understanding debilitating ambivalence, you see that it occurs when you cling to all the options in a situation. The clinging arises because your mind is caught in some combination of greed, aversion, and delusion. These mind states are not personal, they don't constitute a "you," rather they are habitual thought patterns that have become established in your mind. For example, when greed is the primary source of your ambivalence, you want the benefits of all your options. Therefore you're ambivalent about making any choice because it means that in choosing one you won't receive the benefits of the other options. A classic example of ambivalence based on clinging due to greed is the "promising" young person who is so talented that they seduce everyone with their potential, but who so loves their options that they can never choose one because that would mean letting loose of the others. Thus, they never actually manifest the potential for which they were so valued.

If aversion is the underlying reason for your ambivalence, you don't want to pay some price, take some risk, or endure some unpleasantness in order to make a decision and move on in your life. Therefore, even if you want to say yes, it is neutralized by your aversion. When this happens repeatedly, the mind becomes conditioned not to open to the feelings of yes, which brings frustration. Oftentimes this means you give up your enthusiasm or vital energy in that part of your life.

If delusion is at the root of your ambivalence, you're unable to distinguish between skillful and unskillful choices or discern the true cause of happiness and unhappiness in a particular situation. You may repeatedly make wrong choices and lose your confidence, thus becoming ambivalent. Or you may have such anxiety in one area of your life—relationships, finances, or work—that you can't think clearly and therefore become ambivalent.

In most cases, debilitating ambivalence results from a combination of greed, aversion, and delusion. Just seeing and naming these conditions in the mind, without adding self-judgment, brings immense relief.

BUDDHIST INSIGHTS AND PRACTICES FOR ATTENUATING DEBILITATING AMBIVALENCE

The Buddhist approach to resolving debilitating ambivalence doesn't focus on eliminating it, but rather emphasizes being mindful that this difficult mind state is present. Mindfulness allows you to see that the ambivalence is just one more conditioned mind state that arises and passes and to acknowledge, "Ambivalence is like *this*." Sometimes it's quite strong and other times not so much. You attend to ambivalence by observing its characteristics, its effects on your internal experience, and its effects on others and then by cultivating compassion for yourself and others. You then work to balance your emotions and energy by not allowing your mind to fixate on the subject of your ambivalence. This is called *right effort* in the Eightfold Path of the Fourth Noble Truth.

Mindfulness also helps you avoid judging or chastising yourself for experiencing ambivalence and understand that it has come about because of *karma*. The "seed" of this experience was planted earlier and now conditions are right for the seed to blossom.

An important step in the mindfulness process is investigating mind states that arise; therefore in working with ambivalence, you might ask: "Is this ambivalence actually a message that I need to hear? Is there something I don't want to face?" For example, your ambivalence may be telling you not to take a new job, get married, or make a particular decision before you're ready. Or the message might be that you have unfinished business regarding something in your past or that you haven't developed sufficient clarity, therefore you need to delay making a decision or continuing in a certain direction. You might also ask yourself if your ambivalence is a sign that what you're wanting is unskillful or if you're not being genuine or generous.

As your mindfulness capacity develops, the ambivalence is gradually penetrated and you experience a series of insights that brings freedom and ease in the mind. You may finally accept a decision you made in the past, which allows you to fully commit to the present, or you realize that there never really was a decision to be made because there was only one choice for you. Or the insight may be that you don't need to fear uncertainty or the disapproval of others. Your insights can manifest in any of the following ways:

- You may still feel ambivalence, but you don't identify with it therefore it no longer creates suffering.
- You gain clarity and the ambivalence dissipates.
- You develop the ability to make decisions.
- You cease clinging to the idea that there is such a thing as a "right" decision because you had the insight that with the passage of time it isn't always clear what was and was not a good decision.
- You have the insight that everything is constantly changing, just as the Buddha taught, and that your ambivalence is a delusion so it just drops away, seemingly on its own.
- Your ambivalence disappears because you have insight into how unskillful and pointless it is to be attached to getting what you want.
- You have the insight that your ambivalence is just a series of thought moments, and your mind spontaneously lets loose of its pattern of clinging to ambivalence.[3]

---

3   Obviously vipassana insight is not the same as what in psychotherapy is sometimes called *anosognosia* and is often used as a synonym for "poor insight," meaning that the client lacks the insight that would allow them to recognize that they were or are mentally ill and therefore must take their prescribed medications. Such insight into illness is considered crucial for compliance in taking prescribed drugs for schizophrenia or mood disorders. There are tests for measuring this insight ability such as the Scale to Assess Unawareness of Mental Disorder. When teaching silent meditation retreats, a teacher takes care with students on medication to see that they continue in compliance, but developing this particular insight is not a focus of teaching *samma sati*. However, an individual trained in insight would seem to be more receptive to accepting this fact about himself or herself.

THE DUKKHA OF AMBIGUITY

Ambiguity is characterized by uncertainty, confusion, and doubt and occurs when a situation or a person's actions can be interpreted in more than one way. *In contrast to ambivalence, which is the inability to decide, ambiguity is the inability to comprehend and is the result of lacking clarity regarding your values and priorities.* Ambiguity shows up in your speech in the following ways: "I don't know what I think," "I don't know what matters in this situation," "I don't know where to begin," "I don't know what s/he wants," or "I don't know what to say."

Ambiguity is easily confused with ambivalence; therefore, in order to effectively deal with either, it is essential that you be able to distinguish between them. When you are ambivalent, you have mixed or fluctuating feelings about what you value most, so it's hard for you to make a decision, but you know what your choices are and what you value. With ambiguity, you lack a basis for making a decision; your feelings, goals, perceptions, or values are so unclear that you don't even have mixed feelings!

Unfortunately, these two mind states are often coupled. There are times when you may be feeling ambivalent about a situation, but as you become mindful of your ambivalence, you discover that underneath the ambivalence is ambiguity that you have never confronted or even knew existed. The ambiguity prevents you from resolving your ambivalence. For instance, when one partner in a relationship is ambivalent about the other, sometimes it has little or nothing to do with the other person; it may be coming from ambiguity about intimacy, or sexual identity, or commitment. In my view, Hamlet's ambivalence about what action to take stemmed from his ambiguity. He lacked a clear moral basis on which to act. His ambiguity led him to helplessness and madness.

Like everyone, you experience episodes of ambiguity in different areas of your life at various times. Such ambiguity is normal and usually means you are still developing clarity about a situation or the situation itself is ambiguous. There are times when you may even deliberately be ambiguous in your speech or other form of communication in order to wisely avoid conflict or to create a collaborative atmosphere for brainstorming. You may employ ambiguity in a tense situation to buy time for compromise to emerge. Ambiguity can be a helpful messenger, letting you know that you don't have the information you need to make a decision or that you're not emotionally ready to decide. Diplomats, good brainstorming leaders, effective mediators, artists, and creative people of all types often consciously cultivate skillful use of ambiguity.

How Ambiguity Obscures Reality

You can experience ambiguity regarding persons, objects, or situations such as work and relationships due to not knowing what you want, what's possible, what's a priority, or what's essential. You can communicate in an ambiguous manner that is vague, ineffective, frustrating, and anxiety creating for others and yourself. You can be ambiguous about how you feel about yourself or how you feel about others.

You may experience appropriate feelings of ambiguity about your goals or values when some of your old goals and values have ceased to be relevant, but new ones are still in the process of being formed. However, if you are consistently lost and unclear about what's important to you or how to decide which direction to go in, then you may be developing debilitating ambiguity. Likewise, if you refuse to reappraise what matters to you because you don't want to face certain difficulties or make changes, you are in danger of succumbing to debilitating ambiguity. I've seen this happen to many middle-aged people who refuse to listen to their intuition telling them that they need to reappraise their lives. The goals they had when they were younger are no longer appropriate, but they refuse to do the inner work necessary to create new goals that will be relevant and add vitality to their lives. In many such instances, they have unconsciously drifted into debilitating ambiguity and feel lost and hopeless.

Trying to resolve a problem or make a decision when you're caught in ambiguity can be debilitating because you don't know on what basis you are to gather information and start the evaluation process. You can become so lost in ambiguity that you cannot assess situations effectively, prioritize your time, or set goals. Debilitating ambiguity occurs also when you can't access your emotions or don't know how to interpret them for making decisions.

The Causes and Effects of Debilitating Ambiguity

Debilitating ambiguity can result from early developmental issues, adolescent challenges, or physical or emotional trauma. It can also be the result of having compromised your values and not acknowledged that you've done so. It may develop after experiencing a major disappointment that caused your ego to feel defeated. It can arise in confusing situations that you lack the maturity or wisdom to confront. You may have started using ambiguity as a means to avoid addressing difficult situations, and it became a habit that slowly eroded your ability to have discernment.

Of course, the transitive nature of life and the existential dilemma that it creates can also cause debilitating ambiguity. We are all faced with answering the question implied by the First Noble Truth: If life involves so much physical and emotional pain and is so short and uncertain, how do I find joy, peace, meaning, and purpose? Answering this question is a lifetime's work, and it's easy to get lost in the ambiguity that is an unavoidable part of the search for your personal answer. Moreover, your answer to this question at any moment is often ambiguous. You can become mired in existential ambiguity such that it starts to hinder your clarity in making daily life decisions. Even people who don't seem to give much thought to this existential question can unconsciously suffer the effects of debilitating ambiguity without recognizing the cause. Fortunately, as you develop the capacity to stay mindfully present with your discomfort concerning this existential question and not grasp for answers, your mind learns to let go. When your mind is relaxed, you intuitively know what your priority is at the moment; therefore, the mind doesn't demand a definitive answer to the larger question. Of course, you still wrestle with ambiguity regarding what gives meaning to your life, but your struggle isn't debilitating to your immediate life.

Buddhist Insights and Practices for Working with Ambiguity

Buddhist psychology with its emphasis on mindfulness offers a sophisticated and skillful means for resolving debilitating ambiguity. You don't have to rid yourself of ambiguity, but rather attend to it mindfully and see the role it plays in your life and the choices you have in responding to it. In time this means you develop a new, healthy relationship with the ambiguity, one in which you are able to make decisions, maintain goals, and live from your values despite its presence. This empowered relationship to ambiguity evolves from developing mindfulness, and it inevitably reveals new insights about the nature of ambiguity, its origins, and the ways you can be more effective in dealing with it.

The same mindfulness skills that you use to resolve ambivalence can also be applied to working with ambiguity. When you are caught in ambiguity, you stay present to it and notice that the ambiguity changes moment to moment and that sometimes it's not there. You observe that the degree to which it dominates your mind varies tremendously. You use mindfulness and compassion to avoid judging yourself. If you start to label yourself as inept or hopeless because you are caught in ambiguity, you interrupt the thought stream and move your attention to other areas of your life where you do not suffer from ambiguity.

As with ambivalence there is a series of questions you might ask yourself as you investigate your ambiguity: Am I suffering from general ambiguity or is it specific to a particular situation? Is it part of a pattern or has it been triggered by a specific event? Are my values or goals unclear? Is the ambiguity coming from fear of the unknown or dread of a certain outcome? Is there a message in this ambiguity, suggesting that I'm not prepared to face up to this situation? If so, what should I do? By answering these questions, the ambiguity starts to resolve on its own.

You can also utilize humor to break apart the seemingly solid presence of ambiguity in your mind. For example, you might say to yourself, "Here I am being ambiguous about my ambiguity!"

When you are in the throes of debilitating ambiguity, the wise response is to be extremely kind to yourself, without being indulgent or self-pitying. Treat ambiguity as you would any other problem, simply as a mind state that has come as a visitor and will depart on its own accord if you don't hold onto it by demanding that it leave. You may utilize psychotherapy, a good friend, or your various practices to help you through the worst times.

Also, when you are caught in debilitating ambivalence, you can reframe the situation and make it a practice opportunity instead of just feeling stuck. Name it as ambivalence and commit to learning and developing from it. For instance, you may need to develop patience or more determination or more willingness to let loose of your need to be in control. Of course you would prefer not to be ambivalent in the first place, but if you have to pay the price of discomfort, then why not derive value from it?

You can also consciously work with ambiguity and not wait for it to show up by focusing on an area of your life where your ambiguity isn't dominant. Or choose an area where you've had a strong positive experience in the past that helped you move beyond the ambiguity. By repeatedly noticing all the areas and situations in your life where you are not ambiguous, you dispel the seeming dominance of ambiguity.

THE ROLE OF AMBIGUITY IN DEPRESSION

Mild-to-moderate, temporary depression accompanied by feelings of meaninglessness often creates ambiguity. The ambiguity is caused by a general condition of the mind, rather than any specific situation or question of what gives life meaning. A person suffering from this form of ambiguity may fail to recognize the depression and keep trying without success to resolve the various situations where the ambiguity is manifesting. Over many years of teaching meditation, I've encountered a number of people who outwardly seem to function well, but who exhibit symptoms of ambiguity—they feel directionless, apathetic, or inauthentic. As they learn to be more mindful, they reach the realization that they have low-grade depression. Once they have this information, they can start to address the depression.

In my experience, compassionate mindfulness can prevent someone from identifying with the emotions of hopelessness and meaningless that often accompany depression. Therefore, even though the depressive feelings are present, they don't deprive the individual of perspective. One meditation student described watching himself sink into depression and having terrible thoughts arise in his mind, but because he was anchored by his mindfulness, he never believed his terrible thoughts, although they were dominating his mind. He was also able to observe objectively what he was feeling in his body and his mind, even though he was helpless to do anything to relieve his depression. To this day he believes that being present with his feelings and aware of what was happening saved him from getting lost in despair.

AMBIVALENCE AND AMBIGUITY IN VIPASSANA PRACTICE

Mindfulness practice is slow and repetitious and often seems to be going nowhere, so you can easily start to doubt your practice. The same is true with all of the other vipassana practices; they require patience and persistence. Therefore, almost everyone practicing the Eightfold Path experiences ambivalence about their practice at various stages. For this reason, every dedicated vipassana student must learn to live with and wisely respond to feelings of ambivalence that will inevitably arise. You learn to do so by being mindful of the ambivalence and utilizing the many practices that are offered to interest and inspire the mind. Two examples are the practice of gratitude meditation and reflecting on the benefits of wholesome mind states—there are many, many more.

As you become more mindful, you naturally become more aware of all of your negative emotions, which can create feelings of ambivalence about the practice! From a Buddhist psychological perspective, however, difficult emotions are not setbacks to your practice. Instead, they are "grist for the mill" of your mindfulness. The process of grinding them up with mindfulness yields insights and will free you from their power to hold the mind hostage. You will also gain insight regarding the nature of mind and the Four Noble Truths.

In Theravada Buddhism periods of ambivalence are considered key steps in what's called *the progress of insight*. In this map of practice, a specific insight will arise during a certain stage of practice and evoke so much negative feeling that you become ambivalent about practice and want to just quit. The reason is that this particular insight is breaking you free from illusion, and the ego becomes temporarily discouraged by what it now knows. But with more practice, you experience yet another insight, and this one brings renewed aspiration. The journey to liberation involves a number of these episodes of ambivalence.

Ambiguity is also unavoidable in vipassana practice. You can't be sure which practice is right for you, whether you're doing it correctly, or whether it's worth it. How could there not be ambiguity? But as your mind becomes more still and you see deeper into your mind states, you start to encounter the many ambiguities that are part of your personality—from trivial vagueness to core questions about how to live your life—therefore it's important that you have patience with yourself and persist in your practice. The single biggest danger is that your ambiguity might evolve into skeptical doubt and you quit, without ever giving yourself a full chance at realizing insight.

You can also experience mundane ambiguity such that you don't know how you want to practice or what your practice goals are. The good news is that by repeatedly being mindful of ambiguity, your ambiguity not only starts to diminish, but your capacity to work skillfully with whatever ambiguity remains increases dramatically. The end result is that ambiguity ceases to have the power to be your predominant experience in an ongoing way because you have clarity about its existence and can contain it so effectively with your compassion. Said another way, you are no longer attached to comprehending every situation, you can rest in "don't know mind."

THE JOY OF HAVING A MIND THAT'S FREE OF AMBIVALENCE AND AMBIGUITY

When the mind ceases to be caught in ambivalence or ambiguity, you may experience the feeling of being *grounded in nongrasping awareness that simply knows what's true in the moment, but isn't reactive to it*. The venerable Ajahn Sumedho refers to this ease of mind as "taking refuge in awareness knowing it is *like this.*" Being grounded in this awareness, you can identify what matters to you and you have an inner reference point from which to make decisions when difficult situations arise in your life. All the moments of ambivalence and ambiguity don't magically disappear from your life, but they become less frequent, don't last as long, and don't dominate the mind so much. When your mind is at ease with itself in this manner, your challenges become more manageable although your life may remain difficult.

Even when confronted with ambivalence or ambiguity, if you have let loose of reactivity and stopped grasping for definitive answers, your mind doesn't collapse into reactive mode. Instead, you're able to respond with a certain amount of ease. You have a healthy, relaxed relationship to the challenge that the ambivalence or ambiguity presents. You begin an inquiry: What's this? Who is thinking this thought? What is this awareness that knows these mind states are occurring and can observe their nature? At this level of inquiry, ambivalence and ambiguity become empowering rather than disempowering. Thus, you're no longer being defined by either ordinary or debilitating ambivalence and ambiguity.

As you begin to feel more grounded and less identified with ambivalence and ambiguity when they arise, another deeper capacity opens up in you. This is the capacity of the heart to respond to ambivalence and ambiguity with compassion, loving-kindness, and equanimity. When the mind is not being reactive or clinging, compassion, loving-kindness, and equanimity arise as natural responses to the suffering caused by ambivalence and ambiguity. At first you have to cultivate these responses because they are the opposite of how you've been conditioned to respond when confronted with difficult mind states. But gradually they become a spontaneous response. Once these responses become spontaneous, episodes of ambivalence or ambiguity that once would have created suffering for you are reduced to just mind moments that arise and pass.

When your mind ceases to be defined or controlled by ambivalence and ambiguity, a feeling of joy arises because the mind is no longer contracting into suffering. Thus, the mind is able to rest in its natural state of calm and buoyancy. The hindrances no longer cloud your mind, and you are free of greed, ill will, and delusion for the moment. Of course, this joyful mind state will not last. New external challenges will arise for which you lack the capacity to respond to without first going through ambivalence or ambiguity. Also, as you continue your insight practice, you will discover deeper, subtler levels of clinging embedded in your mind, which will engender more ambivalence and ambiguity. But now when you encounter them, you recognize them for what they really are—temporary mind states arising due to conditions and passing when conditions change. Therefore, they are "not self" and not to be identified with. You know your goal—to rest in the joy and freedom that lies beyond all conditioned states of mind.

ACKNOWLEDGMENTS

I am infinitely indebted to the Buddha as well as the many teachers and practitioners who have kept his teachings alive to the present day. In an immediate and personal way, I am most grateful to Joseph Goldstein, Sharon Salzberg, and Jack Kornfield for their teaching and guidance. For generously sharing his wisdom with me and for encouraging me to teach from my experience, I especially wish to acknowledge the Venerable Ajahn Sumedho, whose teachings I have tried to faithfully represent here.

To the many vipassana students who have graced me with the sincerity of your practice and the opportunity to work with you in individual interviews, I offer my deepest thanks. In so many ways this is your book. It reflects the insight you've gained through the courageous exploration of your individual suffering. My thanks also goes to the members of the Marin Sangha, the meditation group I have taught most Sunday evenings for the past 10 years. You have witnessed the development of the teachings in this book and have contributed in many ways to its formation.

I credit my longtime friends on the spiritual path, David V. White, for acquainting me with the work of Helen Luke and for stimulating my deep interest in T. S. Eliot's *Four Quartets*, and Victor Byrd, for introducing me to vipassana 25 years ago.

The actual creation of this book could not have occurred without the unstinting support and skillful editing of my friend and colleague Kathryn Arnold, who helped bring clarity to my prose while preserving my voice. My friends and teaching colleagues, Gil Fronsdal and Guy Armstrong, who are both Buddhist scholars, gave generously of their time to read the draft manuscript and provide me with feedback. Their vast knowledge and candid criticism have yielded a better book, for which I am most grateful. The creation of www.dancingwithlife.org, which I hope will provide ongoing support to readers, is due to the efforts of Wendi Gilbert, director of the Lifebalance Institute.

And also indebted to my literary agent Amy Williams for her unshakable faith in me and to my editors Leigh Haber and Shannon Welch at Rodale, who gave me a free hand and without whose efforts this book could not exist.

I also wish to acknowledge my companion Pawan Bareja, who has been an enthusiastic supporter throughout the three years of writing this book.

Any historical inaccuracies or misperceptions concerning the dharma contained in this book are my responsibility alone. All of the individuals named above did more than their share in supporting my journey or in helping to create the best possible book.

Finally, I wish to acknowledge you the reader. I hope this book will benefit you on your journey to liberation. In gratitude, I offer the following Dedication of Merit:

> May any understanding that arises from the creation and reading of this book be to the benefit of all those with whom we come in contact.
>
> Any merit that arises from these efforts of practice we offer freely to the liberation of all beings.
>
> May all beings everywhere be free from suffering.

INDEX